Democratizing Technology

Science in Society Series

Series Editor: Steve Rayner
James Martin Institute, University of Oxford

Editorial Board: Gary Kass, Anne Kerr, Melissa Leach, Angela Liberatore, Jez Littlewood, Stan Metcalfe, Paul Nightingale, Timothy O'Riordan, Nick Pidgeon, Ortwin Renn, Dan Sarewitz, Andrew Webster, James Wilsdon, Steve Yearley

Democratizing Technology
Risk, Responsibility and the Regulation of Chemicals
Anne Chapman

Genomics and Society
Legal, Ethical and Social Dimensions
Edited by George Gaskell and Martin W. Bauer

Nanotechnology
Risk, Ethics and Law
Edited by Geoffrey Hunt and Michael Mehta

Democratizing Technology
Risk, Responsibility and
the Regulation of Chemicals

Anne Chapman

London • Sterling, VA

First published by Earthscan in the UK and USA in 2007

ISBN: 978-1-84407-421-1

Typeset by Composition and Design Services, Belarus
Printed and bound in the UK by TJ International, Padstow
Cover design by Susanne Harris

For a full list of publications please contact:

Earthscan
8–12 Camden High Street
London, NW1 0JH, UK
Tel: +44 (0)20 7387 8558
Fax: +44 (0)20 7387 8998
Email: earthinfo@earthscan.co.uk
Web: **www.earthscan.co.uk**

22883 Quicksilver Drive, Sterling, VA 20166-2012, USA

Earthscan publishes in association with the International Institute
for Environment and Development

A catalogue record for this book is available from the British Library

Library of Congress Cataloging-in-Publication Data

Chapman, Anne, 1964-
  Democratizing technology: risk, responsibility, and the regulation of chemicals / Anne Chapman.
     p. cm.
  ISBN-13: 978-1-84407-421-1 (hardback)
  ISBN-10: 1-84407-421-8 (hardback)
  1. Chemical industry--Government policy. 2. Chemical industry--Environmental aspects. 3.
Chemical industry--Law and legislation. I. Title.
  HD9650.6.C52 2002
  363.17'91--dc22
                              2007004092

The paper used for this book is FSC-certified and
totally chlorine-free. FSC (the Forest Stewardship
Council) is an international network to promote
responsible management of the world's forests.

Contents

Preface

In the mid 1990s I was working for an environmental consultancy and used to read the monthly magazine, *The ENDS Report*, to keep up to date with developments in environment policy. Almost every month there was something related to the newly discovered phenomenon of oestrogenic chemicals. Synthetic chemicals suspected of mimicking the female hormone oestrogen were turning up in the linings of tin cans, in baby milk formula, and leaching from babies' dummies. There were also reports of the effects that such chemicals could be having: sperm counts in many countries had declined over the past few decades, and male fish with female characteristics were being found in rivers downstream of sewage discharges. In 1996 *Our Stolen Future*, by Theo Colborn, Dianne Dumanoski and John Peterson Myers, was published. *The ENDS Report* did a feature on this book, which brought together the evidence that a large number of synthetic chemicals can interfere in complex ways in the hormone systems of humans and of other animals, affecting development, health and reproduction. The fact that synthetic chemicals can mimic oestrogen was discovered in the 1930s. Why then did it take until the 1990s for us to realize the implications of this? Why has so little been done since then to reduce the production and use of chemicals that may be endocrine disrupters?

Our Stolen Future convinced me that we should be much more worried about synthetic chemicals than we generally are. So when I decided to do a PhD in philosophy in 2000, I chose to look at the regulation of chemicals, to see why the regulatory system was so ill equipped to deal with the issues raised by endocrine disruption. I felt that treating chemicals as isolated entities was part of the problem, so my research became an investigation into how we think about and publicly assess technologies, taking synthetic chemicals as an example. This book is the result of that research.

Acknowledgements

I would like to thank:

Professor John O'Neill for much helpful criticism and advice.

Caroline Lucas MEP for information on the REACH negotiations.

Professor Andrew Dobson for advice on getting books published.

The Safer Chemicals Campaign team at Friends of the Earth for their thought-provoking campaign about 'risky chemicals'.

The Arts and Humanities Research Board who funded my research.

Chapter 7 and parts of Chapter 10 are an amended version of 'Regulating chemicals: From risks to riskiness', *Risk Analysis*, vol 25, no 3 (2006).

1

Introduction

Technology at a Turning Point?

New technologies have long been a contentious issue. From the 18th century riots precipitated by the introduction of machinery into the textile industry to the mass demonstrations against nuclear power in the 1970s and the destruction of genetically modified crops in the 1990s, people have protested against certain technological developments. What is new is that, with the rejection of genetically modified food by the European public, for the first time the protesters may have won a significant, if local, victory, resulting in severe restrictions being put on a technology that had the backing and support of governments and major companies. This has perhaps created a space in which it may be possible to change the forces controlling the development of new technology; to think differently about technology, its significance and meaning, and how we should assess it and make decisions about it.

In recent decades protests have generally been regarded as being about the risks associated with a technology: industry and government portray the public as being concerned about the risks of physical harm, to people or to the environment, posed by a technology. Risk assessment has become the dominant framework within which regulators consider technological developments. However, while people often are concerned about risks, it is apparent from the debates about genetic engineering that risks of physical harm are not the limit of their concerns. Debates have also raised issues about the power of multinationals, the direction of agricultural development, food security, the preservation of biodiversity and how we should be relating to other living organisms.

It is therefore clear that we need to break out of the narrow confines of risk assessment and develop an enlarged framework for thinking about and assessing technology in the context of public policy.

Towards a New Framework for Making Public Decisions about Technology

For some, changing how decisions about technology are made (or perhaps *become* made) involves challenging and changing the social forces and interests at work. The problem is identified as the distribution of power between those interests and the solution a matter of changing that distribution: reducing the power of capital and increasing the power of deliberative democratic institutions, for example. By contrast, the focus here is on the intellectual underpinnings of the current framework and the development of a possible alternative framework. Social and political institutions need intellectual justification if they are to endure. Cogent criticisms of that justification, and the provision of intellectual justification for alternative institutions, is part of how change happens.

To examine the intellectual underpinnings of the current dominant approach to technology, I look at contemporary UK government policy on technology and the relationships implied by that policy between science, technology and the economy. This discussion is informed by a review of the philosophy of technology that considers the various answers that have been given to the question 'What is technology?' To give focus to my examination of decision making about technology I look in some detail at policy in a specific area of technology: synthetic chemicals.

From my review of the philosophy of technology, in Chapter 2, I conclude that technology is not merely useful machines and tools, rather that it orders and structures human life. I suggest in Chapter 3 that we should think of technology as 'world-building': it is both how we add material things to the world and the things we have added to the world that we use. That world is public, in the sense of being shared or had in common by different people, each of whom has a different perspective on it. As well as technology, it consists of human-constructed laws, institutions and cultural norms. The nature of the world that people share affects the scope for human action and the possibilities for human relationships. It is a condition of our existence: it conditions us, affecting, if not determining, who we are. The world should be a home for its inhabitants and is the proper concern of politics. It is the context for human life that gives life human meaning. So aside from biological necessities, what the interests of individuals are depends on the world that they live in.

This world is constructed on the earth. And the earth consists of the totality of life, including our own, together with all the non-living elements that play an active part in that life: the seas, air, soils and rocks. The earth is in a sense what is 'given' – it is not of our making. We build a world using materials taken from the earth, a taking that necessarily involves doing some violence to it (mining, quarrying or the felling of trees, for example). More recently we have started creating new types of matter, such as novel synthetic chemicals, that interact with the materials of the earth to start new processes. And these processes put at risk the earth itself, including the life of our own species, not merely the human-constructed world or human relationships.

The nature of the world that technology creates and constitutes is obviously important for the quality of human life and the future of the earth. From the perspective that I present it should be at the heart of thinking about technology. In contrast, as I show in Chapter 4, government policy on technology does not acknowledge such a shared human world, but is concerned with the economy and with science.

Science is seen as perhaps the most important source of new technologies, and the development of new technologies the primary role of science. Within public policy discourse science and technology are linked together to such an extent that what are in fact concerns about technology are regarded as concerns about science. I argue that this privileges scientific understandings over other types of knowledge, narrows legitimate concerns to those that can be addressed by science and effectively closes down what should be an open public political debate.

Science and technology obviously are related, but what is the nature of that relationship? I argue that when one looks at science one does not find an integrated single entity but many different sciences, each with their own methods, domains and theories, and relationship to technology. Some sciences lead to technological innovation, others reveal the effects of technology on natural systems, while others simply give us a better understanding of the world. The theories, models and laws of a science apply only within the domain of that particular science, so no one science provides a complete account of the world, or of a particular technology within it. To predict the effects of a new technology we have to know what domains we should consider, and thus what sciences need to be involved. This is often only revealed after the introduction of a technology, when effects have become apparent.

Government policy on technology is concerned with the economy; the desire to maintain economic prosperity is the primary reason the government gives for its promotion of technological innovation. Innovation is seen as necessary for national economic competitiveness. In Chapter 4 I argue that the primary responsibility of the government should be for the world, rather than for the economy. And in Chapter 8 I argue that current methods of assessing the impact of new legislation related to technology, such as the new European regulation on chemicals, REACH, misconceive the relationship between technology and the economy. Technology and legislation are usually seen as causes of changes in levels of economic activity, whereas I argue that technology, along with other aspects of the world, such as laws, institutions and cultural norms, are the framework or structure in which the causes of economic activity (human desires and needs) have effects. Technology changes the nature of economic activities and the effects that our economic activities have. Government should therefore have a more discriminating approach to technological innovation: it should consider whether the innovation in question would make for a better world. In contrast, the current approach regards innovation as inherently good because it is thought to lead to economic growth and increased competitiveness. The only possible downside to technological innovation that is recognized in government policy is risk of physical harm, either to human health or to the environment.

Synthetic chemicals are one area of technology where such risks have been of concern. In Chapter 5 I review European legislation on synthetic chemicals. Synthetic chemicals have been around rather longer than genetically modified organisms, so there is experience of producing, using and regulating them. It is also an arena in which risk assessment plays a central role, but in which, as I show, the problems and limitations of risk assessment are increasingly apparent. Risk-based regulation requires that there is good evidence that a chemical is likely to cause harm to human health or to the environment before actions to restrict its production or use are taken. However, as I discuss in Chapter 7, the current methods of investigating and assessing the risks from chemicals do not succeed in providing evidence of sufficient weight to command the agreement of the scientific and regulatory communities as to whether or not harm is likely to be caused. Furthermore, limitations to our knowledge mean that we can never be sure that we know all the ways in which novel chemical substances may cause harm. The result is that risk assessment for chemicals has been characterized by procrastination and delay. And during such delay, the manufacture and use of suspect chemicals is allowed to continue unrestricted.

I argue that, rather than just known risks, regulation should consider the *riskiness* of a technology, a concept I introduce in Chapter 6. While risk is a matter of the probability of a harmful outcome, riskiness is a feature of a thing, situation or action relative to our knowledge about it. Situations of uncertainty and ignorance, in which risks cannot be calculated because we do not know the probability of harm, or cannot identify the harm that may be caused, are nonetheless risky situations if what we do know does not enable us to rule out significant harm occurring. To assess riskiness we do not have to be able to identify the type of harm that something might cause: something may be risky simply because there is much that we do not know about it, or because it puts at risk something of great value, or because its consequences are irreversible. The riskiness of a technology depends on the technology, whereas the probability that it will cause harm also depends on how people behave as a result of it. That behaviour may change as a result of the dangers presented by the technology, so that no harm actually occurs, but people's lives have been restricted. I suggest that the riskiness of synthetic chemicals depends on how novel they are, whether they start new processes in nature, their persistence and bioaccumulation, and their mobility, as well as their known capacities to affect biological or geochemical systems.

The focus on physical harm, to the exclusion of other considerations, is no doubt a result of the influence of the political philosophy of liberalism. One of the tenets of that philosophy is that government should not interfere in the actions of individuals unless those actions cause harm to others. In the arena of technology regulation this is in effect a reverse precautionary principle: technologies are assumed to be safe unless there is evidence that they cause harm. In Chapter 8 I examine liberalism and utilitarianism, the latter being the ethical theory that most influences public policy. I argue that neither recognizes the existence of a public world shared by individuals, both being concerned only with individual people – their welfare or the distribution of goods and rights between them. The republican tradition, I suggest, offers an alternative, as it is concerned with the preservation of a public realm – the world shared by the public in question – as well as with individual liberty. However, whereas liberalism tends to conceive of liberty in terms of non-interference, for republicanism it is more a matter of non-domination or independence. Being a free person is a matter of possessing the capacity to think for oneself and to take responsibility for what you do. It is a matter of having the virtues of a good citizen, the development of which requires that one take an active part in sharing responsibility for the public realm with others. One of the most important of these virtues is a sense of responsibility for the public world.

In contrast, the approach to technology in contemporary society has been characterized as 'organized irresponsibility' (Beck, 2000). In Chapter 9 I discuss responsibility and argue that this organized irresponsibility has two sides to it.

The first is that public decisions about technology are made without consideration being given to the nature of the world that the technology would bring into being, neglecting responsibility for the human-constructed world. The second is the fact that, despite technology clearly being something that humans are causally responsible for, rarely is anyone held responsible for the damaging effects of technology, such as the destruction of the ozone layer or the ill-health of humans and wildlife caused by synthetic chemicals.

In Chapter 10 I present proposals for reforming the way we make decisions about technology. These aim to put responsibility for the world at the heart of public decisions and to enable responsible individual choices about technology. I suggest that the UK system for control of built development – the planning system and building regulations – provides a possible model for public decision making about technology. Within that system the existence of a shared, public realm is recognized and the nature of that realm is seen as having an effect on individuals' quality of life, the wellbeing of communities, the environment and the economy. I suggest institutional arrangements for public decision making about technology and principles from which policies to inform the decisions made in those institutions could be developed. I further suggest ways of encouraging individual responsibility, such as by a levy on commercial advertising of products to provide a fund for 'public interest advertising'. Such advertising would allow public airing of concerns about the effects of particular types of products, thereby encouraging public debate and putting pressure on businesses to make products that contribute to making the world a better, rather than a worse, place for human life.

Chapter 10 also includes my proposals for reform of the regulation of chemicals. Chemicals should be regulated on the basis of their riskiness, rather than just of known risks, but we should also take a wider view: synthetic chemicals are not just isolated substances but things that have been made, whose making requires particular technologies and that are used for particular purposes. I therefore suggest that we should consider the nature of the world constituted by the process of production of a synthetic chemical, compared to that of alternative substances, and that each practice that uses synthetic chemicals should develop an 'ethic' of that practice to regulate its use of chemicals. Such an ethic would set out principles to inform the development of acceptable and recommended methods and materials for the particular tasks and functions involved in the practice. Those principles should require that, where possible, risky chemicals are not used, but they should also set out criteria in other domains, so that methods have positive effects when considered from a variety of perspectives. A current example of such an ethic is that of organic methods in agriculture.

The importance of multiple perspectives, which provide different descriptions of the same thing and different criteria by which it is to be judged, is one of the key conclusions of this book. There are many different conditions that must be met if human life is to be lived well. Recent times have perhaps become dominated by meeting the condition of providing material comfort and convenience. This has been at the expense of a world in which responsible human action is possible. It has also meant that we are living in a way that cannot be sustained on this earth. We now need to think about what sort of world we should be building with our technology.

Philosophical Sources

Thinking about technology requires both a political philosophy and a philosophy of science: the latter because of the obvious importance of science in the development of technology *and* in the assessment of its effects; the former because technology constitutes part of the public world and thus is of political concern.

It is in the work of Hannah Arendt that I have found a political philosophy adequate to the task of thinking about technology. Hannah Arendt was a pupil of Martin Heidegger in the 1920s, fled Germany in the 1930s and became a citizen of the US in 1951. Her work is an outcome of her attempt to come to grips intellectually with what happened to the world she was born into, and to herself as a Jew, during the first half of the 20th century. In many ways she stands alone as a philosopher, though depending on what aspect you consider she can be considered a phenomenologist, Aristotelian, Kantian or Republican. From Arendt's thought I have developed my view of technology as 'world-building' and derive principles for assessing whether technology will help to make the world a fit home for human life on earth. Linked with Arendt – he was her life-long friend – is Hans Jonas, whose work on responsibility is central to Chapter 9.

My main source for a philosophy of science is Nancy Cartwright. In contrast to that of Arendt, the work of Cartwright is very much within a particular 'school' of the philosophy of science, the 'Stanford school'. This school includes Ian Hacking and John Dupré, whose work I also draw on.

While having very different concerns, there are commonalities between Arendt and the Stanford school. One is that the origin of events lies in the natures, or capacities, of things or people, not in 'laws' imposed on things from the outside. Arendt's concern with politics means that she generally considers only human beings as having this capacity to act, though in one of her later works she notes how studies of the behaviour of animals have shown that much of what we previously thought only occurs in humans, and that we know about precisely because we are human beings, also occurs in animals (Arendt, 1970, pp59–60).

A second commonality is the importance of a plurality of perspectives. In Cartwright's view of the world as 'dappled' (Cartwright, 1999), the limitedness of scientific laws and theories – the fact that they only apply under particular circumstances, in particular domains – means that to get a complete picture (or as complete a picture as possible) a phenomenon, problem or issue must be investigated by the many different disciplines that make up what we call science, perhaps also drawing on knowledge and experience that is external to science. Similarly, in the conclusion to his book *Human Nature and the Limits of Science*, Dupré says that his argument has been that:

> *a proper understanding of a domain as complex and richly connected to diverse factors as that of human behaviour can only be adequately approached from a variety of perspectives.* (Dupré, 2001, p154)

In the work of Arendt the presence of a plurality of perspectives on the common world is vital to our sense of reality and objectivity, as well as to politics. She also gives us different perspectives: the different conditions of human life mean that there are a number of different perspectives from which it is possible to 'think what we are doing' (Arendt, 1958, p5). The three activities of human life that she identifies – labour, work and action – are descriptions of what we are doing that take into account different conditions of our existence (Chapman, 2004). They are thus 'what we are doing' seen from different perspectives.

A third commonality is the importance of attention to phenomena, to what appears. For Cartwright this means studying what actually goes on in laboratories, how experiments are done, what they are intended to achieve. It means an approach to science where what is important is the evidence we have for our beliefs. For Arendt, it means trying to discover the essence of the experience that is being articulated by ideas and concepts. Cartwright is opposed to 'fundamentalism' in science (Cartwright, 1999, pp23–24), Arendt to ideology in politics (Arendt, 1966, p468). Fundamentalism and the ideologies of totalitarian governments involve logical deduction from what are thought to be fundamental laws, of nature or history, regardless of reality. Where reality conflicts with these deductions the fundamentalist or ideological response is to attempt to remake the world according to the ideal contained in the law. Thus Hitler's 'prediction' in 1939 that the Jewish race in Europe would be annihilated were there to be a world war was one that he set about making into a reality (Arendt, 1966, p349). At the mundane level of kitchen renovation Cartwright points out the disaster that can be created if we start from our ideal kitchen, rather than the kitchen that we actually have (Cartwright, 1999, p13).

Outline of Chapters

Chapter 2 considers the question 'What is technology?' I examine the origins of the word 'technology' and how its meaning has changed over the centuries, from a description or study of arts, where arts refers to the means by which artefacts are produced, to those means themselves. Philosophical accounts of technology have regarded it in various ways. I discuss accounts that see technology as the following: knowledge, artefacts, the extension of human capabilities, a means for improvement, a substantive force, devices, a social construction and a contingent social structure. From these accounts I draw out what I think is useful for thinking about technology in the context of its public assessment. Technology involves knowledge of how to produce things, the artefacts that are used in production and, to a lesser extent, artefacts that are used for doing other things. It is a matter of doing that involves both things and knowledge. It is often a means to ends, but it is not simply this. Rather, technology affects the structure and pattern of human life, including what ends it is possible to have. The everyday word that best encompasses that which orders and structures human life is the word 'world'. Technology forms part of the world that we inhabit together, the outcome of the activity of past and present generations, and that we can change.

Chapter 3 sets out my view of technology as 'world-building'. I suggest two definitions of technology: how we add things to the world, and the things that we have added to the world that are used, where 'things' are either material things or are embodied or realized in material things. The world is always to some extent public, in the sense of being shared by more than one person. In that decisions about technology are decisions about the world, they are always of public concern. I suggest that the goal of public policy should be to make the world a fit home for human life on earth. Because we are biological beings (and therefore part of the earth), moral beings and beings who make aesthetic judgements, the human world should not significantly change the natural processes and cycles of the earth; it should be a place for responsible human action, and it should be beautiful rather than ugly. I consider the first two of these requirements in some depth to translate them into principles on which more concrete policies to inform decisions about technology could be based.

Chapter 4 considers the relationships between technology, science and the economy. I critically review UK government policy on science and technology. This regards science as leading to technological development and technological innovation as necessary for a competitive national economy. I consider arguments about the nature of science and introduce Cartwright's 'dappled world' view of science. I argue that although science, like technology, can be considered to be 'world-building' it adds knowledge, rather than material things, to the world. The norms and criteria of judgement that apply to the acceptance of that knowledge are quite different to those that are appropriate for judging whether a technology should form part of the world. I criticize the contemporary framing of debates about technology as debates about science. This framing narrows the debate, excluding important concerns and perspectives. Finally, I develop the account of technology introduced in Chapter 3 by considering the relationship between the world and the economy and the connection between technological innovation and economic growth.

Chapter 5 introduces synthetic chemicals as a technology and summarizes the European system of controls over the manufacture, importation and use of synthetic chemicals. Major problems for regulation have been the lack of data on the long-term health and environmental effects of most of the chemicals currently in use and the delays in carrying out risk assessments. Out of several tens of thousands of synthetic chemicals marketed in Europe since before 1981 and still in use, risk assessments have been carried out for less than 100 substances. To address these problems a major new European Regulation, REACH (Registration, Evaluation, Authorization and restriction of Chemicals), was brought into force in 2007. I outline this new system and discuss the key issues that emerged in the debates about it.

Chapter 6 explores the concept of risk. In technical risk assessment, risk is often conceived to be the probability of harm. The harm is not a property of a technology, but an unwanted event that it causes. So one problem for risk assessment is the establishment of a causal connection between a particular event and the technology. I suggest that rather than trying to assess risks we should ask how risky a technology is, where the riskiness of a technology is a matter of the possibility of it causing harm. This possibility is a function of our knowledge: as we do not know how things are independent of our knowledge of them, we have to recognize that something is possible if it is not ruled out by what we do know. In technical risk assessments it is generally concluded that there is no risk if it is not possible to identify a specific type of harm caused by the technology. This means that where there is a great deal of ignorance about a technology and its effects (as there is if it is a novel technology) the assessment concludes that there is no risk. In contrast, assessments of riskiness would conclude that the technology is risky: it is risky because, for all we know, it is possible that it causes harm. Finally, in this chapter I discuss how the context of a risky situation affects our evaluation of it. Risks are 'taken' in exchange for benefits and our moral evaluation of the risk-taking depends on whether the person who makes the decision is the one who is put at risk. Our attitude to a risk is also dependent upon whether those put at risk have any agency in the situation to affect the outcome, as well as whether the risk-taker will take responsibility if harm occurs.

Chapter 7 describes how risks from chemicals are assessed. It concludes that the many uncertainties mean the assessment process generally does not succeed in providing evidence that commands agreement as to whether or not a chemical poses a risk. Hence the frequent disputes as to whether restrictions on chemicals are justified. Rather than trying to assess the risks from a chemical, I suggest we should aim to assess how risky a chemical is in a more everyday sense. Risky chemicals are ones where, given our state of knowledge, it is possible that they cause harm. I discuss four things that make a chemical more risky: (1) its capacity to cause harm, (2) its novelty, (3) its persistence and (4) its mobility.

Chapter 8 considers the ethical theory (utilitarianism) and the political philosophy (liberalism) that underlie the existing regulatory system. I use Cartwright's concept of a nomological machine to critique the socio-economic impact assessment of REACH and consider Arendt's view that the world has interests which are not reducible to the self-interests of individuals. I then examine the arguments for the harm principle of liberalism. This restricts the legitimate use of coercive government interference in the actions of the individual to instances where those actions cause harm to others. I claim that neither utilitarianism nor liberalism recognizes the existence of a public world shared by individuals. That world is the context in which individuals have interests, and individual life has value and meaning. I suggest that the classical republican tradition offers a better basis for a public technology assessment process that has the nature of the public world at the centre of its concern. As well as being concerned for the preservation of the public realm, republicanism values the freedom of the individual, where that freedom is conceived as consisting in the possession of the virtues of citizenship, including a sense of responsibility for the world.

Chapter 9 is about responsibility. I look at the various ways in which the word responsibility is used. One of those ways – responsibility *for* things – I discuss in some detail, using the work of Hans Jonas. We are responsible for things that are good but vulnerable, where we have some power to protect or nurture what is good about the thing or person. Governments and citizens are responsible for the public world. I examine how, in making decisions about technology, that responsibility is neglected. I examine why, with respect to synthetic chemicals in particular, there is a lack of accountability for technology and what could be done to remedy this. Finally, I consider whether basing decisions on the outcomes of risk assessments itself constitutes responsible conduct. I argue that assessments of risks must be supplemented by at least two other considerations: the completeness and degree of certainty of our knowledge and who or what is put at risk.

Chapter 10 sets out my conclusions with respect to how we should make decisions about technology, synthetic chemicals in particular. Using the UK system of controls over built development as a model, I argue that controls over technology should consist of two types of systems: technical standards equivalent to building regulations and a system of political oversight over technological development equivalent to the planning system. In both systems decisions should be made on the basis of policies that outline the attributes or features that technology should have if it is to make for a better world, and I suggest that the principles derived in Chapter 3 could inform the development of such policies. I also present proposals for the reform of chemical regulation and suggest ways of enabling responsible individual decisions about technology. In conclusion, I draw some lessons from synthetic chemicals: our knowledge is limited, if we introduce novel things into the world we cannot know what will happen, and we should avoid solving old problems in ways that create new ones. Finally, to provide the many conditions needed for human life to be lived well, we must consider what we are doing from many different perspectives.

References

Arendt, H. (1958) *The Human Condition*, University of Chicago Press, Chicago, IL

Arendt, H. (1966) *The Origins of Totalitarianism*, Second Edition, Harcourt, Inc, New York

Arendt, H. (1970) *On Violence*, Harcourt, Brace & World, New York

Beck, U. (2000) 'Risk society revisited: Theory, politics and research programmes', in B. Adam, U. Beck and J. Van Loon (eds) *The Risk Society and Beyond: Critical Issues for Social Theory*, Sage Publications, London

Cartwright, N. (1999) *The Dappled World: A Study of the Boundaries of Science*, Cambridge University Press, Cambridge

Chapman, A. (2004) 'Technology as world building', *Ethics, Place and Environment*, vol 7, nos 1–2, pp59–72

Dupré, J. (2001) *Human Nature and the Limits of Science*, Clarendon Press, Oxford

2
What is Technology?

Introduction

Thinking about technology inevitably requires having an understanding of what technology is. Before examining public policy to discover how it conceives technology, I want to develop an account of technology from philosophical thinking. In this chapter I examine the origins of the word technology and how its meaning has changed over the centuries. I then consider philosophical accounts of technology according to what they take technology to be: knowledge, artefacts, the extension of human capabilities, a means for improvement, a substantive force, devices, a social construction and a contingent social structure. I conclude by drawing out from these accounts what I think is useful for thinking about technology in the context of its public assessment, and in Chapter 3 I propose two definitions of technology. My aim is an account that sheds light on the meaning of technology in everyday life and points to what technology should be, an account that can inform the public assessment of technology. In future chapters this account will provide the basis of my critique of the current dominant approach to technology implicit in public policy.

A Brief History of Meanings

The word 'technology' is derived from the Greek words *techne* and *logos*. *Techne* is commonly translated as art, craft or skill. *Logos* can be translated as word or utterance, but also as reason or logic; thus, something with a logos is something that you can give an account of. However, *techne* itself involved *logos*: Aristotle defined it as 'a state involving true reason [*logos*] concerned with production' (Aristotle, *Nicomachean Ethics*, Book VI, Chapter 4, 1140a, lines 21–22). The 'state' referred to here is of the rational part of the soul that is concerned with contingent things, as opposed to things that are how they are by necessity, or by nature (ibid, VI.1.1139a). Production consists of activities that are done for the sake of an end outside themselves, and is distinguished from action, whose end 'is acting well itself' (ibid, VI.5.1140b, lines 7–8). *Techne* involves inquiry, understanding, knowledge and deliberation about production. However, not all elements involved in production can be understood in a rational way by the mind. While reason grasps the form (*eidos*) to be taken by the artefact being made (and can be said to originate in the mind of the artisan, as an idea – Aristotle, *Metaphysics*,

VII.7.1032b1), it cannot grasp the matter: the matter is not part of the concept of the product (ibid, VII.10.1035a) and a consistent and accurate account of matter cannot be given because matter is subject to change (Plato, *Timaeus*).

The terms *techne* and *logos* were first joined together by Aristotle, in his treatise on rhetoric. The exact meaning of the term is not clear, but Carl Mitcham suggests that he meant something like 'the *logos* of the activity of the *techne* of persuasion' (Mitcham, 1994, p129). This use became embedded in the ancient world with technology coming to mean the study of grammar or rhetoric. It was not until the late 16th century that the word came to have something like its present meaning, resulting in a 1706 dictionary defining it as 'a Description of Arts, especially the Mechanical' (quoted in Mitcham, 1994, p130).

The idea that technology is a description, or study, of arts remained until well into the 20th century. The 1944 *Concise Oxford Dictionary* gives two meanings of the word technology: 'science of the industrial arts' and 'ethnological study of development of arts'. But, like a number of other '-ology' words, the meaning of technology has altered in the past half century to come to refer to the object of study, rather than the study itself. Thus one of the definitions in the 1969 *Little Oxford Dictionary* is the 'practical arts collectively' and a 1972 Chambers dictionary defines technology as 'technical means and skills characteristic of a particular civilization, group or period'. Another definition given by the Chambers dictionary is 'the practice of any or all of the applied sciences that have practical value and/or industrial use'. In this definition technology has become the application of science, rather than a science that gives knowledge about 'arts'.

Technology as Knowledge

In some philosophical accounts technology is principally a form of knowledge. More specifically, it is knowledge of a practical kind, of *how* to make and use things, not knowledge that is simply concerned with describing what *is* (Feibleman, 1966; Jarvie, 1972). This view of technology as knowledge seems to be related to the older view of technology as a study, or description, of the arts. However, the latter implied that technology was knowledge *derived* from studying arts. The more recent philosophical accounts consider it to be the knowledge that is *used* in arts; it might or might not have been obtained by studying them.

Some consider that there is something systematic, scientific and objective about the knowledge that is technology, so that technology is a specifically modern phenomenon, distinguishable from the crafts and techniques that went before (see, for example, Cardwell, 1994, p4). For Mario Bunge those crafts and techniques were guided by 'rules of thumb' derived from experience and often justified by myth, whereas technological rules are grounded in the laws of science. Bunge considers technology to be knowledge derived by the application of science to practical problems with the aim of increasing the effectiveness of the control or manipulation of matter (Bunge, 1972).

If science is regarded simply as 'generalized, objective knowledge', then Tim Ingold, an anthropologist, has a basically similar view of technology to Bunge, although, unlike Bunge, he does not think that it has a simple clear aim. Ingold takes technology to mean 'a corpus of generalized, objective knowledge, in so far as it is capable of practical application' (Ingold, 2000, p315). Such generalized, objective knowledge is associated with an epistemology that seeks an objective, external view of nature in order to assert control over it, and is a distinctly modern concept (Ingold, 2000, p314). This means that there was no such thing as technology in pre-modern societies. In such societies technical accomplishments were associated with skills, rather than necessarily with the production of complex artefacts. Ingold discusses how the simple tools of hunter-gatherers, such as lassos, digging sticks or boomerangs, required a great deal of skill to put them to their many uses, whereas a complex machine such as a food processor requires very little skill to use (Ingold, 2000, pp366–369). Where technical accomplishment consists of skills, rather than of codifiable, discursive, generalizable knowledge, it is inseparable from skilled persons. It is therefore inseparable from the other aspects of those persons such as their relationships with families and friends and with the place they inhabit. The technical is thus embedded in social relations. As the importance of skill in the making and using of objects has declined, so has the degree to which the technical is embedded in the social. Technology, as a separate sphere of human activity, is the product of 'externalization' – the 'withdrawal of the producer, in person, from the centre to the periphery of the production process' (Ingold, 2000, p289).

Technology as Artefacts

The problem with regarding technology as a form of knowledge is that it is artefacts, not knowledge, that most readily come to mind when the word 'technology' is mentioned (Mitcham, 1994, p161). Although technology certainly used to mean a type of study, and thus knowledge, this is no longer the common understanding of the word. However, it does not seem sufficient to simply say that technology denotes artefacts. Not all artefacts are equally 'technological'. At one end of the spectrum are works of art, which we simply gaze at,[1] at the other end automatic machines that produce other artefacts. This suggests that the degree to which an artefact is technological depends on the degree to which it does things, or to which we can do useful things with it. The more an artefact can do things without humans being involved (a machine as opposed to a hand tool) the more we think of it as technology. Technology thus appears to be linked to doing – particularly with doing that transforms or produces things – as well as to artefacts. Thus Robert McGinn suggests that technology is 'material product-making or object transforming activity' (McGinn, 1978, p181) and Mitcham that technology is 'the making and using of artefacts' (Mitcham, 1994, p1).

Technology as the Extension of Human Capabilities

One way to see technology as a combination of artefact and doing (though sometimes the artefact slips from view and does not seem to be essential) is to regard it as essentially a means by which humans extend their capabilities. For example,

Donald Schon defines technology as 'any tool or technique, any product or process, any physical equipment or method of doing or making by which human capability is extended' (Schon, 1967, p1). This definition implies that there are identifiable basic human capabilities prior to the tools, techniques and so forth that comprise technology, an assumption that Ingold would take issue with (see Ingold, 2000, pp373–391). These basic human capabilities are generally taken to be those of the human body, leading to the idea of technology as 'organ projection' (Kapp, 1877). Mitcham suggests that a hammer can be seen as extending the power of the arm muscle and the form and hardness of the fist (Mitcham, 1994, p177), but can a tool such as a hand drill, which does something of a different nature than that which can be done by the human body alone, be similarly regarded as a projected organ, let alone artefacts such as televisions, vacuum pumps or synthetic chemicals? It seems rather convoluted to explain these in terms of the human capabilities that they are extending as Marshall McLuhan (1964) and Paul Levinson (1988) try to do.

Defining technology as an extension of natural capabilities also implies that technology does not really do anything new, it simply stretches out the boundaries of what was possible without it. Thus James Beniger's definition of technology as the 'intentional extension of a natural process, that is, of the processing of matter, energy and information that characterizes all living systems' (Beniger, 1986, p54) naturalizes technology. Technology must be 'natural' if it is merely an extension of processes that go on in living things. But the significance of many technologies lies in the fact that the manner in which they process 'matter, energy and information' is radically different from how it is done in living things. Living things do not make organo-chlorine chemicals (Commoner, 1971), nor do they generate energy by bombarding radioactive elements with neutrons (as happens in a nuclear reactor). To see them simply as extensions of processes in living systems requires them to be re-described in more general terms, which involves a loss of precision and clarity.

Technology as a Means for Improvement

The idea of technology as extending human capabilities begs the question 'For what purpose?' Some philosophers address this question by making the purpose of technology central to their definition of what it is. Thus Nathan Rotenstreich writes that technology 'represents the set of means by which man puts the forces and laws of nature to use, in view of improving his lot or modifying it as may be agreeable to him' (Rotenstreich, 1967), and José Ortega y Gassett that technology can be defined as 'the improvement brought about on nature by man for the satisfaction of his necessities' (Ortega y Gasset, 1972). Technology is conceived here as how human beings use or alter natural things, to 'improve' them, so they are more suitable for, or amenable to, human needs and purposes.

Such improvements are often conceived in terms of problem-solving. Thus Neil Postman recommends that the question 'What is the problem to which this is the solution?' be asked of any new piece of technology (discussed in Graham, 1999, p4). The fact that he did not find a satisfactory answer to this question with respect to electrically-controlled car windows suggests that technological development is not always driven forward by the need to solve practical problems. Gordon Graham suggests that the problem-solving that played a part in the development of the internet was the intellectual interest of computer programmers in solving particular technical problems. These are problems of how to do something, the solutions to which are sought out of curiosity rather than because being able to do that thing will solve particular problems. This may, of course, be a symptom of the specialist nature of modern technological development, and the separation of its development from its use, rather than a general feature of technology. However, Graham's point that technology may solve problems that are only revealed once the technology is put to use is probably more general. For example, that the wounds created by conventional surgery take a long time to heal was only revealed as a problem by key-hole surgery, when it was found that patients recover from key-hole surgery quicker than they do from conventional surgery (Graham, 1999). The significance of technology, argues Graham, is not a matter of its instrumental usefulness at solving pre-existing problems, but in the fact that it changes what is possible.

Graham suggests that the question we should ask of new technology is not 'What problem does it solve?' but 'What does it make possible that was not possible before?' (Graham, 1999, p41). New possibilities are often, of course, thought of as inherently a good thing. Emmanuel Mesthene expresses the traditional liberal view that equates new possibilities with increasing human freedom:

We have the power to create new possibilities, and the will to do so. By creating new possibilities, we give ourselves more choices. With more choices, we have more opportunities. With more opportunities, we can have more freedom, and with more freedom we can be more human. (Mesthene, 1972, p111)

Mesthene does point out that technology destroys as well as creates possibilities, and that it can lead to evil, but in that 'technology spells only possibilities' it is neutral.

Technology as a Substantive Force

The idea that technology is a neutral means is countered by 'substantive' views, which argue that technology is a force that shapes human life and values: technology is not simply a means to ends determined external to technology, but has a substantive effect on those ends, even to the extent of determining them completely.

Martin Heidegger considered the essence of technology to be that it frames things (including humans) as 'standing reserve', as stock piles of raw material for the enhancement of human power (Heidegger, 1954).[2] This is the culmination of Western metaphysics since René Descartes; a metaphysics that has regarded the reality of the self-conscious human subject as primary, and nature as an object *for* the subject, to be manipulated and controlled. Everything, including ultimately the human subject, is seen as simply instrumental to something else, leaving only the 'will to power'. The danger of technology is thus nihilism: the collapse of values (Zimmerman, 1979). Enframing as 'standing reserve' is the essence of modern technology, not of traditional crafts and techniques: the silversmith 'brings-forth' (*poiesis*) the silver chalice, by carefully considering and gathering together the matter, form and *telos* of the chalice. Modern technology, on the other hand, 'sets upon' nature, in the sense of challenging it to yield some general thing, such as energy, that is then transformed, stored and distributed (Heidegger, 1954).[3] Heidegger is generally regarded as pessimistic and fatalistic when it comes to the possibilities of changing our situation. The technological framing of the world blocks other ways in which the being of things is revealed and is 'irresistible' – a destiny (Heidegger, 1954, p314). It does not seem that we have the capacity to reject technology, rather that a 'saving power', if it is to be revealed, will grow out of the danger that is technology. However, at the end of 'The question concerning technology' Heidegger considers whether there is a 'more primally granted revealing that could bring the saving power into its first shining-forth' (Heidegger, 1954, p315) and suggests that this may be the poetic revealing of art – something that was once called *techne*, along with other forms of making, and that therefore is related to technology.

That technology is an autonomous force that determines its own ends, in opposition to human freedom, is generally perceived to be the claim made by Jacques Ellul. Ellul's major work, *The Technological Society* (which he wrote in the 1950s, but which was only published in English in 1964), is a critique of what he terms '*La Technique*'. One of the problems with Ellul's work is the issue of exactly what *La Technique* is. In the introduction to the 1964 American Edition of *The Technological Society*, Ellul defines *Technique* as 'the *totality of methods rationally arrived at* and having absolute efficiency (for a given stage of development) in *every* field of human activity' (emphasis in original). However, much of the discussion of it in the main book suggests that it should be regarded as a mindset, or way of thinking, rather than as technology itself. On page 19 he gives it a very general meaning: 'nothing more than means and the ensemble of means'. On the following page he says that 'what characterizes technical action within a particular activity is the search for greater efficiency' (Ellul, 1964, p20). *Technique* is the search for 'the one best means in every field', this best means being the one that is most efficient, where efficiency is regarded as an objective matter, one that can be assessed by rational, impersonal procedures. But the idea of efficiency presupposes some externally determined value that it is maximizing. Ellul does not say what that value is, rather he claims that technological development is not oriented towards any external end (Ellul, 1964, p97), that it is a purely causal process, a matter of the 'anonymous accretion of conditions' (Ellul, 1964, p85).

Technology as Device

Heidegger's idea that technology yields some general thing, such as energy, is taken up by Albert Borgmann in his concept of the device paradigm (Borgmann, 1984). The device is the general pattern followed by modern technology. A device provides one thing (such as warmth) – the thing that the device is *for* – in a way that does not require our physical engagement. This one thing provided by a device is a commodity in that it is a quantifiable amount of a general substance or material, not a specific, unique thing, and it is provided in a 'commodious way' (Borgmann, 1984, p42). Because what is important about the device is the commodity it provides, the machinery of the device (its material and structure) can be completely changed while keeping the device functionally the same. Borgmann contrasts devices with 'focal things': things that require our bodily engagement and provide a variety of benefits, rather than simply one commodity. Through that bodily engagement we develop skills which contribute to our character, and through sharing with others the tasks required by focal things we forge relationships. Borgmann's key example of a focal thing is the wood burning hearth or stove, which is contrasted with the device of a central heating system. The hearth provides a focus for the room and the household as well as warmth. It requires daily physical tasks to be allotted to and undertaken by the various members of the household necessitating their interaction with each other and with the hearth and the wood. In contrast, a central heating system merely provides warmth at the flick of a switch, by mechanisms which do not need to be seen or understood. Changing from an oil to a gas central heating boiler would not make a great deal of difference.

The device paradigm highlights the merits of engagement: in demanding something from us focal things encourage activity rather than passivity, strengthen our relationships and enrich our lives, while devices make possible unsatisfying laziness. However, Borgmann has to welcome the device as a support for focal things and practices because he considers that devices 'liberate us from misery and toil' by bringing 'the harsh conditions of nature and culture under control' (Borgmann, 1984, p41). He counsels acceptance of the disburdenments offered by devices in some areas of life to allow time for focal practices in others. Reform of technology should involve the recognition and restraint of the device paradigm, not rejection of it.

One problem with the device paradigm is that of where the distinction between focal things and devices lies. I suggest that this distinction is relative to particular people: the central heating boiler is a device as far as the occupants of the household are concerned, but for the central heating engineer it is a focal thing: it demands his engagement and skills and is the focus of practices. For that engineer, changing from oil to gas may make all the difference. This suggests that whether something is a focal thing for a particular person depends on their agency with respect to it: whether they can understand how it works, maintain it and fix it when it breaks down. Cars are focal things for car mechanics – but they are becoming less so as electronic controls are integrated more and more into car engines and there are more and more specialized components that have to be simply taken out and replaced when anything goes wrong with them. Technological change affects agency and the practices and institutions through which that agency is exercised.

The problem with Borgmann's work is that his predominant perspective is that of the private individual – the consumer. He does not recognize that things that are devices for the individual consumer may be focal things for others. His recommendation that devices should be used intelligently and selectively, merely as means, with space cleared for focal things and practices as ends, is perfectly sensible at the individual level, but it is less easy to see how it applies to the public realm: in the public realm it is not clear what is a device and what is not. Borgmann recommends a two sector economy: a local, labour-intensive sphere for engaging work 'capable of focal depth' and a centralized/automated sphere. His division of labour between the two does not recognize the interdependencies between what he puts in one sphere and what he puts in the other. Thus goods such as food, furniture, clothing, health care, education, music, arts and sports are in the local sphere, while the maintenance and improvement of infrastructure, the production of certain manufactured goods such as cars, and research and development are in the centralized/automated sphere. However, local production of food and other goods may well be threatened by imports from elsewhere, which are only possible because the centralized sphere has provided an infrastructure that promotes long distance over local transport.

Technology as a Social Construction

The idea that technological change follows its own logic and is a purely causal process, unaffected by economic, political or social factors – an idea present in popular myth as well as in the work of Ellul – has been undermined by studies of technological innovation in the sociology of science tradition. These studies have emphasized the contingent nature of technological development and the role of 'relevant social groups' in determining the development of technologies. Relevant social groups are defined as groups of people who share a meaning of an artefact (Kline and Pinch, 1999). Two relevant social groups involved in the development of the bicycle, for example, were the young men riding bicycles for sport, for whom the high-wheeler was a 'macho machine', and the women and elderly men who wanted to use bicycles for transport, for whom the high-wheeler was an 'unsafe machine' (Bijker, 1995). That the artefact can have these different meanings for different social groups, social constructivists label 'interpretative flexibility'. Their relativist stance, taken from the sociology of science, means that no judgement is passed on whether some meanings should be accorded more validity than others – rendering the approach open to the criticism of being morally and politically indifferent (Winner, 1993). The development of artefacts is a matter of the reinforcement of some meanings at the expense of others, and thus can be seen as being a matter of the interaction between those groups: the artefact 'is gradually constructed or deconstructed in the social interactions of relevant social groups' (Bijker, 1993, p119). The artefact as a thing that, once made, has its own independent existence – a thing which is one and the same thing, even though different social groups may describe it in different ways, and which may have consequences that are unrelated to the needs, interests and problems of those groups – is in danger of disappearing in this account, to be replaced by a fluid network of human interactions.

The focus of social constructivists on the necessarily interpretative descriptions, or accounts, of an artefact made by different social groups means the reality of the artefact itself tends to be lost. However, when social constructivists emphasize the inter-relationship between the technical and the social, they seem to imply that artefacts do have their own reality, for if they did not, how could they affect social interactions?[4] Thus Bijker argues that:

> *society is not determined by technology, nor is technology determined by society. Both emerge as two sides of the sociotechnical coin during the construction processes of artefacts, facts, and relevant social groups.* (Bijker, 1993, p125)

The analogy with sides of coins suggests a symmetry between the social and the technical, and that they should each be treated in the same way. This is the method of 'actor-network theory', in which non-human artefacts and humans are regarded alike as 'actants' in the same sociotechnical realm.[5]

Actor-network theory may be a useful methodological tool: in not presupposing a boundary between the social and the technological it can shed light on technological change in a way that emphasizes the inter-relationality of people and artefacts. However, adherence to the symmetry principles may hide as much as it reveals. Thus in a study of attempts to tackle the problems of over-fishing of scallops in St Brieuc Bay, Michel Callon rigorously uses the same terms, such as negotiation, representatives and enrolment, with respect to fishermen and to scallops (Callon, 1986). The researchers, says Callon, negotiated with the representatives of fishermen and with representatives of scallop larvae, the latter being the larvae who, in the initial trial, anchored on collectors intended to protect them from predators and ocean currents. However, both negotiations failed to 'enrol' fishermen or scallops: after the initial trial period the scallop larvae did not anchor on the collectors; the scallops that had been collected in the initial trial and were growing in the bottom of the bay were raided one night by a group of fishermen.

These failures to enrol were very different matters in the two cases, differences that are obscured by the use of the same terms. In the case of the scallops we can only explain the fact that in later years scallop larvae did not anchor on the collectors by saying that the conditions were not the same as those during the original experiments in which the 'representatives' of the scallop larvae had anchored on the collectors, even if we cannot determine what the relevant differences in conditions are. In the case of the fishermen the failure to enrol the fishermen was not due to any difference between the conditions of the raiders and those of the fishermen's representatives who negotiated with the researchers, but to either the breaking of promises or the failure to elicit such promises. Contrary to the impression given by Callon, it is not possible to 'negotiate' with scallops and sea currents in the same way as employers negotiate with unions, or researchers with the representatives of fishermen. Negotiation implies that both parties can have a concept of the future, can evaluate different possible futures and can make promises with respect to their future actions. Scallops and sea currents cannot do any of these.

At the same time as attributing human capacities to non-human objects, the accounts of actor-network theory strip human actors of important aspects of their agency. What counts as an actant is 'an *effect generated by a network of heterogeneous, interacting, materials*' (Law, 1992, p383, emphasis in original) and actants are said to act when the effect of the set of relations that constitutes the node extends to other nodes in the network. There is no difference between causal agency – which is revealed by perceptible effects – and rational agency, where the agent not only causes an effect, but has the capacity to make decisions about whether or not to take a particular course of action. The rational agent, but not the merely causal agent, can be held morally responsible for its actions. The problems with actor-network theory is that doors appear to have as much agency as human beings, and therefore to be equally responsible for the state of affairs (Latour, 1995). This runs the danger of absolving human agents of responsibility, in a similar way to the technological determinist view that technological development is an automatic, autonomous process. Symmetry is thus not something that should be striven for – not between artefacts and human agents, nor between different human beings. A child is not as responsible for their actions as an adult, and those at the margins of society do not have as much influence over technology (though they may be as much affected by it) as those at the centre.

Technology as a Contingent Social Structure

A rather more subtle version of technological determinism than that of Ellul, or of popular myth, is represented by the work of Langdon Winner. His 1977 book *Autonomous Technology* is in many ways a critical exposition of and response to Ellul's work. In it Winner points out that the idea that technological development is an autonomous process can, contrary to Ellul's intentions, result in technology being seen as an 'overwhelmingly powerful destiny with the moral obligations of service and obedience' (Winner, 1977, p51). Winner's conclusion is that technological change is better described by the notion of drift rather than determinism. It is not 'a law-bound process grinding to an inevitable conclusion', but 'a variety of currents of innovation moving in a number of directions toward highly uncertain destinations' (Winner, 1977, p88).

Although we consciously and deliberately choose to use particular technologies, these decisions relate only to their immediate benefits, not to their wider consequences. New technologies have 'lives of their own': they find applications undreamt of by their inventors, call forth new inventions and open up new possibilities, which people may respond to in various ways. These responses in their turn may lead to changes in patterns of travel and social interactions, demands for new infrastructure, or the closure of industries. The result can be a radical change to social structure. One example Winner gives is the effect of snowmobiles on the social structure of the Skolt Lapps of Finland. The snowmobile was introduced in the 1960s and its use caused far reaching changes in Lapp society: it changed the relationship between the Lapps and their reindeer and tied them into a money economy. What had been a highly egalitarian society rapidly became non-egalitarian and hierarchical. The Lapps chose to use the snowmobile, but they did not choose the changes that just 'happened' as the community made a place for it (Winner, 1977, pp86–88).

A technology does not exist in isolation, but requires the conditions needed for its operation – including people who behave in the right way towards it, appropriate resources, and the other technologies that are required for its functioning. In some instances the presence of the 'conditions' – a supply of electricity for domestic lighting, for example – then leads to the invention of technologies which make use of those conditions – a huge range of domestic electrical gadgets. In other cases the supporting conditions have been provided by society following the invention and uptake of a technology: the invention and use of cars has demanded massive investment in road infrastructure, as well as oil refineries, oil tankers (with the oil spills which result when these go aground), and the exploration and extraction of oil in new territories. Winner argues that the transformation required by a technological system occurs prior to any 'use' – it is a consequence of the construction and operating design of the system, before it is used for anything. Technology thus structures and orders human life and activity, and we need to enquire into the structures of technologies, not merely their uses (Winner, 1977, p224).

Winner argues that technology is political because it decides many of the issues that have traditionally been thought to be the prerogative of political decision making: whether power is dispersed or centralized, the best size for units of social organization, and what constitutes authority (Winner, 1986, p49). However, our orientation towards technology is characterized by 'pervasive ignorance and refusal to know, irresponsibility, and blind faith' (Winner, 1977, p314). We are 'passive sleepwalkers' when it comes to how technology reshapes our lives.

Waking up a sleepwalking population is perhaps what writers such as Andrew Feenberg and Richard Sclove are trying to do. Sclove argues that technologies are 'social structures' (Sclove, 1995) and Feenberg that they are contingent social products (Feenberg, 1991), but both acknowledge that they are generally not recognized as such. Making this recognition involves subjecting technology to the democratic decision making that we currently apply to non-technological social structures, such as laws and political institutions (Sclove, 1995; Feenberg, 1999).

Conclusions

The question 'What is technology?' does not appear to have a simple answer. Technology clearly involves knowledge of how to produce things, but it also encompasses the artefacts that are used in production and, to a lesser extent, those that are used for doing other things. Technology is a matter of doing, as well as a matter of things and knowledge, but I do not think it useful to think of technology as merely extending what we can do, as an extension of putative 'natural', pre-technological human capabilities. New technologies may change what is possible for us to do, they may make it easier or cheaper to do what could be done before, or they may solve problems that arose from the way things were previously done or not done. Technology is a means to all these things: to reducing the labour required to sustain human life, to producing new material goods, to making production more efficient. What a technology is and does may be different for different social groups, and the relative power of those groups often determines what a technology becomes.

However, closer inspection reveals that it is not sufficient to say that technology is simply a means to ends. First, the drive behind technological development is not always the desire to achieve a particular end; it may, as in the case of the internet, be internal to the technological development process itself. Second, the effect of a technology is not simply the achievement of a particular end, if one is intended. Not only are there unintended side-effects, like pollution, but the whole structure and pattern of life are affected by technology: how and where people work; the skills needed to find work; who a person sees in the course of everyday life; how people communicate with each other; upon whom or what people are dependent.

I do not think that modern technology is different in this regard from older forms of technology: technology has always structured human life. The rapid pace of technological change is perhaps a recent phenomenon that brings its own problems. There may also be a distinctive pattern to modern technology: it is not concerned with the particular, with making specific unique items, but with producing standard, uniform products – general things that can be sold as commodities in markets.

The everyday word that best encompasses that which orders and structures human life is the word 'world'. The world orders and structures human life, is what we inhabit with others, is the outcome of the activity of past and present generations, and can be changed. Thus Winner suggests that the question we should ask of technology is 'What kind of world are we making?' (Winner, 1986, p13), and Graham that 'improvements' brought about by technology are only improvements in so far as they make for a better world (Graham 1999, p55). To change technology is thus to change the world.

In the next chapter I propose that we should think of technology as 'world-building' and suggest two definitions of technology. For this idea of technology to give guidance on how we should assess technology we need to have an idea of what the world should be like, or at least the principles by which it should be judged. We then need to consider what properties technologies must have if they are to make that world a better place.

Notes

1   One could argue that works of art may be 'used' – for educational purposes, for example. We can, nonetheless, distinguish between works of art and items produced primarily for their utility, and the latter are more technological than the former.

2   Thus the hydroelectric power plant on the Rhine turns the river into a water-power supplier. Heidegger asks us to contrast 'The Rhine' revealed by the power plant with 'The Rhine' revealed by a Hölderin hymn of that name (an art work) (Heidegger, 1954, p297).

3   This is similar to the analysis made by Mitcham: in the ancient Greek concept *techne* was orientated towards particulars, about making a particular thing, out of particular matter, matter that could not be completely known by reason, using skills that also could not be fully articulated. In contrast, modern 'making activities' are about the 'efficient production of many things of the same kind in order to make money' (Mitcham, 1994, p123).

4   They may say, of course, that the artefact is simply the effect of social relations, so that it is not actually the artefact that affects social interactions, but the social relations it embodies.

5   For various perspectives on actor-network theory see Law and Hassard (1999).

References

Aristotle, *Metaphysics*, trans. H. Tredennick (1933), W. Heinemann, London

Aristotle, *Nicomachean Ethics*, trans. T. Irwin, Second Edition (1999), Hackett, Indianapolis, IN

Beniger, J. (1986) *The Control Revolution*, Harvard University Press, Cambridge, MA

Bijker, W. (1993) 'Do not despair: There is life after constructivism', *Science, Technology and Human Values*, vol 18, no.1, pp113–138

Bijker, W. (1995) *Of Bicycles, Bakelite, and Bulbs: Towards a Theory of Sociotechnical Change*, MIT Press, Cambridge, MA

Borgmann, A. (1984) *Technology and the Character of Contemporary Life: A Philosophical Inquiry*, University of Chicago Press, Chicago, IL

Bunge, M. (1972) 'Toward a philosophy of technology', in C. Mitcham and R. Mackey (eds) *Philosophy and Technology*, Free Press, New York

Callon, M. (1986) 'Some elements of a sociology of translation: Domestication of the scallops and the fishermen of St Brieuc Bay', in J. Law (ed) *Power, Action and Belief*, Routledge and Keegan Paul, London, pp196–233

Cardwell, D. (1994) *The Fontana History of Technology*, Fontana, London

Commoner, B. (1971) *The Closing Circle*, Knopf, New York

Ellul, J. (1964) *The Technological Society*, trans. J. Wilkinson, Vintage, New York

Feenberg, A. (1991) *Critical Theory of Technology*, Oxford University Press, New York

Feenberg, A. (1999) *Questioning Technology*, Routledge, London

Feibleman, J. K. (1966) 'Pure science, applied science, and technology: An attempt at definitions', in H. Cairns (ed) *The Two-Story World*, Rinehart and Winston, New York

Graham, G. (1999) *The Internet: A Philosophical Inquiry*, Routledge, New York

Heidegger, M. (1954) *The Question Concerning Technology*, trans. W. Lovitt, reprinted in D. F. Krell (ed) (1977) *Martin Heidegger, Basic Writings*, Harper & Row, New York, pp287–317

Ingold, T. (2000) *The Perception of the Environment, Essays in Livelihood, Dwelling and Skill*, Routledge, London

Jarvie, I. C. (1972) 'Technology and the structure of knowledge', in C. Mitcham and R. Mackey (eds) *Philosophy and Technology*, Free Press, New York

Kapp, E. (1877) *Grundlinien einer Philosophie der Technik: Zur Entstehungsgeschichte der Cultur aus neuen Gesichtspunkten* (*Fundamentals of a Philosophy of Technology: On the Genesis of Culture from a New Point of View*), Westerman, Braunschweig

Kline, R. and Pinch, T. (1999) 'The social construction of technology', in D. MacKenzie and J. Wajcman (eds) *The Social Shaping of Technology*, Open University Press, Buckingham

Latour, B. (1995) 'A door must be either open or shut: A little philosophy of techniques', trans. C. Cussins, in A. Feenberg and A. Hannay (eds) *The Politics of Knowledge*, Indiana University Press, Bloomington and Indianapolis

Law, J. (1992) 'Notes on the theory of the actor-network: ordering, strategy, and heterogeneity', *Systems Practice*, vol 5, no 4, pp379–393

Law, J. and Hassard, J. (1999) *Actor Network Theory and After*, Blackwell, Oxford

Levinson, P. (1988) 'Mind at large: Knowing in the technological age', *Research in Philosophy and Technology*, supplement 2

McGinn, R. E. (1978) 'What is technology?', *Research in Philosophy and Technology*, vol I, pp179–197

McLuhan, M. (1964) *Understanding Media: The Extensions of Man*, Routledge and Keegan Paul, London

Mesthene, E. (1972) 'Technology and wisdom', in C. Mitcham and R. Mackey (eds) *Philosophy and Technology*, Free Press, New York

Mitcham, C. (1994) *Thinking Through Technology: The Path between Engineering and Philosophy*, The University of Chicago Press, Chicago, IL and London

Ortega y Gasset, J. (1972) 'Thoughts on technology', in C. Mitcham and R. Mackey (eds) *Philosophy and Technology*, Free Press, New York

Plato, *Timaeus*, trans. H. D. P. Lee (1965), Penguin Books, London

Rotenstreich, N. (1967) 'Technology and politics', *International Philosophical Quarterly*, vol VII, no 2

Schon, D. (1967) *Technology and Change*, Delacourte Press, New York

Sclove, R. (1995) *Democracy and Technology*, Guilford Press, New York

Winner, L. (1977) *Autonomous Technology: Technics-out-of-Control as a Theme in Political Thought*, MIT Press, Cambridge, MA

Winner, L. (1986) *The Whale and the Reactor: A Search for Limits in an Age of High Technology*, MIT Press, Cambridge, MA

Winner, L. (1993) 'Upon opening the black box and finding it empty: Social constructivism and the philosophy of technology', *Science, Technology and Human Values*, vol 18, no 3, pp362–378

Zimmerman, M. (1979) 'Heidegger and Marcuse: Technology as ideology', *Research in Philosophy and Technology*, vol 2, pp245–261

3
Technology as World-Building

The World and Technology

The previous chapter concluded with the idea that technological change is change to the world. In this chapter I will set out a view of technology as 'world-building'. I use the term 'building' rather than 'making' because it suggests that what is made is something that we inhabit, rather than simply use, and that it endures, probably beyond the lifetime of the builders. Buildings, rather than machines, are the paradigm technological products, and architects, rather than engineers, the paradigm technologists. If a 'definition' is needed, I suggest the following two (two seem to be needed as technology is not a word that is used in just one simple way):

1 Technology is how we add things to the world; and
2 Technology is the things that we have added to the world that we use.

The how in the first definition includes techniques, knowledge, skills and processes, as well as tools and machines. The things are material things themselves or are embodied or realized in material things. Thus the internet, it might be argued, is not a material thing, but it certainly needs a whole host of material artefacts to exist – computers, modems, phone lines, as well as power stations, pylons and transformers. It is embodied in material artefacts, though like a novel that is embodied in the material book, a description of those material artefacts does not give a full account of what it is. The restriction of technology to things that have some materiality as artefacts preserves the connection found in everyday understanding between technology and material artefacts. We live in a world with a great many artefacts, though I am not claiming that the world consists only of material artefacts. Using Richard Sclove's terminology, the non-technological social structures of laws, political and economic institutions, languages, and systems of cultural beliefs are also part of the world (Sclove, 1995, p23). Like technology they provide 'a framework for public order that will endure over many generations' (Winner, 1986, p29).

Because technology is how we add things to the world, the common idea that technology is a means to ends has some truth in it. However, it is a narrow truth that applies only to the production process itself. In that technology forms part of the world that we inhabit it is not merely means. Unlike the production process, which can be judged in terms of how well it serves the end of producing a product, instrumental, means–ends thinking is not appropriate when thinking of technology as part of the world. How we should think about technology 'as world' is the main topic of this chapter.

The ideas in this chapter owe much to the work of Hannah Arendt, in particular her book *The Human Condition* (Arendt, 1958).[1] Arendt emphasized the publicness of the world: it is always to some extent public in the sense of being shared by more than one person. The things of the world are not like private thoughts and feelings; rather they appear to and can be experienced by multiple people, from a plurality of perspectives. My claim that technology is world-building therefore means that technology is no mere private matter, but is always of public concern.

The World and the Earth

Before going on to discuss what sort of world we should be building with our technology, we need to note the difference between the world and the earth.[2] Although these terms are sometimes used interchangeably there are important differences and the distinction between them will be critical to my argument. Note first that we could not speak of 'earth-building', and the things that I have mentioned above as being part of the world (material artefacts, laws, institutions, languages, systems of beliefs) are all products of human activity. Second, we have organizations such as Friends of the Earth and Earth First! that are concerned about the natural environment. 'Friends of the World' or 'World First!' would have very different connotations.

The world, in the sense that I intend to use it, thus refers to things that are produced by humans, that together form a home for human life. Arendt talks of the things of the world both separating and relating individuals, as a table both separates and relates those who sit around it (Arendt, 1958, pp52–53). It 'gathers us together and yet prevents our falling over each other, so to speak' (Arendt, 1958, p52). The world is the place that human individuals inhabit with others, providing both a context and a structure for our relationships with each other. Human identity is a matter of a person's place in the world.

Being 'produced' can be interpreted in two ways. The most straightforward is that things produced by humans are the product of human work: they result from a production process that starts with raw materials and an idea in the mind of the producer and ends with a finished product (an artefact). That finished product then forms part of the world, and has an existence that is independent of that of its producer (the producer may die but the product endures). The other way recognizes that how things appear to us is the product of our minds as well as of what our senses receive. This derives from the philosophy of Immanuel Kant: we have no access to things as they are (the noumena), because how things appear to us (the phenomena) depends on our categories of thought as well as on what is given to the senses by the noumena. In this sense natural things such as trees, rivers and mountains, or at least their appearance to us, are part of the human world because how they appear is constructed by us from what is given to our senses, just as we construct buildings with materials provided by the earth. What appears to us, and how, may depend on our artefacts (things that are part of the world in the first sense): microscopes, Geiger counters, thermometers, and a myriad of other detectors all reveal aspects of the noumena which are not apparent without them.

The earth is what is given, as opposed to that which is produced by humans. It can be thought of as being the natural environment, including all living things and rocks, soils, sea and air. In the short term (in other words from the perspective of a human in the world), the earth is characterized by cyclical movement: the basic elements of life, such as carbon, nitrogen and water, move from one medium to another and back again. The organisms that inhabit the earth go through 'endless cycles of growth and decay, one generation of animals or plants replacing the previous generation in a natural movement that is indifferent to individual specimens' (Canovan, 1992, p106). As far as the earth is concerned it no more matters that the individual people alive now are different from those alive 100 years ago, than that the ants I find in my garden this year are different individuals from the ones that were there last year. We are all simply members of one species, our differences matters of variations in biology, not matters of personal identity or moral excellence. Hence 'death is no respecter of persons': the biological processes that result in the death of an individual are indifferent to the status of that individual within the human community.[3] For the human individual in the world there is a linear progress from birth to death, a start and an end to life. But on the earth 'life goes on'. Death is simply the replacement of one form of life with another: the life of the herbivore is replaced by that of the carnivore who kills it and the scavengers who finish off the carcass; the life of the tree with that of the beetles and fungi which degrade the wood.

Making a Home Fit for Human Life on Earth

As the world is built by humans it is obviously within human capacities to change it. This is what technological change does, and a key question is how we are to judge whether those changes are for the better or worse. To make these judgements we need some principles that can be applied, or some idea of what sort of world we should be building. I suggest that our goal should be to make the world a fit home for human life on earth. The question that then arises is 'What sort of home do we need?' I propose to answer this question by considering what sort of beings we are, and therefore what sort of world we need to live in if we are to flourish and have at least the possibility of a good life.

There seem to me to be three aspects of human existence that are relevant. The first is that we are biological organisms, materially dependent on our environment: we are part of the earth. Like other animals, we have needs for food and shelter. And because we are social animals we need the presence of other human beings. Human life is as liable to extinction as that of other organisms: we are vulnerable to being harmed by a wide range of physical, chemical and biological agents. Because we are part of the earth our consumption of food and excretion of wastes is part of the natural cycles of the earth, though the ways we currently obtain food and dispose of our wastes often disrupt or dislocate these cycles (discussed later in this chapter). Because we need to consume food we have to labour to produce it: by tilling the soil, tending animals, gathering, cooking. Like life on earth itself, this activity of labour has neither beginning nor end.

The earth provides the raw materials for the building of the world. The world protects us from the ravages of nature: we build houses to give us shelter and make clothes to protect our skin from the sun or cold. While as biological organisms we are part of the earth, as fabricators of a human world we wrest natural materials from the cycles of the earth and try to hold at bay the natural processes that lead to their decay and disintegration, so that what we build lasts. Holding natural processes at bay requires further labour: the never-ending task of cleaning and maintenance, without which our buildings and other artefacts would become the substrate for the growth of bacteria and fungi, finally becoming overgrown by vegetation as they sink into decay.

In recent decades we have not only been using the materials provided by the earth, but making new matter: new elements (by nuclear fission) and new chemicals (by organic synthesis). This new matter takes part in the processes of the earth: it enters our bodies, soils, the water and air, where it interacts with the natural chemicals it encounters, transforming them and itself. Its novelty means that the processes in which it takes part can be considered to be 'new natural processes' (Arendt, 1968, p58). The complexity of the environments in which these take place means that there is great uncertainty as to their outcomes.

The second aspect of human existence is that we are moral beings: persons responsible for our actions. As part of the earth we are a species of animal among other species, but as moral beings we are, as far as we know, unique.[4] A person is responsible for their actions to the extent that the person, rather than 'the system', economic forces, history or nature, is the cause of what that person does. A person's actions reveal something of *who* they are – the person that they are, whether kind and generous or spiteful and mean – rather than the biological organism that they are – their skin colour, blood group or genotype. That revelation is always to other moral persons, who may then act in response. Human actions thus start boundless and unpredictable processes of action and reaction: we can never say that the consequences of our actions are complete, let alone predict what they will be. Actions result in the formation of relationships between people, in people getting to know each other for who they are. They always take place in a context – a world of things, institutions, knowledge and so forth – that is shared by the interacting persons. The nature of this shared world affects people's scope for action – the choices available to them and the power they have to change things – and the relationships that they form.

The third aspect of human existence is that human beings have some sort of aesthetic sense, and make aesthetic judgements. Things appear to us as beautiful or ugly, not merely as useful or functional (Arendt, 1958, p173). One could, of course, have a long debate about whether something is beautiful rather than ugly, but it is generally agreed that, other things being equal, the beautiful is to be preferred to the ugly.

These three aspects of human existence mean that:

1   the human world must not significantly change the existing natural processes and cycles of the earth since, as biological organisms, we are part of the earth;
2   the world should be a place for responsible human action; and
3   the world should be beautiful rather than ugly.

There is a hierarchy to these criteria. First, if there is to be human life at all, in any form, then the natural systems and processes of the earth must not be significantly changed from those that gave rise to human life, as the chances are that humans would not be adapted to the new conditions and, like most other species before us, would become extinct. Second, if humans are to have a life worth living, one in which they are able to exercise their capacity for responsible action, then the human-constructed world must enable rather than repress such action. Finally, if humans are to take pleasure in their world, to love and care for it, then that world should be beautiful rather than ugly.

The third of these criteria obviously means that technology should produce and be constituted by things that are beautiful rather than ugly. The other two need rather more examination to uncover how they translate into features that technology should have. These features are not necessarily essential features of all technology, rather they are dimensions along which we should consider technology when deciding whether it contributes to making the world a fit home for human life on earth.

Creating a World that does not Endanger the Earth

Our consumption of food and the burning of biomass (such as wood) are part of the natural cycles of the earth (and because they are consumed food and fuel do not need to be durable). So too, in a more extended way, is our use of natural materials to build the world. Materials such as cotton and wool, wood and metal are liable to decay or corrode, even if they are part of artefacts. When we stop actively protecting these materials by keeping them dry or cleaning, natural processes take hold and the materials are returned to natural cycles.

Many current problems are caused by dislocations to these natural cycles: materials are taken from one place but discharged in another where they cannot be transformed in the way they should be and thus cause pollution. For example, when cattle are fed in lots with food imported from elsewhere the excretions of the cows are not able to replenish the soil that grows the plants that feed them. Instead the excretions pollute water supplies, and where the plants are grown artificial fertilizers have to be used. These do not provide the humus to maintain soil structure so soils are vulnerable to erosion. In burning fossil fuels, formed from vegetation that grew millions of years ago, we are, in effect, stepping outside the contemporary carbon cycle, simply putting more and more carbon dioxide into the atmosphere at a rate much faster than current vegetation can take it out. This action from the outside, as it were, is increasing atmospheric concentrations of carbon dioxide which in turn causes climate change. Altering the effects we are having on the cycles of the earth requires changes to the world: the use of different technologies, the construction of different infrastructures.

Obtaining the raw materials from which we make artefacts often involves being violent to the earth: the felling of trees, mining of ores or extraction of oil are all inevitably destructive and damage-causing activities. We can, however, reduce this damage by making our artefacts last, so we do not need so much raw material. This will also reduce the waste resulting from discarded products. Technology should therefore produce and consist of durable things.

These concerns, which are about reducing the environmental impact of technology, can be seen in the discourse of sustainable development, which talks of the need to reduce resource use, increase energy efficiency and use renewable rather than non-renewable sources of energy. Sustainability is at heart about how to live in a way that can last – where the demands made on natural systems do not exceed the capacity of those systems to meet those demands indefinitely. There is, however, a way in which we act as if we were outside the earth's natural cycles which is little recognized in sustainable development discourse. This is through the use of materials that are unnatural and therefore are not consumed by the natural processes of the earth. Such materials, though not necessarily the objects made of them, are often not destroyed by natural processes, so they create a new type of waste problem, which to solve we need to set up our own systems of recycling, systems that can never be complete and capture all the synthetic material. The non-captured material has to go somewhere: for example, plastic fragments and synthetic fibres are accumulating in the marine environment, where they are ingested by marine organisms (Thompson et al, 2004). Where these unnatural materials interact with natural systems, they in effect start new processes in nature – processes that would not occur were it not for the novel materials made by humans. These processes have all the uncertainty and boundlessness of processes within the realm of human affairs (which is constituted by human relationships) started by human action, but they take place in and change the natural earth, rather than just the human world and human relationships.

Creating a World that is a Place for Responsible Action

The human capacity for action can be thought of as the capacity that a person (a moral being) has to cause things. As moral beings, people are more than just living bodies that can react to stimuli. If someone hits me below the knee and my foot swings out and knocks over a glass on the floor, my foot, but not me as a moral being broke the glass. I as a person cannot be held responsible: it was not an action of mine, simply a reaction of my body. At the other extreme, I as a person can be held responsible if I tell a lie when I could just as easily not have done so. The fact that an action can consist of speech shows that actions do not necessarily affect the physical disposition of matter, rather they affect relationships between people. Action in this sense would not be possible if there were not other people who are like me in that they are also moral beings, but who are different from me, each having a unique history and perspective on the world. Action would also not be possible if those people never knew of what I did. Action is always potential interaction. Even if other people are not present when an action is performed, it is the fact that there are other people who may recount it, and perhaps pass some sort of judgement on it, that makes what I do an action.

Actions take place in the world. As discussed above, the world provides both a context and a structure for our relationships with each other. Thus the technologies that form part of the world affect where we go, how we get there and whom we see and communicate with in the course of our everyday lives. They determine the possibilities for interaction and thus action. For example, the car and the television are implicated in Robert Putnam's study of the decline in social interaction and civic participation in the US (Putnam, 2000). The car and the television are both technologies of the private sphere: the television because it keeps people at home, increasingly watching alone; the car because it means that even when people go out they do not encounter others while travelling. Designing urban areas on the basis that people travel by car results in a spatially fragmented world, where people often live in one suburb, work in another and shop in a third. Not only do people spend more and more time 'shuttling alone in metal boxes among the vertices of [their] private triangles' (Putnam, 2000, p212), but the sense of identity that the inhabitants of a place have with that place is weakened by their lives being spread over several different places. The urban sprawl that the car makes possible is thus harmful to civic life, as well as to the environment (Dagger, 2003).

Technology should facilitate genuine human interaction as this is a precondition for responsible action. The responsibility of persons for their actions is a matter of fact, but responsibility is also a virtue. As I discuss in Chapter 9, acting responsibly involves recognizing that you are the cause of what you do, being prepared to be held to account for the consequences of your actions and acting in the interests of what you are responsible for. If people are to do this, the world must provide space for each individual to take responsibility for themselves, for others and for the world.

This space is a matter of being able to choose to do what is right.[5] It is possible, unfortunately, for the world to be such that only wrong choices are available, so the only choice is between lesser or greater evils. This is the situation when the dominant technologies that individuals cannot help using if they are to be part of society are ones that cause significant damage. Building designs that make air conditioning essential[6] and public infrastructure designed for high-energy-consuming modes of transport both effectively force people into making choices that involve the substantial consumption of fossil fuels, leading to climate change. Deciding not to use air conditioning or drive a car in such circumstances is a difficult, heroic decision. Decisions about technology made in the past affect the choices available to us today, and, as David Nye points out, there was nothing inevitable about these past decisions. Although cars are found in both the US and The Netherlands, in many parts of the former individuals have no choice but to travel by car, but they did have a choice of different modes of transport 100 years ago when the train, bicycle, horse and trolley bus were all viable options for many journeys. In contrast, in The Netherlands a real choice of different modes of transport has been preserved: many journeys can be made by mass transit or the bicycle as well as by car (Nye, 2006, pp219–220).

In the development of technologies there is often a phase when lots of different possibilities are open, but after a while one particular type becomes dominant and other options are not realistically available because the costs of switching to them are too high once everyone has adopted the dominant option. The classic case of this technological 'lock-in' is the qwerty keyboard – the keyboard layout that has now become standard, even though one could type faster on alternative layouts (once one had learned to use them). Other examples are the VHS video recorder, which won the marketing war over the technically superior Sony

Betamax system, and Microsoft software (though open source software is perhaps mounting a challenge) (Nye, 2006, pp50–51).

Our choices about the world are never entirely open because the world that is built by technology outlasts its creators. So we never start with a blank sheet of paper, but with the choices made by our predecessors. What we have to decide is how to continue the story of the past into the future. The endurance of artefacts, social practices and institutions gives the world a degree of stability, and although this may lead some to feel trapped by choices others have made (Nye, 2006, p20), that stability is important if the world is to provide a home for human life. Think what life would be like if the institutions of government were changed every year, or if the furniture in your home was thrown out and replaced with new stuff, differently arranged, every day. Negotiating such a world so that one could act in it and form stable relationships with others would be very difficult. The existence of meaningful things that last for longer than our own lifetimes provides a connection to the past and the future. These things give us a sense of historical continuity that is important for the identity of individuals and communities. They help us to understand who we are. Our technology should therefore produce at least some such things that are made to last both by being made of durable quality and through being designed so that they can be taken care of by regular cleaning, repair and maintenance. Our technological choices should acknowledge the past, not try to erase it, and ensure that what is of value and significance is taken forward into the future.[7]

Human action is always to some extent unpredictable; technology should allow for this unpredictability. With technologies such as nuclear power and large chemical manufacturing plants, the consequences if people do not follow the rules and act in unexpected ways are potentially catastrophic: they are highly risky technologies. The scale of the hazards associated with them legitimates authoritarian enforcement of the rules, which in turn erodes civil rights and threatens the basis of democratic politics (Beck, 1992, p80). Rather than being designed for infallible humans who always follow instructions, technology should be designed for humans as they are, and allow for them to make mistakes or act in unexpected ways, sometimes maliciously, without the consequences being catastrophic. Catastrophic is obviously a relative concept here that depends on the situation: in some contexts serious injury or a single death is catastrophic, while in others the loss even of many lives is not.[8] A measure of the degree of catastrophe is perhaps the ease with which the agent (the human individual, local community or nation state, depending on the situation) would be able to cope and respond positively in the situation. Rather than aiming for the unachievable ideal of total prediction and control, we should aim to preserve this ability to cope and to respond even to the worst possible outcome. We should thus choose technologies where the worst possible outcome is something that we would be able to cope with.

The impact of risky technologies, from cars to chemicals, is not merely the harm they may cause. Even if they in fact cause no harm directly, their presence in the world means that people have to change the way they behave to avoid harm. Fast traffic on a street, for example, endangers the lives of pedestrians and means the street can no longer be a place for convivial human interaction. Pollution of the Arctic by persistent organic chemicals means it may no longer be safe for the Inuit to consume Arctic wildlife (Colborn et al, 1996). This change to the nature of the street and the Arctic wildlife is independent of whether any pedestrians are actually injured by traffic or Inuit harmed by chemicals in their food. The fact that pedestrians and Inuit change their behaviour to avoid injury is enough.

An important factor that can limit the scope for individual and collective action is economic dependence. The individual who is not economically independent can be forced into certain courses of action by the need to earn their living. There is an important difference here between dependence on our natural environment (entailed in sources of economic support that rely on natural processes) and economic dependence on other people or human institutions. While with the former we have to do certain things if our activities are to be successful (such as plant seeds in the spring rather than the summer), whether we are successful or not at obtaining a living does not depend on our political opinions or support for one person over another. In contrast, with the latter there is the possibility that our livelihood will be withdrawn in response to our actions (such as trying to organize a trade union). Technological development has often made livelihoods based on the utilization of natural products and processes unviable, and in their place people have become dependent on human institutions.[9] This economic dependence is a strong disincentive to political opinions and actions that are critical of such institutions and those in control of them.

Conclusions

Technology is world-building: technology is how we make the material aspects of the world we inhabit and the resulting artefacts that are put to use. This account of technology is true to the everyday use of the word in that it preserves the idea that technology is about material things and in particular artefacts that do things (such as machines). It clearly does not just apply to modern technology: for as long as humans have made artefacts there has been a *how* they did this. Because technology in part constitutes the world that we live in, however, it is more than simply means. Decisions about technology are decisions about the world; and since the world is always to some extent public in the sense of being shared by a group of people, so technology is a matter of public concern.

How are we to make decisions about the world? I have suggested that our goal should be to build a world that is a fit home for human life on earth. Humans are biological beings and moral beings and they make aesthetic judgements. The world should therefore not damage the systems of the earth because as biological beings we are part of the earth; it should be a place for responsible human action, and it should be beautiful rather than ugly.

From my discussion of what these criteria mean for technology, I suggest the following as principles on which more concrete policies to inform decisions about technology could be based. These are not rules for decision making, but indicators of what should be considered in deciding whether a technology helps to make the world a fit home for human life on earth.

1   technology should use materials that can be incorporated into the natural cycles of the earth without changing those cycles or starting new 'natural' processes that would not exist without human action;
2   technology should not dislocate natural cycles but enable human activities to be accommodated within them;
3   technology should facilitate human interaction;
4   technology should allow for human unpredictability and fallibility – of designers, engineers and risk assessors, as well as of operators – and not lead to catastrophic consequences if people make mistakes or act maliciously;
5   technology should not make the world more risky, and thus restrict what it is safe for people to do;
6   technology should enable responsible individual action and should not enforce irresponsibility or increase dependency (of some people on others or on institutions and organizations); and
7   technology should produce and consist of durable, beautiful things.

How does this view of technology compare with that implicit in contemporary policy debates? In the next chapter I examine the current dominant view of technology, as exemplified by UK government policy. In that policy technology is intimately related to science and to the economy: the role of science is technological innovation and the role of technological innovation the enhancement of economic competitiveness. As a result, new technologies are frequently seen as being a matter of science, privileging scientific understandings over other types of knowledge and narrowing legitimate concerns to those that can be addressed by science. The perceived relationship between technology and the economy means that technological innovation is promoted indiscriminately, without concern for how new technology will change the world. In the context of the view of technology presented in this chapter, how should we conceive the relationships between science and technology and between technology and the economy?

Notes

1   For an account of the relevant aspects of Arendt's thought, including a discussion of the distinctions she makes between the human activities of labour, work and action, see Chapman (2004).
2   For a fuller account of the world/earth distinction see Chapman (2007).
3   Though there may be differences between people of different social strata that are biologically relevant, such as differences in nutrition, exposure to pollution, amount of exercise, etc., it is these factors, not the social status itself, that causes differences in life expectancy between different groups.
4   Whether we are unique or not is not really critical to the argument. Certain other animal species may be moral beings. The point is that humans definitely are.
5   Note that in any particular situation there is almost always more than one right thing that can be done, these different options realizing different goods. To have choice, wrong options do not have to be available – indeed there is probably no benefit to be had from having them available – though their existence cannot be eliminated as they include the option of not making an effort, this probably being the most common way in which we do not do the right thing. The things that are right for any one individual are often more limited than what, objectively, are within the range of possible right choices – so choosing what is the right thing for me reveals who I am.

6   See Shove (2003) for how the traditional design of houses in the US, with large eaves and porches to make the summer heat bearable, has given way to houses designed to be cooled by air conditioning systems. This entails a significant use of energy for cooling, as well as reducing the social interaction that formerly took place between neighbours on porches.

7   See discussion of the stability of the world in Chapman (2004).

8   The film *The Fog of War* (2004) starts with Robert McNamara, US Secretary of Defense in the 1960s, saying that military commanders always make mistakes and errors of judgement which can lead to the loss of hundreds of thousands of lives. However, with modern nuclear weapons those mistakes would destroy nations. In the extreme situation of war it is possible to regard the loss of many lives as not catastrophic, but destruction of the nation fighting the war is.

9   For example, the replacement of wool by synthetic fibres makes the independent way of life of the sheep farmer less viable.

References

Arendt, H. (1958) *The Human Condition*, University of Chicago Press, Chicago, IL

Arendt, H. (1968) *Between Past and Future*, Viking Compass Edition with additional text, New York

Beck, U. (1992) *Risk Society: Towards a New Modernity*, trans. M. Ritter, Sage Publications, London

Canovan, M. (1992) *Hannah Arendt: A Reinterpretation of her Political Thought*, Cambridge University Press, Cambridge

Chapman, A. (2004) 'Technology as world building', *Ethics, Place and Environment*, vol 7, nos1–2, pp59–72

Chapman, A. (2007) 'The ways that nature matters: The world and the Earth in the thought of Hannah Arendt', *Environmental Values*, forthcoming

Colborn, T., Dumanoski, D. and Myers, J. P. (1996) *Our Stolen Future*, Little Brown and Company, London

Dagger, R. (2003) 'Stopping sprawl for the good of all: The case for civic environmentalism', *Journal of Social Philosophy*, vol 34, no 1, pp44–63

Nye, D. (2006) *Technology Matters: Questions to Live with*, MIT Press, Cambridge, MA

Putnam, R. (2000) *Bowling Alone: The Collapse and Revival of American Community*, Simon & Schuster, New York

Sclove, R. (1995) *Democracy and Technology*, Guilford Press, New York

Shove, E. (2003) *Comfort, Cleanliness and Convenience: The Social Organization of Normality*, Berg, Oxford

Thompson, R. C., Olsen, Y., Mitchell, R. P., Davis, A., Towland, S. J., John, A. W. G., McGonigle, D. and Russell, A. E. (2004) 'Lost at sea: Where is all the plastic?', *Science*, vol 304, p838

Winner, L. (1986) *The Whale and the Reactor: A Search for Limits in an Age of High Technology*, MIT Press, Cambridge, MA

4
Technology, Science and the Economy

Introduction

If we want to understand the view of technology that informs public decisions about technology in contemporary society, we need to look at government policy on technology. What we find is that policy is rarely about technology alone, but about 'science and technology', or 'science and innovation'. Scientific research is regarded as resulting in technological innovation and that innovation is considered essential for the competitiveness of the national economy. This raises questions about what science is, whether science is inherently technological and the role of science in technological innovation. Does the relationship between science and technology mean that science, like technology, should be subject to political control? What is the role of technological change in economic growth? How should we conceive the relationship between the economy and the world of which technology is a part?

In this chapter I start with an examination of two UK government White Papers on science and technology, one produced in 1993 by a Conservative Government (DTI, 1993) and the other in 2000 by a Labour Government (DTI, 2000). Both see technological development as an outcome of science and as essential for economic prosperity. I then critically examine the supposed relationships between science and technology and between technology and the economy. This leads first to an account of what science is and second to a critique of the priority given to the economy by government policy.

UK Government Policy on Science and Technology

The 1993 White Paper 'Realising our potential: A strategy for science, engineering and technology' (DTI, 1993) linked science and technology with free trade and prosperity: the prosperity of the UK, it claimed, has been based on free markets and on the application of science to tradable products (paragraph 1.2). This is even more the case today:

> The United Kingdom's competitive position rests increasingly on our capacity to trade in goods and services incorporating or produced by the latest science and technology. (DTI, 1993, paragraph 1.14)

In keeping with the Conservative Government's desire to minimize the role of government, the White Paper emphasized private funding of science (paragraph 2.20), but also that there should be greater links between industry and the scientific expertise of British Universities:

> *steps should be taken [...] to harness that strength in science and engineering to the creation of wealth in the United Kingdom by bringing it into closer and more systematic contact with those responsible for industrial and commercial decisions.*
> (DTI, 1993, paragraph 1.16)

Public spending on science is justified where the benefits of scientific research will 'accrue to society at large and the economy generally' (paragraph 1.4), where such research will contribute to 'improved public services and the quality of life' (paragraph 1.5) or where market forces do not work in a satisfactory manner, so that 'investments in commercial research and development which offer a good economic return to the nation' do not give such returns to the individual firm (paragraph 2.20).

The Labour Government's White Paper 'Excellence and opportunity – A science and innovation policy for the 21st century' (DTI, 2000) is based on the same assumptions about the relationship between science, technology and the economy as the 1993 White Paper produced by the Conservative Government. Science is 'a driving force for progress' (executive summary, paragraph 1) that 'feeds innovation' (executive summary, paragraph 3), so that 'science will soon breed new families of products and with them new global markets' (executive summary, paragraph 2). However, 'scientific breakthroughs are often not exploited to the full because universities and businesses operate at arm's length' (executive summary, paragraph 9). A difference is the greater emphasis placed by the Labour Government on the contribution 'scientific know-how' should be making to 'health care, public services and the environment', as well as to 'business and jobs' (chapter 1, paragraph 12).

A more significant difference between the two White Papers is that the 2000 document included a chapter on regulation – a topic that was not addressed at all in 1993. Regulation of the application of science is necessary if the public are to have confidence in the results of innovation. It is thus linked, along with competition policy, to the creation of markets for innovative products. Creating such markets 'is as vital as investing in basic research' (chapter 1, paragraph 15). For there to be a market for a new product, consumers must be prepared to buy it, and this is unlikely to happen if 'a new product seems to offer only minimal improvements to the quality of life or the range of choices available, at an unacceptably high level of risk' (chapter 4, paragraph 4). The response in the White Paper is two-pronged: benefits must be promoted and spread as widely and quickly as possible by a vigorous competition policy and the enlargement of markets (chapter 4, paragraphs 8–9) and risks from new technologies must be assessed. Risk assessment must be 'open to public scrutiny at every stage' because 'consumers will feel confident only if risks from new technologies are questioned and challenged in an open and informed way' (chapter 4, paragraph 17). If they know the risks, consumers can then make their own, informed decisions:

When consumers feel the risks and benefits are clear and properly assessed it is up to them to make their own judgements about whether to buy and how to use a product. Government cannot eliminate risk. But where Government does have a role is in assuring consumers that risks have been properly assessed and controlled, and in communicating those risks clearly and simply, and at the right time. (DTI, 2000, chapter 4, paragraph 16)

In buying and using new technologies, consumers are active parts of the innovation process. They often discover or create new uses for products not predicted by the original inventors: 'Active, intelligent and even creative consumers are a vital part of the cycle of innovation' (chapter 4, paragraph 2). Government policy to encourage this cycle needs to address consumers: 'The consumer's role in fuelling innovation has to be as effective as the other components of the process' (chapter 4, paragraph 3).

The government sees objections to new technologies as objections to science:

Consumers will support investment in science if it helps to deliver products they value. But, in addition, public confidence in the whole notion of science must be strong and well founded. People must feel that science is serving society and that it is properly regulated, open and accountable. The BSE crisis and the controversy over GM foods have raised questions about the value of scientific progress in society. [...] We need a more systematic and independent approach to satisfy public concerns about the risks created by scientific innovation. (DTI, 2000, chapter 1, paragraph 16)

The government does want people other than scientists to take part in the debate about risks from new technologies, but the subject matter of that debate is considered to be science, not technology:

science is too important to be left only to scientists. Their knowledge, and their assessment of risks, is only one dimension of the challenge for society. When science raises profound ethical and social issues, the whole of society needs to take part in the debate. (DTI, 2000, chapter 4, paragraph 27)

A further White Paper on enterprise, skills and innovation (DTI, 2001a), and a science and innovation strategy (DTI, 2001b) were produced by the Department of Trade and Industry (DTI) in 2001. These documents identify particular technologies that should be developed through government investment in research and development and in infrastructure to enable business to 'exploit new technologies and markets' (DTI, 2001a, paragraph 4.5). These technologies include genomics, e-science, nanotechnology, renewable energy, waste reduction, broadband internet connections and digital television. That the government regards scientific research and technological innovation as central to the UK's future prosperity was further demonstrated by the 'Science and innovation investment framework, 2004–2014' produced jointly by HM Treasury, the DTI and the Department of Education and Skills (DfES) in July 2004. This commits the government to increasing spending on science with the clear expectation that a better funded 'public science base' will benefit business research and development activities, increase innovation and thus make the UK economy more competitive on the global stage.

To conclude, there seem to be three main assumptions underlying government policy on science and technology:

1 that science leads to technological innovation, this being the primary role of science;
2 that technological innovation is inherently good, and continual innovation and uptake of new technology essential for economic prosperity; and
3 that public concerns about new technologies are about risks and are expressed through consumer choice. Thus the purpose of government assessing risks of new products becomes the provision of information to consumers so they can make informed decisions, thereby creating a more ideal market.

In the following sections I will principally focus on the first two of these assumptions. These are a matter of the relationships between science and technology and between technology and the economy. Is science inherently technological in the sense of leading inevitably to technological innovation? Is technology applied science? If so, does this mean that technology is within the domain of science? What is the relationship between technological change and economic prosperity? My arguments in Chapters 8 and 9 will challenge the third assumption.

Science and Technology

Is science technological?

Successive UK governments have seen the purpose of scientific research as being the creation of new technology. The implication is that scientific knowledge is not so much a matter of 'knowing-that' but of 'know-how': it is intrinsically technological. This is a widely held view, by critics as well as by supporters of science. Below I examine and criticize two versions of the idea that science is technological: that of the Frankfurt School theorists and that of Hans Jonas. From this examination I develop what may be termed a pluralist account of what science is, drawing on the work of Nancy Cartwright.

For the Frankfurt School theorists, science is a matter of seeking to manipulate and control the object of scientific investigation. However, rather than welcoming science as the engine of human progress and increasing prosperity, they denounced it as an ideology that dominates and exploits humans and nature (Marcuse, 1968; Horkheimer and Adorno, 1972; Habermas, 1971). Domination is not the result of the 'misuse' of essentially neutral and value-free knowledge obtained by science, but is inherent in the scientific method itself.

In Herbert Marcuse's account this is because science is concerned with establishing predictive laws of nature – and thus takes as real only properties that can be measured and mathematically specified, because only such properties can appear in predictive laws. Such laws enable the manipulation and control of nature: science is thus constituted by an interest in the technical control of nature. This technical control can be applied to humans as well as to nature and is a form of domination. However, Marcuse claims that the constitutive interest of science in technical control is historically specific: it is a result of the capitalist social context in which science has developed. A different society could give rise to a different type of science, not constituted by an interest in control. Marcuse wants a science that regards nature as 'a totality of life to be protected and cultivated' (Marcuse, 1972, p61). Such a science would arise in a transformed, peaceful society and would result in different scientific facts and understandings (Marcuse, 1968).

Jürgen Habermas shared Marcuse's analysis of the basic constitution of modern science as one orientated to technical control. However, he did not think that there could be a new science not so constituted. In a development of Hannah Arendt's distinction between work and action, Habermas distinguishes between instrumental and communicative action (Habermas, 1977 and 1984; Canovan, 1983). Science is concerned with instrumental action. In it we seek prediction and control of nature, but in the communicative action that takes place between people we seek common understanding. Habermas criticizes Marcuse and others for thinking that our dealings with nature should be subject to the same norms as our dealings with each other (Habermas, 1971). Science becomes problematic for Habermas when its norms of instrumental action are extended to the domain of meaningful everyday life, in which the interest that constitutes knowledge should be that of successful communication, not of technical control (Habermas, 1978).

At first glance the motivations of early scientists seem to conform to the ideas of Frankfurt School theorists: Francis Bacon wanted to be able to understand nature in order to 'conquer and subdue' it (Robertson, 1905, p843). C. S. Lewis argued that science, like magic, was born of the desire to 'subdue reality to the wishes of men' through technique, a desire that arose in the 16th century (there was little magic in the preceding Middle Ages). Both were prepared to do things previously regarded as disgusting and impious in pursuit of that technique (Lewis, 1943). However, when it comes to the motivations of most individual scientists, it seems likely that they simply desired to distinguish themselves through their intellectual achievements and were not greatly concerned with the practical usefulness or otherwise of their discoveries (Hall, 1981, p153). In reply to this the Frankfurt School theorists' argument would be that if their science was essentially concerned with discovering predictive laws, which then (perhaps by others) could be used to manipulate and control nature, it was nevertheless constituted by an interest in the technical control of nature.

However, science is not just about predictive laws. It also seeks to understand and explain: models, or theories that provide a conceptual framework for understanding some aspect of reality, are as important to science as predictive laws. The theory of electricity, for example, explains lightning strikes; molecular theory explains diffusion and the relationship between the pressure and temperature of gases; the theory of evolution explains the various similarities and differences between different species, as well as how they came into being. These theories postulate the existence of entities and processes and how these are manifest in phenomena that can be observed, directly or via instruments. Mathematics, quantification and measurement play a large part in some theories (in quantum mechanics, for example) but almost none at all in others (for example in evolution).

Explanation is related to prediction: the models or theories that explain phenomena sometimes enable predictions to be made about what would be observed in specific circumstances. The making of such observations is the essence of scientific experimentation. However, the complexity of the real world means that it is not always possible to make predictions. We may, in retrospect, be able to explain an event such as a hurricane or a crop failure, but we cannot predict whether there will be a hurricane or crop failure in a year's time. Conversely, there are instances when we can make reliable predictions (for example that a medical treatment will be effective) but cannot explain why. These predictions are based on repeated experience and are not derived from an explanatory theory.

Even if we can predict and explain, we cannot necessarily manipulate something to change what happens: we can predict and explain the movement of the planets but can do nothing to change them. Neither does being able to manipulate mean we have control, in the sense of being able to achieve the outcome we envisage: genetic engineering can insert foreign genes into developing organisms, but the outcome in the form of the mature organism is often not what the genetic scientist envisaged.[1] Finally, being able to control does not necessarily constitute domination: forms of control do not dominate nature if they are receptive to the qualities and properties of natural processes, materials or organisms and allow these to influence and constrain the desired outcome, rather than imposing an independently conceived outcome.

A slightly different argument for science being technological by nature was made by Jonas. For Jonas practical use is integral to modern scientific theory because it is a matter of the 'analysis of *working* nature into its simplest dynamic factors' (Jonas, 1966, p200, emphasis in original). Science seeks to explain wholes in terms of their component parts: how things are made up and thus how they can be made up out of their elements. Scientific knowledge is thus a matter of 'knowing how' not of 'knowing what', even if in practice the making up cannot be done:

> *Man cannot reproduce a cosmic nebula, but assuming he knows how it is produced in nature, he would in principle be able to produce one too if he were sufficiently large, powerful, and so on, and this is what to know a nebula means.*
> (Jonas, 1966, p204)

The relationship between scientific theory and the active making of things is more than that the former provides the knowledge to do the latter: active making, in the form of experimentation, leads to theory. Jonas suggests that for theory to be a means to practice it must have practice among its own means. In a later essay (Jonas, 1974) Jonas distinguishes between the controlled experiment of science, in which, he says, 'an artificially simplified nature is set to work so as to display the action of single factors', the observation of '"natural" nature in its unprocessed complexity' and 'any non-analytical trying-out of [nature's] responses to our probing interventions' (Jonas, 1974, p63). Jonas's paradigm for the controlled, analytical experiment is Galileo's inclined plane, because this 'made the vertical component in the motion of the balls clearly distinguishable from the horizontal'.

The critical thing about Galileo's concept of motion, according to Jonas, was that, unlike the preceding Aristotelian concept, it considered a motion as being analysable into discrete components, each with their own direction and velocity. This new mechanics was developed at the same time as the collapse of a cosmology which had divided nature into different spheres: a corruptible terrestrial, or sub-lunar, sphere and an incorruptible celestial sphere. The Copernican revolution turned the earth into just another planet, and the planets merely other earths: nature is the same everywhere and one set of laws is valid for all phenomena. Thus terrestrial mechanics could explain the movement of the planets. Jonas suggests that sciences become technological – that is they make possible a scientific technology – when they are assimilated to physics, in other words to an analytical view of nature, where wholes are merely composites of parts and the laws that describe the behaviour of the most fundamental of those parts can, in principle, be used to predict the behaviour of the whole (Jonas, 1974, p73). This happened to chemistry in the 19th century and to biology in the latter half of the 20th.[2]

This view of science as explaining things from the 'bottom up' – so that physics explains chemistry which explains biology, which explains psychology and thence sociology – is no doubt a common view of the relationship between the sciences, but is it what science is really like? Nancy Cartwright has labelled this view 'fundamentalism' (Cartwright, 1999): science here is an ideology because it purports to explain everything by deduction from a single premise (Arendt, 1966, pp468–474). Like the political ideologies on which totalitarian governments are based, contradictory evidence from the complex world of reality is ignored.[3] But this is not good empirical science, the essence of which should surely be attention to empirical evidence. That evidence reveals that scientific laws and theories are only valid in particular circumstances: quantum physics has not replaced classical physics, rather it is valid in circumstances in which classical physics is not; classical mechanics is not a good model for the motion of a $1000 note blown by the wind, but fluid mechanics may be – though the latter is even better for the flight of aeroplanes which we have built to conform to the fluid mechanics model (Cartwright, 1999, pp2 and 27). Science gives us a 'patchwork of laws' (Cartwright, 1999, p31).

If science does not tell us how to make things up out of their elements, as Jonas suggests – or at least not 'all the way from the bottom' – perhaps it is not inherently technological? Paradoxically, however, Cartwright explicitly says that her concern is practical: with 'how the world can be changed by science to make it the way it should be' (Cartwright, 1999, p5). Her point is that the practical use of science is more successful if we apply theories and laws which are appropriate to the situation, rather than trying to stretch them out to cover situations in which they are not valid. The latter approach, however, is the current trend in economic theory, and it has the serious consequence of the world being forced into conformity with models – such as when the International Monetary Fund requires the restructuring of the economies of developing countries according to the dictates of neo-classical economic theory – rather than models being devised and adapted to fit the world. It is also apparent in the current emphasis on genetics in medical research: Cartwright suspects that the hunt to find the genes for breast cancer get the funding and attention it does not because genetics offers the best chance of preventing or curing breast cancer, but because genetics happens to be the latest likely 'theory of everything' within biology (Cartwright, 1999, p18).

The solution is to realize that there is not an integrated whole called 'Science', but only a number of different 'sciences' – the different scientific disciplines. What they have in common is a systematic, empirical approach to investigation, not a single model of reality; and it is perhaps overstating the similarities to call that approach 'the scientific method'. Each science has its own methods: sometimes these are based on the classical model of controlled experiments which test hypotheses, but in many disciplines, such as epidemiology or atmospheric chemistry, investigation proceeds primarily through the collection and interpretation of data – controlled experiments are not always possible, though what data is collected may be informed by hypotheses. In others, such as botany, classification is of prime importance. A science may use conceptual models to understand the domain that it is concerned with and sometimes laws that give a precise account of what regularly happens can be formulated. These models and laws, however, are not universal, though generally they are consistent with one another.[4] The relatedness of disciplines is revealed when insights in one suggest fruitful lines of investigation in another, but this relatedness does not derive from some logical relationship between the models and laws in the two disciplines, but from the fact that they are both trying to account for the same material world (Cartwright, 1999, p6).[5] Cartwright is thus exploding the myth of the possibility of complete, perfect, theoretical knowledge – of science as a unified project that, when complete, will explain and be able to predict everything. Abandoning this myth means paying more attention to what happens in the world, rather than trusting to our theory-based predictions of what will happen.

This pluralist account, of sciences rather than Science means that it does not make a great deal of sense to argue that Science is inherently technological. Each science has its own relationship with technology. Some sciences lead to new technological developments, some reveal the effects of technology on natural systems and are important in the regulation and control of technology, while others simply give us a better understanding of the world.

Technology and the application of science

Implicit in the idea that science 'feeds innovation' and 'will breed new families of products' (DTI, 2000) is that scientific research produces new knowledge, which is then exploited in the creation of new technologies. Is this a true picture of how sciences lead to technological development?

While not denying that theories and concepts derived in basic scientific research can lead to new types of technology,[6] there is another important way in which science can be applied to technology: through technology (rather than nature) as the object of science. In this spirit the Royal Society was established to improve the knowledge of 'all useful Arts, Manufactures, Mechanick practices, Engynes and Inventions' as well as natural things (Hall, 1981, p132). Tools and machines were fitting objects of scientific investigation because their development so often preceded a scientific explanation of how they worked (Nye, 2006, p10). Charles Gillispie argued that in 18th-century France the scientific development of an industry was measured not by whether it made use of scientific theories but by the extent to which it could be explained by science. The scientists were educators of artisans, in the hope that if artisans understood their methods better, they would improve them (Gillispie, 1957). In Britain there was a similar, though less centrally organized, application of scientists to industry: more a matter of personal contacts between scientists and industrialists rather than of government policy. These happened in what Sungook Hong calls 'boundary spaces' – the coffee houses and pubs of London or philosophical and literary societies in the emerging industrial cities – where scientists, engineers and businessmen met and discussed scientific and technical issues (Hong, 1999, p298). In these spaces engineers and manufacturers learned about the latest scientific theories, and sometimes these suggested ways to develop their technology. But also scientists sought to explain manufacturing processes that had been developed independently of science. Manufacturers then used those explanations to improve the processes, while also contributing to the development of science (Schofield, 1957).[7] There was thus a 'science of the industrial arts': what used to be called technology (see Chapter 2).

This sort of science – now mainly engineering science – has of course continued to this day. It has enabled the skill and judgement of workers to be replaced by precise measurement and mechanical control, resulting in de-skilling and its social consequences.[8] However, it is rather eclipsed in government strategy by the sort of science that 'will breed new families of products' (DTI, 2000, executive summary, paragraph 2). The government here seems to be thinking of something more radical than the gradual improvement of the manufacture and design of products of the type that has been going on over the centuries. It wants entirely new sorts of products, presumably based on new scientific knowledge. 'Genomics', making use of recent advances in the science of genetics, is the prime example of this.

However, it is not the case even here that there is a simple sequence of the discovery of scientific knowledge followed by its application in new technology – new types of things added to the world. Rather, technology and science are interwoven: the discovery of enzymes that can cut DNA at specific base sequences (restriction endonucleases), and of enzymes that catalyse the synthesis of a strand of DNA using an existing strand as a template (polymerases), were crucial in the development of techniques of DNA replication, sequencing and recombination. However, also of prime importance for the ability to rapidly replicate fragments of DNA (and thus to produce enough copies for its sequence to be determined) was the development of the programmable thermocycler, a piece of hardware with which rapid and precise temperature changes can be made in the reaction tube. This enabled the automation of replication methods that used a thermostable polymerase enzyme,[9] a critical component of polymerase chain reaction (PCR), which has revolutionized DNA sequencing (Dale and von Schantz, 2002, pp143–148). The ability to replicate, sequence and recombine lengths of DNA has led to many further scientific discoveries about the genome and about protein structure.

It has also made possible the technology of genetic engineering, which can add things – organisms whose genes have been modified by direct intervention at the level of the DNA – to the world outside the laboratory.

However, inventions are frequently neither the outcome of scientific investigation nor of the application of new scientific knowledge. Rather they are the implementation of ideas for how artefacts can be improved that arise in the course of practical dealings with artefacts. Recent examples of such inventions include the wheelbarrow with a spherical wheel, the water-filled lawn roller and the cyclone vacuum cleaner, all invented by James Dyson (see Dyson, 1997), the Freeplay wind-up radio, and beakers for toddlers that do not spill their contents when up-ended (such as Any Way Up Cups). The inventors of these practical, useful artefacts were not scientists, but people who engaged in practical activities and reflected on how they could be made easier. Their inventions do not make use of any new scientific knowledge, but only of well-known and understood principles. The story of James Dyson's development of the cyclone vacuum cleaner is the opposite of the idea that scientific models reveal how something is made up, and thus how to make it. Dyson found the mathematical models of how particles behave in cyclones to be no use at all in designing his cyclone vacuum cleaner because they applied only to situations where all the particles entering the cyclone were of the same size, whereas his cyclone had to be able to cope with particles of all sizes and shapes entering the cyclone at once. Instead he went through a painstaking process of methodically testing prototypes, changing one thing at a time.[10] He argues that the essence of invention lies in this process of iterative development, not in 'quantum leaps' made by individuals of genius (Dyson, 1997, pp112–113 and 168–169). Making things and testing them, not theoretical insights, are what is important in developing new technology.

Even where new technology does arise from the insights of recently acquired scientific knowledge, making things and testing them is just as important, because the scientific knowledge on which the technology is based is not a complete account of the world. This is the implication of Cartwright's view of science as giving us a patchwork of laws: the models and laws of any particular science at best describe one aspect of the world under particular conditions (Cartwright, 1999). Whether the technology is going to work in the 'real world' – and how it is going to affect the other components of that world – is not something that can be known a priori. Theory can point to what may happen, and to which aspects should be considered, though to give the fullest account, of course, all theories, in all disciplines, need to be brought to bear on the situation, as well as everyday knowledge and common sense, particularly with regard to how people behave. However, even when we have drawn on all the available knowledge, something still needs to be tried out in practice before we can be sure that it will work and what effects it will have.

Science, technology and world-building

Sociologists of science tend not to distinguish between science and technology because they focus on how science, like technology, is a social practice. Scientific knowledge is 'made' by this practice. There are indeed important symmetries between science and technology: science adds knowledge to the world while technology adds things. Scientific knowledge is as much part of the world as are houses, so science, like technology, is a world-building activity (Arendt, 1978, p57). However, houses and scientific knowledge are different types of things, the one clearly a material object, the other not; we can therefore distinguish between the activities that make them. My suggestion in Chapter 3 that we should think of technology as 'world-building' is not meant to imply that technology is how we build all the things that form the world. This would give far too wide a meaning to technology, taking it away from the connection with material artefacts implicit in our everyday understanding of the word. Technology is how we make material things, not how we make knowledge, though of course technology is also used in activities that make knowledge.

That science and technology are different activities can be seen in the fact that they answer to different norms and we use different criteria when judging them: how we judge whether or not the outcome of a scientific investigation should be added to our stock of knowledge about the world is quite different from how we judge a material object that is the product of technology. With regard to the former we ask questions about the extent to which evidence supports the conclusions drawn. Of course, the answer is rarely a simple yes or no, and it is quite reasonable to require stronger evidence in some cases than in others, depending on judgements about the implications of that knowledge. However, one cannot reject scientific knowledge simply because of its implications: the oil companies who opposed action to reduce greenhouse gas emissions could not object to the scientific theory that such emissions are causing climate change on the basis of the implications of this knowledge – that they should reduce production and use of oil. Rather they had to argue that the evidence supporting the theory was not sufficiently strong to take action.

With regard to the material objects produced by technology, questions about evidence only have relevance with regard to claims of non-self-evident facts about the object (such as whether it is toxic). Other questions can be asked about the object – such as whether it is beautiful or ugly, and how useful it is – the answers to which are not matters of fact but of opinion.[11] Opinions have to be supported by reasons, not evidence (though the reasons may take the form of facts for which evidence can be demanded). It is also legitimate to inquire into how a technology will affect social relations and the structure of society and to argue against the use of the technology on those grounds. To allow scientific knowledge to be scrutinized in this way, and for this to be a criterion for its acceptance, is the approach taken by totalitarian regimes.

The limits of political control over science

The above distinction between the norms and criteria of judgement that apply to the acceptance of scientific knowledge and those that are appropriate for technology means that scientific knowledge should not be subject to the democratic control that I argue should be applied to technology. However, this is not to argue for the complete autonomy of science as a practice. There are at least three arguments against such autonomy and in favour of political control over the practice of science.

First, the technology used within science to gain knowledge, technology that constitutes the world of the laboratory, is of legitimate public concern. The pursuit of knowledge is not a justification for the use of any method whatsoever. Thus there are controls over the use of laboratory animals in experiments and over investigations in which human beings are the objects of the research.[12] These controls are intended to prevent the unjustified use of animals and to ensure that the rights of the human subjects of experiments are respected. We perhaps also should be concerned about the world of the laboratory because it may serve as a model for the 'real' world outside it if technologies used there then find wider application (Arendt, 1978, p57). Concern over the methods of science is also justified where the effects of those methods are not confined to the laboratory. Testing things out – as objectors to nuclear weapons tests and farm-scale trials of genetically modified crops have made clear – involves actually doing them – exploding the bombs, or growing the crops, and thus causing the effects that are being investigated.

Second, science cannot be the judge of whether scientific investigation has provided sufficient evidence to support a particular course of action, or what the burden of proof should be. That judgement involves evaluation of the possible consequences of alternative actions, including that of non-action, and of non-consequentialist reasons for the action – an evaluation that is not the job of science. The practical acceptance of knowledge, in the sense of acting upon it, is therefore not a matter for science alone.[13] What the burden of proof should be depends on the institutional setting in which science is used (Cranor, 1993, p9). Within the institutional setting of academic scientific research, the standard of proof normally required is equivalent to the 'beyond reasonable doubt' standard of criminal cases: just as it is more important that the innocent are acquitted than that the guilty are found innocent, it is more important that propositions are not accepted as true when they are not than that they are (provisionally) rejected when they are true. The aim is to avoid adding erroneously to accepted knowledge. The result is that epidemiological studies or animal tests on the toxicity of chemicals are only considered to provide 'statistically significant' results if the probability of a false positive is less than five per cent. However, Cranor points out that if this data is evidence in civil cases, or used for regulatory purposes, this standard of proof is inappropriate. In civil cases, for example, a case only has to be proved on the 'balance of probabilities', equal weight being given to both sides of the dispute. This means designing tests and analysing data to give as much weight to guarding against false negatives as against false positives (Cranor, 1993).

And third, science cannot decide what it is worthwhile to know, and thus to what ends scientific investigation should be put. Whether it is worthwhile knowing something depends on its meaning in the context of human life in the world. In *The Life of the Mind* (Arendt, 1978) Arendt makes a distinction between the processes of cognition that lead to knowledge, and thought which leads to the understanding of what something means. The process of cognition 'leaves behind a growing treasure of knowledge that is retained and kept in store by every civilization as part and parcel of its world' (Arendt, 1978, p62). In contrast, the understanding of meaning is intangible and never final. Thinking and understanding do play an important role in science, but here they are means to an end, the end being the type of knowledge sought. Science may seek knowledge of something because that knowledge would resolve problems and questions internal to the science, but ultimately the meaning of scientific knowledge has to involve reference to things and concerns that are external to science. And at that point science is not the judge of what it is worthwhile to know (Arendt, 1978, p54).

Thus there is scope for democratic control over what science investigates, the methods of investigation it uses, and whether action should be taken as a result of those investigations. However, there should not be political control, democratic or otherwise, over adding scientific knowledge to the stock of knowledge that forms part of the world we inhabit.

The confusion between science and technology

A striking feature of much recent policy debate on science and technology is that this distinction between science and technology does not seem to be made. Thus the 2000 White Paper (DTI, 2000) talks about 'risks from science' (chapter 4, paragraph 26), when it does not mean risks from scientific investigation or knowledge, but risks from the technological fruits of those investigations. Similarly, the House of Lords' third report on science and technology was concerned with the processes whereby positions are taken on issues such as nuclear waste and genetically modified food (paragraph 1.22), but saw these issues as a matter of the relationship between 'Science and society' – the title given to the report (House of Lords Select Committee, 2000). Likewise, the government consultation on the 'biosciences' was not about sciences such as biology, zoology, biochemistry and genetics, but matters such as cloning, genetic testing and genetically modified crops (DTI, 1998). While these are associated with biological sciences, these are in fact technologies, not the sciences themselves, but by calling them 'sciences' the government can label as 'anti-science' those who oppose their introduction.

The idea that concerns about technology are concerns about science, or 'risks from science', perhaps arises because the kind of technologies that raise these concerns are ones developed from recent advances in science: people are concerned about genetic engineering, but not about Dyson vacuum cleaners. However, opponents of genetically modified food are not opponents of genetic science: Friends of the Earth, for example, which has campaigned against genetically modified food, has welcomed the 'biomedical revolution' for the insights it will give into the effects of chemicals on the human body. They regard the sequencing of the human genome as the first step towards a much better understanding of how the body works at the molecular level, and thus how chemicals affect health (Friends of the Earth, 2000).

Another reason why debates about technologies seem to be debates about science is that concerns about those technologies are seen as being concerns about their safety – the risk of physical harm. And whether something will cause harm or not is considered to be a matter that science should decide. Scientific investigation is obviously very important in establishing what the effects of a technology are, though that investigation is often done by disciplines other than the one that gave rise to the theories on which the technology is based: the investigation of the effects of genetically modified crops and food is not done by geneticists, but by field ecologists and toxicologists.[14] But it is not just different scientific disciplines that need to be involved: a great deal of relevant knowledge, particularly with regard to how things are done in practice and how people, or animals, behave, is not held by scientists but by workers, mothers, farmers and so on (see, for example, Wynne, 1996).

Situating technology within science, as is done in current policy, leaves unaddressed concerns that are not about safety but are about, for example, the corporate take-over of food production, animal suffering or whether due respect is being shown for other species – all concerns raised in connection with the use of genetic engineering in agriculture. If the dialogue that the 2000 White Paper (DTI, 2000) says the government seeks is about science, it will privilege scientific understandings, implicitly excluding others from the debate. Technology, not just science, is 'too important to be left only to scientists'.

Technology and the Economy

Technological change and economic growth

New technologies produce new sorts of products, and in a market economy these are generally offered for sale. If these products are things someone wants to buy there is a market for them. If they are bought in addition to what was bought before there is an increase in the amount of goods purchased – in other words there is growth in the economy.[15] It can be argued that in developed capitalist economies, where markets for existing products are already saturated, technological innovation is the only way that the economy can grow (see, for example, Gorz, 1976). The production of new products is potentially more profitable because it is monopolistic: patents and intellectual property rights allow their owner to stop others from using the invention, provided they can pay the costs of legal action. The argument for allowing such monopolies is that developers of new products need to recoup the investment that had to be made to develop the new product, an investment that competitors did not have to make. Nevertheless, it is clear that innovations reduce the amount of competition in a market economy, in the sense of competition between different businesses producing the same product.

Why then do the White Papers on science and technology clearly link competitive markets with innovation? One answer is that competition policy is intended to ensure that it is possible to market new products – and thus that there is competition between different products, not between different people selling the same product (DTI, 2000, chapter 1, paragraph 15). The second answer is that the competitiveness the government is concerned about is that of the British economy in global markets. Hence the government is interested in products that have 'new global markets' (DTI, 2000, executive summary, paragraph 2) and not in products that are culturally or environmentally specific with only local markets. The White Paper reported on 'how Britain stands' in the global competition that is science and technology (DTI, 2000, chapter 1). The concern is how British organizations, or people working in Britain for international companies, can get some of the income from the sale of new products.

According to this view, technological innovation in the UK is a good thing because it increases the amount British companies or individuals receive from the global sale of products: new products are more profitable than old ones, so the more new rather than old products British companies produce, or own the patents of, the greater the profitability of British business; if such products are not produced in the UK, they will be produced elsewhere, increasing the profitability of foreign companies relative to UK ones. Foreign companies, rather than ones in the UK, will then receive investment by international capital. Producing new, innovative products is in fact seen as the only option for British industry: it cannot compete on the basis of labour costs against low wage countries such as China, so must instead try to compete 'through the exploitation of new ideas' (DTI, 2003). This argument assumes an international trade in goods and international capital markets. Such a global economic system does exist, of course, but only because it has been constructed through deliberate choices made by governments.

Technological change, which I argued in Chapter 3 is change to the world, is thus seen by the government as essential for economic growth. With the exception of occasional acknowledgements of the need for products and services to have less impact on the environment, the government promotes technological innovation for the sake of the economy.

The economy and the world; labour and work

Why should economic growth be given this priority? We should perhaps note here that 'growth' is a biological term (though in nature growth is not unlimited, but is followed by death and decay). Also, we use the term 'consumer' for the ultimate purchaser of goods and services as though they are consumed (destroying them in the process) like we consume food. In reality, however, things like cars, fridges and carpets are not consumed: when we cease using them they become waste. The fact that we have needs ultimately derives from the fact that we are living organisms, who must consume food and drink to maintain the dynamic process that is life. Like our need for food, then, the economy seems to be a necessity, and the priority given to economic growth in government policy can be seen as deriving from a view of humans as primarily biological beings with needs – originally for food, shelter and comfort, but now also for computers and mobile phones, trips to the cinema and holidays. What is missing is a recognition of humans as moral persons and a concern for the world that we all share.

The distinction made by Arendt between the activities of labour and work may be useful here (Arendt, 1958; Chapman, 2004). Labour is done to provide for our needs as living organisms. It consists of all the repetitive tasks of daily life, from cooking to cleaning, but also what we do to 'earn a living'. Work is the making of products that then form part of the world. These two activities can coincide: a craftsman works in that he makes a durable product, but labours in that he makes it repeatedly to earn a living. Because he is doing two things at once, there are two objectives that must be met: one is that he must earn a living, the other, which we tend to forget, is that the product made must make a contribution towards making the world a better place.

This second objective is not in conflict with the interests of the craftsman, as long as the craftsman desires to create something that is *good*, as well as to earn his own living. The former is part of the satisfaction that is to be had from work, which can be as important to a person's wellbeing as the consumption that earning their living makes possible (Keat, 2000, p135). And this is not only available to the craftsman: it is a satisfaction that does not derive from the nature of the work process but from a judgement that what has been created, perhaps with others, is good. What has been created forms part of the world: it appears to others, not just to the creator, and those others may judge it as good or bad. Thus the important role that Russell Keat identifies for recognition of a person's work by others: it confirms the goodness of the thing created, as well as acknowledging the role of the particular person in making it (Keat, 2000, p107). In situations of paid employment, recognition may take the form of increased pay or status. Keat's argument suggests that people's desire for these is partly a matter of the recognition that they provide.

On an institutional scale, a focus exclusively on the need to earn a living, disregarding the needs of the world for good products, equates to a concern with short-term financial returns to the exclusion of interest in the product itself. What happens when those in control of businesses are only interested in profits and not in the product they are making is depicted in David Lodge's novel *Nice Work*, set in the English Midlands of the 1980s (Lodge, 1988). Productive industry is shut down, leaving an industrial wasteland, while those involved in finance, who produce nothing, become super-rich. British industry's lack of interest in making good products and its domination by accountants concerned only for the short-term 'bottom line' is also a complaint of James Dyson: as a result he found it impossible to get existing vacuum cleaner manufacturers to take up his new design. Instead of investing in new products, industry spent money on advertising to sell more of what it was already making (Dyson, 1997).

This focus on financial returns to the exclusion of concern with the product itself, and whether it is good regardless of its ability to generate profits, is not a necessary feature of companies in a market economy. Many companies are interested in making a good product, or of doing something that makes the world a better place, not just in making money. Such companies are perhaps more likely to be owned by a small number of identifiable people, rather than by large numbers of anonymous shareholders. Owners of private companies, whose shares are not publicly available, are free from the pressure of the stock market and therefore more able to pursue their particular interests, as long as they make a sufficient profit. However, even in large companies with many shareholders, the fact that the business as a whole has an overriding concern for profits does not mean that this is the overriding concern of all the individuals within the company (Keat, 2000, p118). Indeed, Keat argues that the success of a company may best be served if financial rewards are not the main motivation of the individuals within it. Rather, companies need people who see themselves as engaging in a common enterprise, admire and respect each other's contribution to this, and have the skills and virtues of character needed to do their job well (Keat, 2000, p118). An interest in the product being made and a desire that it be a good product is a motivating concern that it is important for many people to have if they are to do their job well.

In a market economy a company must make a profit to stay in business.[16] However, this does not mean that the maximizing of profits has to be the motivating force of companies, and certainly not of individuals within companies. Many companies may in fact operate as 'profit-*satisficers* rather than *maximizers*', concerned with earning sufficient profits to survive, but not abandoning their 'core activities' for the sake of possibly greater returns elsewhere (Keat, 2000, p121). We need to earn a living, but we also need the satisfaction of having made something that is good. The motivation for work itself is the making of a good product, whose goodness is recognizable by others. The possibility of that recognition comes about because the product forms part of the world inhabited by others as well as ourselves.

Just as companies should not be profit maximizers, governments should not be 'economy maximizers': the government should ensure that the economy of the nation suffices to provide its people with the 'necessities of life' – what they need to live as part of that society[17] – but this does not mean that a bigger economy is necessarily better for people's wellbeing. Just as the overall wellbeing derived from work – the income it provides and the satisfaction from the work process itself – may be reduced if income is increased but other contributions to wellbeing from work decline, so increasing the size of the economy in monetary terms (as represented, for example, by GDP – gross domestic product) does not necessarily lead to greater levels of wellbeing. Studies of indicators of wellbeing, which include non-financial measures, show that these diverge considerably from GDP:[18] GDP may increase but wellbeing decline.

A key influence on the wellbeing of individuals is the nature of the world that they live in. The government's primary duty, I would argue, is for the world shared by all its citizens. The government may be right that to compete in the global economy, as it is currently constituted, British industry needs to be more innovative, including developing new technology.[19] But government should be concerned with the nature of that technology and whether it makes for a better world. It should therefore have a more discriminating approach to new technologies, rather than considering innovation to be inherently good simply because it leads to economic growth.

What is critical for the world, and for the earth, is not the size of the economy but the nature of the activities by which people 'earn a living' – which depends very much on the technology we use – because this activity of 'earning a living' so often coincides with building or caring for a world.[20] In providing for the 'necessities of life', we also have to build and care for a world in which human action can take place, and do both in a way that does not destroy the capacity of the earth to maintain life. The important relationship between technology and the economy is therefore not the effect of technological innovation on the size of the economy but the effect of technological change on the nature of economic activities.

Conclusions

Official policy sees science primarily as something that generates new ideas and knowledge that lead to new technology. I have questioned whether science is inherently technological in this way and concluded that the error lies in thinking that there is an integrated thing called 'Science'. Instead, there is a multiplicity of different sciences, each with its own domains, theories and models. There is no internal, logical relationship between the theories and models of the different sciences, rather they are related by virtue of the fact that they are all trying to account for the same material world and have in common a systematic, empirical approach to investigation.

An important implication of this multiplicity of sciences is that no one science gives a complete account of the world. Where technologies are developed on the basis of the knowledge produced by a science, that knowledge is not adequate to the task of predicting whether the technology will in fact work in the real world or what its effects will be. Knowledge from other sciences, and from experience gained in other ways (that of farmers, workers or mothers, for example), will all help to make predictions more reliable, but in the end, as in the development of all technology, things have to be tried out, tested and monitored.

Science and technology are interwoven in that particular technologies often play a crucial role in scientific discoveries and those discoveries may then lead to further new technologies. However, although both science and technology may be considered to be 'world-building' activities, what they add to the world is different: science adds knowledge whereas technology adds material things. They answer to different norms and criteria of judgement, so should not be confused. Much official discourse, however, does seem to confuse the two, situating controversial technologies such as genetic engineering within science. This may be because these technologies obviously rely on relatively new scientific insights, or because the concerns about those technologies are regarded as being about the risks of physical harm, on which science is considered to be the authority. This placing of technology within science implicitly excludes non-scientists and limits the debate about technology in two ways: first, concerns that are not about safety and risks of harm are not addressed; second, a great deal of non-science knowledge relevant to whether there are such risks is ignored.

Finally, in this chapter I have considered the relationship between technology and the economy. The government regards technological innovation as essential if Britain is to compete in the global economy, and therefore promotes such innovation. Technological innovation is considered to be inherently good, and the only legitimate basis of restrictions the risks of physical harm. I have argued that because the government's primary responsibility is for the world that its citizens inhabit, not for the economy, it should have a more discriminating approach to technology: technological innovation is not necessarily good but should only be promoted and welcomed if it makes for a better world. The aspect of the economy that is of public importance is not the size of the economy in monetary terms but whether the activities by which people earn a living, the nature of which depends on technology as well as on other aspects of the public world, also build and care for a world that is a fit home for human life on earth.

The issues examined in this chapter, concerned with science, technology and the role of technological innovation in economic prosperity, are all important in the particular area of technology that I will turn to next: the manufacture and use of synthetic chemicals. The importance of science here is obvious, not only in the development of chemicals but also in our knowledge of their effects. The chemicals industry is regarded by government as an important part of the economy, but it is subject to regulation because chemicals can cause harm. The next chapter outlines the current regulatory system and proposals for its reform. I then take a close look at the concept of risk (Chapter 6) and how risks from chemicals are assessed (Chapter 7). In Chapter 8 I examine the political and ethical framework of the current system of regulation and take up some of the themes explored here. In particular I give an account of the relationship between the economy and the world, and suggest why public policy on technology does not consider how technology will affect the public world.

Notes

1   Most commonly the added gene or the process of genetic engineering has effects on several aspects of the organism, only one of which is intended. For example, the addition of a cow growth hormone gene to the genome of a pig resulted in a fast growing but deformed, arthritic animal (Wheale and McNally, 1988, p164).

2   'Only when [zoology and botany] were transformed by geneticism from morphological into causal systems and subsumed under the norms of classical mechanics (in a bold extension of its terms) could the idea of a science-informed biological technology arise' (Jonas, 1974, p73).

3   For example, Nancy Cartwright discusses the work of Daniel Hausman on evidence in economic theory. He claims that many economists believe that equilibrium theory provides a complete theory of the whole economic domain and thus dismiss as ad hoc any generalizations about human behaviour that constitute additional causal factors to those considered relevant by equilibrium theory (Cartwright, 1999, p16).

4   Perhaps the exception to this is the wave and particle theories of light.

5   Critics of Cartwright's view, such as Lawrence Sklar (Sklar, 2003), accept that there are many sciences, each with its own conceptual framework, models, laws and so on, which apply only to the aspects of the world with which the science is concerned. Sklar, however, argues that this ineliminable plurality of explanatory schemes does not imply a plurality of ontologies: the account of the world given by fundamental physics (currently relativistic quantum field theory) is how the world really is, other explanations being 'convenient fictions' (Sklar, 2003, p438), useful for predictive and explanatory purposes. Sklar acknowledges the difficulties of 'deciding which descriptive schemes are to be taken as straightforward and which as useful fictive modes of characterizing the world', this being a matter for science (Sklar, 2003, pp438–9). However, saying that the laws of quantum mechanics do not apply to the behaviour of fluids in motion (so that laws explaining the latter cannot be deduced from the former) is not necessarily to commit oneself to saying that the fluid is not made up of atoms that, if placed in suitable conditions, would conform to the laws of quantum mechanics. One does not have to resort to distinguishing between 'straightforward' and 'fictional' descriptive schemes to avoid a plurality of ontologies, just to recognize that scientific models are just that – models for understanding the world that must continually be refined and adapted in the light of evidence.

6   Though note that the scientific theories that are most useful for industrial development are not necessarily the ones that are most fruitful scientifically. Thus late 18th-century French chemical manufacturers were guided by the theory of affinities and not the then latest theory of combustion. The former was little more than 'a tentative classification of substances according to their relative chemical activity […] devoid of abstract interest' but it gave the manufacturers the knowledge of the chemical properties of substances that they needed (Gillispie, 1957, p404). It is claimed that Josiah Wedgewood was indebted to chemistry for improvements he made to processes of ceramic production, but the theory he made use of was that of phlogiston, a theory that was later discredited in favour of the theory of oxygen (McKendrick, 1973).

7   Jonas makes a similar point about the relationship between technology and classical mechanics: 'For the long first phase of the growth and perfection of classical mechanics, it generally

holds that the artificial that happened to be there served to further the understanding of the natural, and not the scientifically understood natural to promote the inventive expansion of the artificial' (Jonas, 1974, p72).

8   For example, an account of bread making in *What Industry Owes to Chemical Science* (Council of the Royal Institute of Chemistry, 1945) describes how the judgement of the dough by the bread maker, a judgement that was 'a matter of personal evaluation, and led to considerable confusion' has been replaced by dough-testing machines which 'make these evaluations with precision and record the results with scientific accuracy, uninfluenced by the personal bias of the operator' (p21). The systematic analysis and measurement of how work was carried out led to the 'scientific management' methods of Taylorism (Taylor, 1911). These increased efficiency and productivity through the standardization of work and the separation of the planning of work from its execution.

9   An enzyme that is stable at high temperatures because it is from a bacterium that lives in hot springs, so is not destroyed by the temperature required to denature the double helix of the DNA molecule into two strands.

10   One could of course argue that in his insistence on changing just one thing at a time Dyson demonstrated a good understanding of scientific method. However, what he was doing was not science: he was not trying to contribute to a body of knowledge, to develop theories and models to describe and account for phenomema, rather he was trying to make something that worked in the real world.

11   The distinction between fact and opinion is taken from Arendt's essay 'Truth and politics' (Arendt, 1968, pp227–264).

12   In the UK, the use of animals is regulated by the Animals (Scientific Procedures) Act, 1986. For a general account of controls over the use of animals in science see Monamy (2000). For restrictions on the use of humans in medical research see World Medical Association (2000).

13   So, for example, the European Commission rebuked a group of its scientific advisers for pub- licly disagreeing with its decision to ban the use of phthalate softeners in certain baby toys. The scientists on a committee that advised on phthalates did not consider that the evidence of harm was sufficient to warrant a ban, but the Commission retorted that this decision was not one for the scientists, as 'the conclusion that there is a serious and immediate risk is a responsibility of the commission. This concept is not scientifically defined' (from *ENDS Environment Daily*, Friday 26 November 1999).

14   Including the right disciplines is important: chlorofluorocarbons (CFCs) were, when they were invented in the 1930s, thought to be safe as they did not have the problems of toxicity or flammability of alternative refrigerants. They have now been banned because of their effects on the ozone layer in the upper atmosphere: in the 1930s nobody would have thought that atmospheric chemistry was a relevant discipline for the assessment of the effects of a refriger- ant.

15   New technologies may also, of course, increase the efficiency of production processes, reducing the costs of products, or freeing resources that had previously been employed in that process so they can be employed elsewhere. This increase in productivity has perhaps traditionally been seen as the source of economic growth, though may now be less important than the creation of new products, and is certainly given less prominence in government policy.

16   One could defend this need to make a profit because it provides the company with some exter- nal feedback as to whether its products are in fact good. But this relies, of course, on the ability and inclination of those who buy the products (usually called consumers) to choose things that are good, an issue that I will take up in Chapter 9.

17   As I will discuss in Chapter 8, what those needs are depends on what the shared world is like.

18   For an overview see McLaren, Bullock and Yousuf (1998, pp60–65).

19   Though it should also recognize its responsibility, along with other governments, for making the world that way: it is something that governments can change, not an inevitable fact of nature.

20   This is not to argue that the scale of many activities is not the critical factor in their impacts on the world and the earth (though the immense scale of many modern activities is only possible because of the particular type of technology used). However, there is no necessary connection between the size of the economy, measured in monetary terms, and the scale of such activities.

References

Arendt, H. (1958) *The Human Condition*, University of Chicago Press, Chicago, IL

Arendt, H. (1966) *The Origins of Totalitarianism*, Second Edition, Harcourt, Inc, New York

Arendt, H. (1968) *Between Past and Future*, Viking Compass Edition with additional text, New York

Arendt, H. (1978) *The Life of the Mind: Part One, Thinking*, Secker & Warburg, London

Arendt, H. (1982) *Lectures on Kant's Political Philosophy*, Harvester Press, Brighton

Aristotle, *The Politics*, translated with an introduction by T. A. Sinclair (1974), Penguin Books, Harmondsworth

Canovan, M. (1983) 'A case of distorted communication: A note on Habermas and Arendt', *Political Theory*, vol 11, pp105–116

Cartwright, N. (1999) *The Dappled World: A Study of the Boundaries of Science*, Cambridge University Press, Cambridge

Chapman, A. (2004) 'Technology as world building', *Ethics, Place and Environment*, vol 7, nos 1–2, pp59–72

Council of the Royal Institute of Chemistry (1945) *What Industry Owes to Chemical Science*, Heffer & Sons Ltd, Cambridge

Cranor, C. F. (1993) *Regulating Toxic Substances: A Philosophy of Science and the Law*, Oxford University Press, New York

Dale, J. W. and von Schantz, M. (2002) *From Genes to Genomes: Concepts and Applications of DNA Technology*, John Wiley & Sons Ltd, Chichester

DTI (Department of Trade and Industry) (1993) 'Realising our potential: A strategy for science, engineering and technology', HMSO, London

DTI (1998) 'Lord Sainsbury announces public consultation on biosciences', press release, 15 December 1998, www.gnn.gov.uk/environment/dti, accessed January 2007

DTI (2000) 'Excellence and opportunity – A science and innovation policy for the 21st century' (Cm4814), July 2000, HMSO, London

DTI (2001a) 'White Paper on enterprise, skills and innovation: Opportunity for all in a world of change' (Cm 5052), February 2001, HMSO, London

DTI (2001b) 'DTI science and innovation strategy', HMSO, London

DTI (2003) 'Innovation report: Competing in a global economy', HMSO, London

Dyson, J. (1997) *Against the Odds*, Orion Business Books, London

ENDS (1999) *ENDS Environment Daily*, Friday 26 November

Friends of the Earth (2000) *Crisis in Chemicals: The Threat Posed by the 'Biomedical Revolution' to the Profits, Liabilities and Regulation of the Industries Making and Using Chemicals*, Friends of the Earth, London

Gillispie, C. C. (1957) 'History of industry', *Isis*, vol 48, pp398–407

Gorz, A. (1976) 'Technology, technicians and the class struggle', in A. Gorz (ed) *The Division of Labour: The Labour Process and Class-Struggle in Modern Capitalism*, Harvester Press, Hassocks

Habermas, J. (1971) 'Technology and science as "Ideology"', in *Toward a Rational Society: Student Protest, Science and Politics*, trans. J. Shapiro, Heinemann Educational, London

Habermas, J. (1977) 'Hannah Arendt's communications concept of power', *Social Research*, vol 44, pp2–24

Habermas, J. (1978) *Knowledge and Human Interests*, Second Edition, Heinemann, London

Habermas, J. (1984) *The Theory of Communicative Action*, trans. T. McCarthy, Heinemann, London

Hall, A. R. (1981) *From Galileo to Newton*, Dover Publications, New York

HM Treasury, DTI and DfES (Department for Education and Skills) (2004) 'Science and innovation investment framework 2004–2014', HMSO, London

Hong, S. (1999) 'Historiographical layers in the relationship between science and technology', *History and Technology*, vol 15, pp289–311

Horkheimer, M. and Adorno T. W. (1972) *The Dialectic of the Enlightenment*, trans. J. Cumming, Herder & Herder, New York

House of Lords Select Committee on Science and Technology (2000) 'Science and society' (third report), TSO, London

Jonas, H. (1966) 'The practical uses of theory', in *The Phenomenon of Life: Toward a Philosophical Biology*, Harper & Row, New York, pp188–210

Jonas, H. (1974) 'Seventeenth century and after: The meaning of the scientific and technological revolution', in *Philosophical Essays: From Ancient Creed to Technological Man*, University of Chicago Press, Chicago, IL, pp45–81

Keat, R. (2000) *Cultural Goods and the Limits of the Market*, Macmillan, London

Lewis, C. S. (1943) *The Abolition of Man, or Reflections on Education with Special Reference to the Teaching of English in the Upper Forms*, Oxford University Press, Oxford

Lodge, D. (1988) *Nice Work*, Secker & Warburg, London

Marcuse, H. (1968) *One Dimensional Man*, Abacus, New York

Marcuse, H. (1972) *Counter-Revolution and Revolt*, Allen Lane, London

McKendrick, N. (1973) 'The role of science in the industrial revolution: A study of Josiah Wedgewood as a scientist and industrial chemist', in M. Teich and R. M. Young (eds) *Changing Perspectives in the History of Science*, Heinemann, London, pp279–318

McLaren, D., Bullock, S. and Yousuf, N. (1998) *Tomorrow's World: Britain's Share in a Sustainable Future*, Friends of the Earth and Earthscan, London

Monamy, V. (2000) *Animal Experimentation: A Guide to the Issues*, Cambridge University Press, Cambridge

Nye, D. (2006) *Technology Matters: Questions to Live with*, MIT Press, Cambridge, MA

Robertson, J. M. (ed) (1905) *The Philosophical Works of Francis Bacon*, George Routledge and Sons, London

Schofield, R. E. (1957) 'The industrial orientation of science in the Lunar Society of Birmingham', *Isis*, vol 48, pp408–415

Sklar, L. (2003) 'Dappled theories in a uniform world', *Philosophy of Science*, vol 70, pp424–441

Taylor, F. W. (1911) *The Principles of Scientific Management*, Harper Bros, New York

Wheale, P. R. and McNally, R. M. (1988) *Genetic Engineering: Catastrophe or Utopia?*, Harvester Wheatsheaf, Hemel Hempstead

World Medical Association (2000) 'Declaration of Helsinki: Ethical principles for medical research involving human subjects', adopted in 1964, last amended 2000, www.wma.net/e/policy/b3.htm, accessed January 2007

Wynne, B. (1996) 'May the sheep safely graze? A reflexive view of the expert–lay knowledge divide', in S. Lash, B. Szerszynski and B. Wynne (eds) *Risk, Environment and Modernity*, Sage Publications, Thousand Oaks, CA, and London, pp44–83

5

The Regulation of Chemicals

Why Chemicals?

This chapter considers policy on a specific area of technology: synthetic chemicals. Synthetic chemicals have been manufactured on a large scale for at least 50 years. Unlike genetic engineering and nanotechnology, they are not considered to be 'new', but despite the decades of production and use there is still a great deal that we do not know about their effects. Time and again novel synthetic chemicals have been found to cause problems that were not expected.

In the late 1990s our lack of knowledge about the long-term effects of most synthetic chemicals was officially recognized. This, combined with mounting evidence that synthetic chemicals are having a significant effect on the health of humans and wildlife (see, for example, European Environment Agency, 1998), led to proposals to reform the system of regulation in the European Union (EU). After several years of negotiation a new regulatory regime, known as REACH, was agreed at the end of 2006.

The general public policy approach to technology, discussed in the previous chapter, can be seen in the attitudes of the UK government and the EU Commission towards synthetic chemicals. The UK government's chemicals strategy (DETR, 1999) and the European Commission White Paper on chemicals (CEC, 2001) both start from the premise that the production and use of chemicals is beneficial, in that chemicals are used in a huge variety of goods and the chemicals industry is an important part of the economy. However, they also recognize that some chemicals cause harm to human health and to the environment. The aim of regulation is to prevent harm while still gaining the benefits which are to be had from producing and using chemicals.[1] Included in those benefits is the financial turnover of the European chemicals industry and its positive trade balance with the rest of the world. One policy aim is therefore that the European industry is not put at a disadvantage compared to its competitors elsewhere. In line with the approach to innovation described in the last chapter – in which technological innovation is regarded as essential for the competitiveness of the national economy, and therefore inherently good – another aim of chemicals policy is that the regulatory regime should stimulate, rather than restrict, innovation in chemicals.

Science obviously plays an important role in chemicals policy. The synthetic chemicals industry is an outcome of the science of chemistry. Many more sciences – including biochemistry, toxicology, epidemiology and atmospheric chemistry – are important in our knowledge of the effects of chemicals. As I argued in the previous chapter, each science is only valid within its particular domain. This has implications for how sure we can be that our knowledge of the effects of synthetic chemicals is complete, an issue that I will take up in Chapter 7.

The lack of knowledge about chemicals that came to light in the late 1990s, and has been a spur to the review of European chemicals legislation, relates not to the inherent limitations of scientific knowledge but simply to the fact that test data on the long-term toxicity of chemicals is not available for most commercially produced synthetic chemicals. A survey by the US Environmental Protection Agency (EPA) in 1998, for example, found that a complete package of basic information was available for only 7 per cent of the 2863 high production volume chemicals, and for 43 per cent of these substances no information was available (DETR, 1999, section 1.7) This appears to have been a surprise to regulators and industry, as they had previously denied the claim, made by the Environmental Defense Fund in 1997, that the Organisation for Economic Co-operation and Development (OECD) minimum data requirements were not publicly available for 71 per cent of the high volume chemicals on the US market (see Environmental Defense Fund, 1997). The UK government, the European Commission and the Royal Commission on Environmental Pollution (RCEP) now all emphasize their concern about the inadequacy of available information on the hazards of chemicals, including those released into the environment in large quantities.[2]

In addition to the lack of basic data, the subtle ways in which, we now believe, some chemicals affect biological systems at very low concentrations, such as by interfering with hormone systems at specific stages in the lifecycle of an organism, add to the difficulties of knowing whether a chemical has a harmful effect (see Colborn et al, 1996, and Cadbury, 1998). There is also the issue that we are not exposed to chemicals individually, but in mixtures. Our bodies now contain several hundred chemicals which did not exist 60 years ago, acquired from the food we eat and the air we breathe or absorbed through the skin. Current methods of testing and risk assessment assume that each chemical acts independently, but the effects of chemicals may be additive,[3] synergistic (more than additive)[4] or antagonistic (less than additive).

To understand the issues involved in chemicals regulation one needs to have some understanding of the different types of chemicals and the development of the chemicals industry. The next section of this chapter therefore outlines the relevant background information. I then go on to describe European legislation on synthetic chemicals (from which UK legislation derives). Finally, I outline some of the relevant issues in the debates that preceded the introduction of REACH.

Chemicals and the Chemicals Industry

Chemicals are what chemistry finds when it looks at matter. In one sense, chemicals are merely one aspect of the ways we can consider matter: matter can be considered in terms of its shape, size, colour, mass, solidity or fluidity, but also in terms of its chemical composition. In the last 150 years we have become adept at identifying, isolating, purifying and synthesizing chemicals. This last process has led to entirely new chemicals. It also means that we can produce large volumes of chemicals identical to those that occur naturally, but in concentrations and forms that do not occur naturally.

Chemicals are traditionally divided into two types: organic and inorganic. Organic chemicals consist of molecules that contain a carbon atom covalently bonded[5] to another carbon atom or an atom of another element (generally hydrogen, oxygen or nitrogen, and sometimes sulphur or phosphorus). The fact that carbon can form four covalent bonds makes possible an indefinite variety of molecules, from methane (one carbon with four hydrogens) to very large and complex molecules, such as proteins and DNA. Organic chemicals take their name from the fact that they are what living organisms are composed of, and in the 18th century it was thought that they could only be synthesized by means of a 'life force' in living cells (Freemantle, 1987, p634). Inorganic chemicals are everything else, though the term is primarily used to refer to salts, metals and minerals.[6]

The manufacture of inorganic chemicals was very important in the development of the chemicals industry and its role in the industrial revolution. Changes in the textile industry meant there was an increased need for soaps, alkalis, acids and mordants. By the late 18th century, meeting the demand for these from the plant sources previously used was becoming difficult. In 1775 the French government offered a prize for the first person to invent a satisfactory industrial process for converting salt (sodium chloride) into soda (sodium carbonate). This prize was won by Nicholas Leblanc in 1790 with a process that treated salt with sulphuric acid, converting it into sodium sulphate which was then roasted with limestone and coal to produce a 'black ash' from which soda could be extracted using water (Williams, 1972, p39). In the 1820s the Leblanc process was brought to North West England, where the environmental devastation it created made it an unpopular neighbour: the chloride from the salt was released as hydrogen chloride gas, which corroded metal and building materials and killed vegetation, and the huge quantities of waste black ash was a source of sulphide pollution of air and water.[7] Complaints to parliament resulted in the Alkali Act of 1863, the first pollution control legislation.[8] That legislation prodded manufacturers into searching for processes and products that made use of the offending wastes, such as making bleach from the hydrogen chloride. Later, methods of producing sodium hydroxide solution from solutions of sodium chloride (brine), produced chlorine gas as a by-product. The need to use this chlorine was one of the factors that lead to the large scale production of organochlorine compounds such as polyvinyl chloride (PVC).[9]

However, despite the importance of the inorganic chemicals industry, the number of useful inorganic chemicals is limited. Also, the chemicals manufactured are found in nature: what was new was not their existence but the ability to produce them reasonably cheaply in large quantities. In contrast, the development of industrial organic chemistry, which started with the production of synthetic dyes in the 1850s (Williams, 1972, p65), has resulted in the production of chemicals not found in nature. The early synthetic dyes were made from the organic chemicals present in coal tar, using reactants such as concentrated sulphuric and nitric acids – products of the inorganic chemicals industry. Large scale production of synthetic organic chemicals began in earnest after the Second World War, using oil, rather than coal, as the source of carbon (Steingraber, 1998, p97).

There are now tens of thousands of commercially synthesized organic chemicals, some of which are identical to compounds found in nature, others of which are not.[10] However, the non-identical ones are often biologically active because their similarity to natural chemicals means they have similar, though not identical, shapes and properties. Their similarity means they participate in biochemical processes, substituting for the genuine biochemical molecules – hence many chemicals are now thought to be able to mimic our hormones, substances that at very low concentrations trigger important physiological pathways. Their dissimilarity, on the other hand, often means that they are not easily degraded by the biochemical pathway that, in conjunction with the pathway for the synthesis of the mimicked molecule, controls the level of that biochemical activity. Thus the body's control mechanisms are thrown off kilter, with complex multiple consequences. The non-degradable molecules persist, accumulating over the lifetime of a biological organism, often in its fat tissue (because organic chemicals are generally more soluble in fat than in water).

The key issues in chemicals legislation are, on the whole, ones around organic chemicals. The sheer number of different synthetic organic chemicals makes it difficult to know what their effects are. Their basic similarities to, but differences from, those made by life mean that they are likely to have effects on living organisms.

European Legislation on Chemicals

Types of legislation

The various types of legislation on chemicals can be differentiated according to what type of thing they consider chemicals to be. Thus pollution control legislation considers chemicals to be substances released into the environment from industrial processes; in health and safety legislation chemicals are hazardous substances in the workplace; in legislation on classification, packaging and labelling chemicals are substances that are sold or transported, about which the right information on hazards must be available; in product legislation chemicals are substances that are used in a particular type of product. Here my main focus will be on European legislation that applies generally to synthetic chemicals available commercially as substances for use in products and controls their classification, labelling, packaging and, in some instances, use. This is the legislative area that is of concern in the UK and EU chemicals strategies (DETR, 1999; CEC, 2001) and which is the subject of the RCEP's twenty-fourth report (RCEP, 2003). The body of law covering it has been built up gradually over the years, starting in 1967 with what has become known as the dangerous substances directive. The European Commission's chemicals strategy (CEC, 2001) proposed a complete overhaul of this legislation. Proposals for a new regulation, known as REACH (Registration, Evaluation, Authorization and restriction of Chemicals), were published in 2003 (CEC, 2003a) and REACH was finally agreed in December 2006.

Below I describe the development of European legislation from 1967 to the late 1990s and contrast some of the principles embedded in it with those contained in some product-specific legislation. I then give an account of REACH and the debates surrounding it.

Dangerous substances

The subject of the first EU directive on chemicals (67/548/EEC) was 'the approximation of laws, regulations and administrative provisions relating to the classification, packaging and labelling of dangerous substances'. The main purpose of this directive was the harmonization of the differing laws of the various Member States so as to enable the establishment of a common market in chemicals, while protecting human health. It was amended many times, to expand its scope to protection of the environment, add new chemicals to the various classifications, and to introduce the concepts of 'new' and 'existing' chemicals.

The dangerous substances directive required that substances falling into one of a number of categories of danger be appropriately packaged and be labelled to inform users of the nature of the danger and of the safety measures which must be applied during handling and use of the substance. The intent was to ensure that those transporting, handling or using chemicals in all countries of the European Community knew of the 'dangers' of those chemicals – whether they were corrosive, flammable, explosive or toxic, for example – so they could handle them in the right way to avoid the threatened danger. The term 'risk' was not used. By the 1990s the categories of danger were as follows: explosive, oxidizing, extremely flammable, highly flammable, flammable, very toxic, toxic, harmful, corrosive, irritant, sensitizing, carcinogenic, mutagenic, toxic for reproduction and dangerous for the environment. In 1999 about 4800 substances were listed in Annex I as falling into one or more of these categories (SLIM, 1999). Other annexes of the directive set out the methods to be used to determine the properties of substances which make them dangerous and criteria for deciding whether a substance is within one of the classes of danger.

In 1979 the sixth amendment to the dangerous substances directive (79/831/EEC) introduced a notification system for 'new' substances and made provision for the publication of an inventory of 'existing' substances, the latter being those substances on the European market by 18 September 1981. The European Inventory of Existing Commercial Substances (EINECS) was published in 1990 and lists 100,106 substances (SLIM, 1999). A decade later some 30,000 or so of these substances were thought to be marketed in volumes of above 1 tonne per year, these accounting for more than 99 per cent of the total volume of all substances on the EU market (CEC, 2001, p6).

Directive 79/831/EEC required that before marketing a new substance (one not listed on EINECS) a company must notify the competent authority in its Member State, giving information about the substance. The amount of information required increased as the volume of the substance marketed exceeded thresholds of 1 tonne, 10 tonnes, 100 tonnes and 1000 tonnes. The notifier also had to suggest 'methods and precautions' concerning handling, storage and transport of the substance and emergency measures in the case of accidental spillage or injury to persons and to propose how the substance should be classified and labelled. A European List of Notified Chemical Substances (ELINCS) was published periodically by the European Commission and by 2006 contained around 3800 substances (European Commission, 2006a). About 70 per cent of these are classified as dangerous (European Commission, 2006b).

It is in this sixth amendment that the term 'risk' makes an appearance in European legislation on chemicals: in the definition of 'dangerous to the environment' ('substances and preparations the use of which presents or may present immediate or delayed risks for the environment' (Article 1, 1(k) of Directive 79/831/EEC)) and in the description of the information that must be included in notifications of new substances, as that which is 'necessary for evaluating the foreseeable risks [...] which the substance may entail for man and the environment' (Article 6.1 of Directive 79/831/EEC). However, no formal assessment of risk had to be carried out until the 1990s when, in 1992, the seventh amendment (92/32/EEC) introduced the requirement for an assessment of the risks of new substances. Then, in 1993, Regulation 793/93 set out a procedure for assessing risks from existing substances. In both instances risk assessment was to be carried out by regulators. How they were to carry out the assessment was set out in Directive 93/67/EEC for new substances and Regulation (EC) 1488/94 for existing substances. Both used the same model of risk assessment, consisting of four stages and described with almost identical wording as follows:

1   hazard identification: 'the identification of the adverse effects which a substance has an inherent capacity to cause';
2   dose (concentration)–response (effect) assessment: 'the estimation of the relationship between dose, or level of exposure to a substance, and the incidence and severity of an effect';
3   exposure assessment: 'the determination of the emissions, pathways and rates of movement of a substance and its transformation or degradation in order to estimate the concentrations/doses to which human populations or environmental compartments are or may be exposed'; and
4   risk characterization: 'the estimation of the incidence and severity of the adverse effects likely to occur in the human population or environmental compartment due to actual or predicted exposure to a substance'. (Quotations are from the definitions in Article 2 of Directive 93/67/EEC.)

These four stages are identical to the four steps of the risk assessment process set out in a key 1983 US publication on risk assessment (NRC, 1983), demonstrating the influence of the US approach on Europe. It is recognized, however, that this model is not always appropriate, with ozone depletion being quoted as an effect for which stages 2 and 3 do not apply. In these cases regulators have to assess risks on a case-by-case basis and give a full description and justification of their assessments in their report to the Commission. In Chapter 7 I discuss how risk from chemicals are assessed in practice.

Assessments of risks are, of course, only as good as the information on which they are based. For new substances, information had to be supplied before a chemical could be marketed. This was not the case for existing substances. Under the Existing Substances Regulation (Regulation (EEC) 793/93) manufacturers or importers of more than 10 tonnes per year of a substance listed in the inventory had to supply information on that substance to the European Commission, and as the amount they manufacture or import increased so did the data requirements. Manufacturers and importers had to make all reasonable efforts to obtain data but 'in the absence of information, manufacturers and importers are not bound to carry out further tests on animals in order to submit such data' (Regulation 793/93, Article 3). This provision effectively meant that industry did not have to provide data on the toxicity of chemicals. Because such data could result in a chemical being classified as dangerous, and thus reduce its market, industry had no interest in providing this data.

Following receipt of data the Commission drew up priority lists of substances that, on the basis of that data, were thought to have the potential to pose a risk of harm to human health or the environment. By the publication of the EU White Paper in 2001, four lists, containing a total of 141 substances, had been adopted by the relevant technical committee (CEC, 2001). The progress of these risk assessments was very slow. Risk assessment of hexabromocyclododecane (HBCD), for example, commenced in 1997 but was still not completed nine years later (ENDS, 2006). In 2006 around 16,700 tonnes of HBCD were produced every year for use as a flame retardant. It may have neurotoxic effects and interfere with the metabolism of thyroid hormone, but because risk assessment of it had not reached a conclusion there were no restrictions on its use. By 2006 final risk assessment reports were available for only about 70 substances (European Commission, 2006b) – less than 0.5 per cent of the 30,000 or so existing substances on the European market at quantities of above 1 tonne per annum.

Lack of data about an existing substance did not prevent it from being produced and marketed. Restrictions could only be put in place if a risk assessment had been carried out by regulators, and that risk assessment would only be carried out if the chemical was put on a priority list because there was data suggesting that it may be a cause for concern. The lack of data on existing chemicals and the slow progress of risk assessments under the existing chemicals regime were seen as major failings of the system that the new system, REACH, is intended to address.

Product-specific regimes

Before going on to examine REACH, it will be useful to briefly look at some alternative approaches to regulating chemicals contained in legislation that is specific to particular products. Pesticides, biocides, cosmetics, pharmaceuticals, veterinary medicines, food additives and animal feeds all have their own legislation at European level (see RCEP, 2003, pp61–62 for a list of the relevant directives). While the controls in the dangerous substances directive operate on the negative principle of allowing use of a chemical unless it is specifically restricted, controls under these product-specific regimes operate on a positive approval system: a substance cannot be used in that type of product unless it has been approved for such use.

For example, Directive 91/414/EEC on plant protection products requires that all the 834 existing active ingredients in pesticides are reviewed using a prioritization procedure similar to that used for existing substances. Substances which pass this review are placed on an EU-wide 'positive' list and only these can be used as active ingredients in pesticides in the EU. The costs of providing the data and evaluations to support a product through the review process have led to many products being withdrawn. It is estimated that by the end of the process 500 of the

834 active pesticide ingredients on the market in 1991 will have been withdrawn, and only around 20 to 30 new substances added (ENDS, 2002).

A further step up from positive approval is comparative assessment. This has long been a principle of the regulation of pharmaceuticals, where it means that treatments which do not offer significant benefits over alternative, lower risk treatments are not approved. The biocidal products directive (98/8/EC) applies it to biologically active ingredients used in products such as disinfectants, preservatives, fungicides and pest control products that are not covered by other legislation. Comparative assessment means that a biocide can be refused approval if there is another active ingredient for the same product type which presents a significantly lower risk to health or the environment, and if this alternative can be used with similar effect without significant economic and practical disadvantages for the user (DETR, 1999, paragraph 5.38).

As can be seen, the various directives and regulations on chemicals differ in the demands they place on the chemicals industry to provide information on the effects of the chemicals that they produce and use. They also vary in where the burden of proof lies – with the regulator to show that a chemical is a significant risk, or with the manufacturer or importer to show that a chemical meets certain requirements. In some cases what has to be demonstrated is not simply whether or not there is a risk, but whether a chemical is or is not more hazardous than alternatives.

REACH

REACH stands for Registration, Evaluation, Authorization and restriction of Chemicals. It is a new system for regulating chemicals that replaces the dangerous substances directive. It has been introduced as a regulation at European level, so comes into force directly, without the need for Member States to bring in their own legislation to implement it. REACH was proposed by the European Commission White Paper 'A strategy for a future chemicals policy', published in 2001 (CEC, 2001). The White Paper was the outcome of concerns within several Member States about the slow pace of progress on assessing chemicals under the existing substances regulation. In addition, the accession to the EU in the mid 1990s of Sweden, with its precautionary approach to chemicals in products, and moves in The Netherlands to institute their own, comprehensive controls on chemicals (see RCEP, 2003, pp70–73) meant that there was a need for radical change at the European level if approaches to chemicals regulation within the EU were not to be fragmented.

The White Paper recognized that certain chemicals may be having significant effects on the health of humans and wildlife and that there is a lack of knowledge about the impacts of many chemicals, described as a 'huge gap in knowledge of substances' (CEC, 2001, p5). With respect to the EU risk assessment process, described as 'slow and resource-intensive' (CEC, 2001, p6), the White Paper made the following specific criticisms:

1   the allocation of responsibilities, with authorities, not enterprises, responsible for the assessment, is inappropriate;

2 only manufacturers and importers of substances have to provide information, not downstream users, so information on uses and about exposure resulting from this use is difficult to obtain and scarce (Information on chemicals in products is often regarded as commercially sensitive, with neither regulators nor the public having a right to access it.); and

3 decisions to require further testing have to go through a lengthy committee procedure and require proof that a substance may present a serious risk. However, without test results such proof cannot be provided. (CEC, 2001, p6)

The objectives of the chemicals strategy outlined in the White Paper were:

1 the protection of human health and the environment (a later paragraph uses the phrase 'the promotion of a non-toxic environment');

2 the prevention of fragmentation of the internal market;

3 increased transparency, so that consumers have access to information on chemicals and can thus make informed decisions and so that enterprises understand the regulatory process;

4 integration with international efforts, because the global nature of the chemicals industry and the trans-boundary impact of certain chemical substances make chemical safety an international issue;

5 promotion of non-animal testing, through the development and validation of non-animal testing methods; and

6 conformity with EU international obligations under the WTO (World Trade Organization), so unnecessary barriers to trade must not be created, nor must imported substances and products be discriminated against. (CEC, 2001, p7)

After a period of consultation on its workability, REACH was published as a proposal for a regulation in October 2003 (CEC, 2003a). It was finally agreed by the European Parliament and the Council of Ministers in December 2006 (Regulation (EC) 1907/2006, Directive 2006/12/1EC) and came into force in June 2007. The components of REACH – registration, evaluation, authorization and restrictions – are outlined below.

Registration

All synthetic chemicals manufactured or imported in quantities above 1 tonne per annum per company have to be registered before they can be manufactured or imported.[11] To register a substance the manufacturer or importer must submit a dossier containing specified information on the substance to a new European Chemicals Agency, which will be set up to manage the technical, scientific and administrative aspects of the REACH system. The data that must be supplied in the dossier is specified in annexes of REACH. It includes information on the identity, properties and uses of the substance, the classification and labelling of the substance, and guidance on the safe use of the substance. As the amount of a substance produced by a company increases above 10 tonnes, 100 tonnes and 1000 tonnes, more information must be supplied. As it will not be possible to register all substances at once there is to be a phase-in period for registration of current existing substances (substances that have been notified as 'new' substances will be deemed to already be registered). High volume substances (over 1000 tonnes per year per company) and certain other substances of high concern have to be registered by November 2010, substances produced in quantities of more than 100 tonnes per year by June 2013 and all other substances by June 2018.

In addition to the technical dossier, registrations for substances produced or imported in quantities of more than 10 tonnes (thought to be only about one third of the 30,000 or so chemicals which will require registration) have to include a chemical safety report (CSR), documenting a chemical safety assessment (CSA). The requirements for these are set out in Annex I of the Regulation. They differ from previous chemicals risk assessment practice in two ways. First, the initial hazard-identification stage of the CSA must include an assessment of whether the substance is persistent, bioaccumulative and toxic (PBT) or very persistent and very bioaccumulative (vPvB). Second, the exposure assessment (which is carried out where a chemical is PBT or vPvB, or if it is classified as dangerous) is based on 'exposure scenarios' for the identified uses of the substance. These set out the conditions of use and the risk management measures that, when implemented, are considered to result in the risks from the substance being 'adequately controlled' (see Chapter 7).

Substances imported into the EU incorporated in articles must be registered where they are intended to be released from the articles during their use and the quantity of the substance incorporated in articles placed on the EU market exceeds 1 tonne per year. Where a substance is not intended to be released from an article the agency should nonetheless be notified, and can require its registration, if the substance is considered to be of very high concern (so it is a candidate for authorization), its concentration in the article exceeds 0.1 per cent by weight and the quantity of it in such articles placed on the EU market exceeds 1 tonne per year. However, this notification is not required if the exposure of humans or the environment to the substance in the article can be excluded during normal conditions of use, including disposal. In these instances safety instructions should be provided.

Evaluation

The evaluation stage is intended to ensure that there is sufficient information about a substance to know whether its use poses a risk to human health or the environment, while avoiding unnecessary testing. Two types of evaluations are carried out:

1 'dossier evaluations' check that the requirements of the legislation have been fulfilled (at least 5 per cent of dossiers will be checked for compliance) and consider any proposals for testing on animals; and
2 'substance evaluations' consider whether further information is required on a substance to decide whether it should be subject to restrictions or authorization procedures.

Substances are prioritized by the European Chemicals Agency for evaluation, carried out by competent authorities in Member States, which may recommend that the substance be subject to authorization or its uses restricted.

Authorization

The authorization procedures effectively reverse the normal burden of proof of regulation: rather than a regulator having to demonstrate that risks from a substance are unacceptable, those wishing to manufacture or use substances subject to authorization have to show that risks from the use are adequately controlled, or that the socio-economic benefits outweigh the risks, taking into account alternative substances or processes. Substances subject to authorization are those listed in Annex XIV of REACH and users of these substances have to apply to the European Chemicals Agency for authorizations for their use. Substances of 'very high concern' are eligible for inclusion in the annex, 'very high concern' being defined (in Article 57) as the following:

- substances that are category 1 or 2 carcinogens, mutagens or toxins to reproduction;
- PBT substances;
- vPvB substances; and
- substances (such as endocrine disrupters) for which there is scientific evidence of probable serious effects to human health or the environment which gives rise to an equivalent level of concern, to be identified on a case-by-case basis.

The European Chemicals Agency is to publish a list of substances matching these criteria that are candidates for Annex XIV. Inclusion in the annex is then agreed by a committee procedure, with priority being given to substances with PBT or vPvB properties that are used in high volumes or in applications which result in significant dispersion to the environment (Article 58).

Restrictions

Member States or the Commission (via the Agency) can propose that the manufacture or use of specific substances is restricted, provided that a risk assessment has shown that the substances pose an unacceptable risk to human health or the environment. The risk assessment and the proposed restrictions must be considered within a set time period by a committee within the European Chemicals Agency (Article 67). The proposed restrictions are subject to a socio-economic analysis, considered by another committee within the Agency, and the opinion of both committees forwarded to the Commission.

Existing restrictions, made under the Marketing and Use Directive (76/769/EEC), are carried over into REACH (Article 64). In addition, REACH makes provision for restrictions of persistent organic pollutants (POPs) to fulfil the EU's obligations under United Nations (UN) conventions[12] to phase out the production, use and emissions of chemicals that, because of their volatility and persistence, are dispersed globally by air and sea currents. Thirteen such substances, listed in Annex XVII, are banned from production and use, though with some derogations.

The Debate about REACH

Introduction

The two most contentious aspects of REACH have been the registration require-ments and the authorization process. While no one has argued that substances should not have to be registered, there have been many arguments about the amount of data that must be submitted in the registration dossiers and about how to deal with substances contained in manufactured articles imported from outside the EU. The public availability of information has also been an issue. The focus of the debate about authorization was whether authorizations should be granted where an alternative was available. The debate here can be seen as an argument between risk-based and precautionary approaches.

Before going on to discuss these issues of contention, I would like to note a couple of issues that have been uncontentious. The first is the role of industry in providing information on its chemicals and assessing their risks, where under the previous system risk assessment was carried out by regulators. Neither industry nor environmental non-governmental organizations (NGOs) have taken issue with this role being given to industry, though NGOs have argued that regulators will nonetheless need significant resources so they are able to scrutinize industry assessments and enforce the system. The second is the positive attitude towards innovation in chemicals. The Commission has argued that one of the benefits of REACH is that it encourages the development of new chemicals by ending the current discrimination against new compared to existing chemicals. For chemicals produced in small volumes REACH is much less onerous than the former notifi-cation system for new chemicals. The consensus on the benefits of innovation is partly a matter of the general positive attitude towards technological innovation, discussed in Chapter 4, but also it is often assumed that new chemicals will be safer than the old ones. This is despite the fact that most new chemicals are classi-fied as dangerous (European Commission, 2006b). The problems for regulation posed by the sheer number of different chemical substances – which will only be increased by the development of new substances – are not considered.

Registration requirements

Perhaps the maim aim of REACH is to 'bridge the knowledge gap': to provide data that is currently not available on the hazards and risks of synthetic chemicals. The problem is that providing that data costs money, and can cost the lives of large numbers of laboratory animals. Thus some of the early debates over REACH saw a strange alliance between the chemicals industry, which wanted to limit requirements because they were going to have to pay for testing, and animal rights organizations, who did not want chemicals to be tested on animals.

A coalition of animal protection organizations, led by the British Union for the Abolition of Vivisection (BUAV), proposed a completely non-animal testing strategy. They claimed that such a strategy, involving consideration of molecular structure, comparison with related compounds, tests on cell cultures and tests on human volunteers (for example for skin irritancy of substances not thought to be irritants), would be scientifically better as well as more humane than existing animal tests (Langley, 2001). In Chapter 7 I compare this strategy with that of animal testing from the perspective of recent debates in the philosophy of science.

The arguments against animal testing had a degree of success in the negotiations over REACH: the sentence 'This Regulation should also promote the development of alternative methods for the assessment of hazards of substances' was added to the first paragraph, and Article 13 states that information on intrinsic properties may be generated by means other than animal tests, and that for human toxicity in particular means other than vertebrate animal tests should be used whenever possible. There is also a commitment to review test methods with a view to reducing testing on vertebrate animals. However, the annexes specifying the information required to register substances do specify tests on animals for substances produced in quantities of above 10 tonnes, and replacing these tests with other data must be justified. But the animal tests specified in Annexes IX and X (for substances produced in quantities of more than 100 tonnes per year and more than 1000 tonnes per year respectively) do not have to be carried out if their results are not already available. Instead the dossier need only include proposals for carrying out these tests, which are to be available for comment by third parties. The aim of this, and provisions on data sharing between registrants, is to ensure that animal tests are not duplicated. While this in itself seems to be a reasonable aim, it does go against the normal practice of science, which is to require repeatable results. If a test is only done once how can we know that the result would be the same if it were done again? Will positive test results be repeated to try to find evidence that the chemical is not hazardous, but tests with negative results not be repeated?

Another issue in the debate about registration requirements was whether the amount of data required should be based on the amount of the substance produced per company, as it was in the new and existing substances regimes. The RCEP considered that tonnage thresholds serve no useful purpose, except at the lowest level to define chemicals produced in too small a quantity to warrant testing, because chemicals vary widely in their behaviour in the environment and in the concentration at which they can have a physiological effect (RCEP, 2003, p18). Tonnage thresholds were criticized by industry groups, who argued that testing should be focused on substances of possible risk rather than on those produced in high volumes. Such a risk-based testing approach ran the danger of replicating the problems with the existing chemicals regime: a lack of data on a substance would mean it would not be considered to be a risk, and so would not be prioritized for further testing. Industry pressure to remove tonnage thresholds was resisted and the debate moved on to how much testing was required, particularly for substances produced in lower tonnages. Here industry did win concessions: the draft regulation published in 2003 proposed much reduced data requirements, compared with the original proposals, for substances produced at less then 10 tonnes per year per company. Around two thirds of the substances covered by REACH are thought to fall into this category.[13] These requirements were subsequently increased for substances with dispersive uses, substances that are incorporated into consumer articles, and substances for which there is evidence that they may be toxic or present risks to the environment. Even so, for many chemicals no information on their toxicity will have to be provided to register them.

A further issue associated with registration was whether each company that manufactures or imports a substance should submit a registration, or whether companies should join together in consortia to submit joint registrations. The former was included in the draft regulation (CEC, 2003a). The latter had implications for commercial confidentiality and raised the issue of how costs should be shared between companies. However, the benefits of 'one substance, one registration' in reduced testing and administrative costs won the argument. A six-month pre-registration phase to enable all those manufacturing or importing existing chemicals to identify themselves was introduced. Companies submit some data, such as their production volume, separately, but test data on the chemical must be submitted by the 'lead registrant' for a chemical on behalf of all the registrants.

European industry will obviously be at a competitive disadvantage if manufacturing industry elsewhere does not have to following the same requirements with regard to chemicals in their products, and can import those products into Europe. There was a great deal of scepticism as to the practicality of the provisions of REACH relating to substances in articles (see ENDS, 2004). These do not give equal treatment to imported and EU-manufactured articles, as substances in the former only have to be registered if they are intended to be released from the article during its use. Furthermore, the 0.1 per cent concentration threshold for the notification of substances of high concern in articles is relative to the whole article (a whole car, for example) not just the part of the article containing the substance (such as the dashboard or seat upholstery), so it is likely that many articles containing such substances will not have to be notified.

Rights to know about chemicals in products

Enforcing requirements about the registration or notification of substances in articles would be more straightforward if the chemical constituents of all articles had to be disclosed. However, the European Commission made it clear that REACH would not require importers to declare the contents of their articles (CEC, 2003a), and similarly there is no right to know the chemical constituents of EU-manufactured goods. Such a right to know was one of the demands of environmental NGOs in the 'Copenhagen Charter'.[14] In Chapter 10 I argue that this information is vital if individuals are to be enabled to act responsibly in the decisions they make regarding their purchase of products. But such a right to know has been resisted by industry. They argue that information on the chemical constituents of products is commercially sensitive, so should be confidential. Some of the information submitted in registration dossiers, such as the precise use of a substance, is indeed regarded in REACH as commercially sensitive and is not publicly available, and registrants can make a case for other information to be treated as confidential.

The one area in which REACH does give consumers the right to know about chemicals in products is with respect to the presence of substances of very high concern. However, products do not have to be labelled to indicate that they contain such substances, rather consumers must be provided with this information if they request it.

Authorization

Another of the demands of environmental NGOs was that manufacturers and users of chemicals should be obliged to use the least hazardous substance or process appropriate for a use. They, and the Greens in the European Parliament, argued strongly that this substitution principle should be incorporated into the authorization process, but only had limited success. Users of substances subject to authorization have to show either that the risks from that use are 'adequately controlled' (Article 60(2)), or that the socio-economic benefits of the use outweigh the risks (Article 60(4)). It is only in the latter case that an authorization will not be granted if suitable alternatives are available, though all applications for authorizations have to 'analyse the availability of alternatives and consider their risks and the technical and economic feasibility of substitution' (Article 55). If they find that alternatives are available then their application for authorization has to include a substitution plan. However, there is scepticism as to the effects of these provisions: the analysis has to be made by the applicant (who is likely to conclude that substitutes are not available if this is what is in their interests), and the technical and economic feasibility of any alternatives are for that particular applicant, not for the use in general.

Adequate control is considered to have been achieved if estimated exposure levels do not exceed 'derived no-effect levels' (DNELs) for human exposure or 'predicted no-effect concentrations' (PNECs) for environmental spheres (Annex 1, section 6). The many uncertainties involved in deriving these levels, discussed in Chapter 7, will be negotiated by the production of guidance setting out how test results are to be interpreted and exposure levels predicted. This will enable decisions to be made, but may not mean that authorized uses do not, in reality, have harmful effects. It is recognized that no-effect levels cannot be defined for substances that are persistent, PBT or vPvB, as well as for some carcinogenic, mutagenic or toxic to reproduction (CMR) substances (European Commission, 2006a, p13). Uses of such substances can therefore only be authorized if socio-economic benefits outweigh the risks. Paragraph 71 of the preamble to REACH signals the intention to develop ways of establishing thresholds for carcinogenic and mutagenic substances. The environmental NGO World Wide Fund for Nature (WWF) therefore concludes that it is only PBT and vPvB substances that will have to be replaced by safer alternatives (WWF, 2006).

A further concern is the limited range of substances that will be subject to authorization. The criteria for PBT and vPvB substances (set out in Annex XIII) are very restrictive and will be met by very few substances. For substances of 'equivalent concern', such as endocrine disrupters, there must be 'scientific evidence of probable serious effects to human health or the environment'. This is a demanding requirement and it could therefore be the case that no substances become subject to authorization because they are endocrine disrupting. The number of substances that will be subject to authorization will also depend on the capacity of the European Chemicals Agency to deal with the applications.

The competences of the Agency were increased during the negotiations over REACH, primarily because industry thought this would result in more consistent decision making, but its funding was yet to be agreed at the end of 2006. How many substances for authorization they will be able to cope with at any one time is therefore very unclear.

Risk versus precaution

Substitution is considered to be a precautionary approach as it requires that a less hazardous chemical or process be used if possible, even if there is no clear evidence that there is a significant risk. The basis for substitution is the possibility that the hazardous chemical may cause significant harm. As I discuss in Chapter 6, considering possibilities rather than probabilities means that the extent of our ignorance, rather than just our knowledge about a chemical, is taken into account. This is a precautionary approach because it takes preventative action when definitive evidence that harm will occur is not available. This use of the precautionary principle was one of the objections to REACH made by the US government in its 'non-paper' on EU chemicals policy, issued in February 2002 (Geiser and Tickner, 2003). The non-paper suggested that the invocation of the precautionary principle where data is unavailable or delayed could provide cover for politically motivated trade restrictions, and questioned whether decisions to require substitution of 'safer' chemicals could be made on a non-arbitrary basis. It argued against authorization on the basis that it could 'remove useful chemicals from the market' and reduce consumer choice.

The US government favours a risk-based approach, by which it means that action to restrict the production, use or import of a chemical should only be taken if that chemical is known to present a risk of harm. The main legislative instrument in the US, the Toxic Substances Control Act, presupposes that industry has the right to produce and market chemicals: the EPA can only restrict that right if it can demonstrate that a chemical poses an 'unreasonable risk'. It must show that the risks outweigh the costs restrictions would impose on industry and the lost benefits of unrestricted use of the chemical (RCEP, 2003, p75). While European legislation demands more from industry in the way of data on chemicals and generally leads to more controls on their production and use, it is nonetheless influenced by the same philosophy as the US system. Thus the RCEP report noted that, despite the lack of progress in assessing the risks of chemicals, 'many regulators and industry bodies continue to argue strongly that control must be on the basis of known risk, regardless of other indications of concern' (RCEP, 2003, p96). And when they proposed REACH, the European Commission emphasized that the authorization requirements are risk-based, in line with the general REACH approach (CEC, 2003a, p16).

The RCEP considered that the current risk assessment approach has the advantage of being evidence-based and transparent, but that a new approach, one that 'balances' precaution with an evidence-based approach is needed (RCEP, 2003, p96). This suggests that precaution disregards evidence, which is not the case. Rather, it is more open to different types of evidence than the often narrow view taken by risk assessment. It considers the 'weight of evidence', the evidence from different, independent sources, which, though none individually is necessarily conclusive, may together form a convincing case. It does not require conclusive proof.[15] Importantly, rather than just focusing on positive knowledge, a precautionary approach takes into account areas of ignorance and considers the potential consequences of that ignorance. In everyday language it considers how *risky* something is, not just the known *risks*.

A work still in progress

Many aspects of REACH are to be reviewed within a few years of REACH coming into force in June 2007. These include Annex I, which sets out the requirements for CSRs (to be reviewed within 12 months); Annex XIII (criteria for identification of PBT and vPvB substances) (within 18 months); the authorization of endocrine-disrupting substances (after 6 years); and the registration requirements for substances below 10 tonnes (after 12 years). These reviews, along with the fact that the implementation of REACH will depend on how its provisions are interpreted and the guidance documents that are produced, mean that it is very difficult to say what REACH will mean in practice for the production and use of synthetic chemicals and the protection of human health and the environment from their harmful effects.

The indications so far, though, are that despite the many concerns expressed, including by the European Commission, about the harm synthetic chemicals are probably doing to us and to our environment, nothing will happen very quickly. The desire for a process that does not restrict the use of a chemical – or even demand information about it – unless this is warranted, has resulted in a complex system that will take years to implement. In 2003 the RCEP recommended that all chemicals manufactured or imported into the UK should be listed on a publicly available database, along with information on their tonnages, properties, uses and so on, within 3 years and that they should be sorted using criteria such as persistence, bioaccumulation and toxicity within a further 3 years (RCEP, 2003, Chapter 4). In contrast, the first deadline for registering existing substances under REACH is not until November 2010, and substances below 100 tonnes per year do not have to be registered until June 2018. No substances will be subject to authorization until 2010 at the earliest and the European Commission apparently estimates that it will take the European Chemicals Agency 65 years to review the 1500–1600 substances that are expected to be on the candidate list for authorization (The United States Mission to the European Union, 2006). Individual applications for authorized uses could take 18 months or more to decide. REACH asks industry to submit all available information in registration dossiers, not just that specified in the relevant annexes, but unless there is a thorough checking process (which seems doubtful given the demands on the agency and the fact that only 5 per cent of dossiers have to be checked for compliance), it is unlikely that they will volunteer information that is inimical to their interests. This approach is similar to that in the existing substances regime. Though more data about chemicals will no doubt be obtained by REACH, there is plenty of scope for the procrastination and delay that has characterized the risk assessment of existing chemicals.

Conclusions

In this chapter I have described the regulatory system for synthetic chemicals in the EU. This system tends to see chemicals as isolated entities that need to be regulated because in some cases they cause harm. The industry that produces them is valued because it is part of the economy – it provides jobs and, through export of chemicals, foreign currency to pay for imports. So regulations to reduce the risks of harm have to be assessed for their effects on that industry and the economy more generally, and these effects compared with benefits from reducing risks. In Chapter 8 I look more closely at how that assessment is carried out and challenge the assumption that it makes with regard to the relationship between a regulation, such as REACH, and the economy.

Chemicals regulation is predominantly 'risk-based', in that only if there is clear evidence that there is a significant risk of a chemical causing a known type of harm is the production or use of the chemical subject to controls; the aim of those controls is to reduce the risks associated with a chemical. The requirement to demonstrate harm, or a risk of harm, before restrictions can be placed on chemical production or use, is in accordance with the 'harm principle', one of the major tenets of the political philosophy of liberalism. The harm principle holds that the government should only interfere with the actions of the individual if those actions cause harm to others. In Chapter 8 I consider the arguments put forward by liberals in defence of the harm principle and conclude that they do not justify its application to the industrial production of chemicals.

The central importance of risk in chemicals regulation warrants an examination of the concept of risk, which I undertake in the next chapter. I argue that rather than trying to assess risks, understood as the probability of harm, we should ask how risky a technology is, where riskiness is a matter of the possibility of harm. It is a way of thinking about precaution. In Chapter 7, after examining the practice of chemicals risk assessment and showing why it is so difficult to obtain agreement on whether a chemical poses a risk or not, I suggest four aspects of chemicals that contribute to their riskiness: their capacity to cause harm, their novelty, and (for novel chemicals) their persistence and mobility. How such assessments of riskiness could function in the regulation of chemicals is discussed in Chapter 10.

Finally, in addition to systems of direct controls on chemicals, we could devise systems of regulation that start from the view of technology as world-building that I set out in Chapter 3. I suggested two definitions of technology: it is how we add things to the world and the things that we have added to the world that we use. Synthetic chemicals are clearly things that we have added to the world that we use. Under the first definition it is the chemical production processes that constitute technology, while under the second it is the synthetic chemicals themselves. This gives two ways of thinking about chemicals: first, in terms of the nature of the world constituted by the technology which makes them; second, in terms of whether a particular use of a chemical is appropriate and justified in its context and in comparison with other means of achieving the same aim. These two alternative frameworks for thinking about chemicals are discussed in Chapter 10.

Notes

1   The EU Commission White Paper (CEC, 2001) says that chemicals 'bring about benefits on which modern society is entirely dependent, for example in food production, medicines, textiles, cars, etc' (CEC, 2001, p4). The EU trade surplus in chemicals and the number of people employed directly and indirectly by the EU chemicals industry are also counted as benefits. These ideas of what counts as a benefit are critically examined in Chapter 8.

2   In the UK chemicals strategy the statement 'The Government is very concerned that we do not have adequate information about the hazards of most chemicals released into the environment in large quantities' is emphasized in bold in section 1.7 (DETR, 1999). The EU strategy states that 'The lack of knowledge about the impact of many chemicals on human health and the environment is a cause for concern' (CEC, 2001, p4). The Royal Commission on Environmental Pollution held an inquiry into chemicals that reported in 2003. They consider that 'our failure to understand the interactions between synthetic chemicals and the natural environment, and most of all our failure to compile even the most basic information about the behaviour of chemicals in the environment, is a serious matter' (RCEP, 2003, p1).

3   In the case of some oestrogenic chemicals (that mimic the effects of the female hormone oestrogen) it has been shown that what should be added to predict the combined effect of a mixture is not the effects of the individual chemicals but their concentrations (Silva et al, 2002). This means that a substance present at a concentration at which on its own it has no oestrogenic effect will contribute to the total oestrogenic effect of a mixture containing other oestrogenic chemicals. For such substances there is in practice no real threshold concentration below which they do not have an effect. Such 'no-effect levels' are a crucial part of chemicals risk assessment, as I will explain in Chapter 7.

4   For example, carbon tetrachloride and ethanol are together more toxic to the liver than would be expected from simply adding their toxicities together (DETR, 1999, Box 1.4).

5   A covalent bond is formed by the sharing of one or more electrons from each of the two atoms that form the bond. Covalent bonds are typically formed by non-metallic elements with each other. The group of atoms so bonded is a molecule. In contrast, metallic elements generally form positively charged ions, by the metal atom losing an electron to the atom of a non-metallic element, the latter becoming a negatively charged ion.

6   Salts consist of positive and negative ions in a lattice crystal structure (until dissolved in water). Minerals are essentially salts, though the negative ion is often a complex one, for example a negatively charged molecule, as opposed to an atom.

7   This pollution is still a significant problem in St Helens in North West England, which had many alkali works. Playing fields, homes and industrial estates have all now been constructed on the tips from those works, but sulphide still leaches into the streams which run through the waste tips.

8   The Alkali Act of 1863 required that 95 per cent of the emissions of hydrogen chloride be abated and a national inspectorate was set up to enforce the legislation (NSCA, 1998). Later acts charged the inspectorate with the regulation of other types of industrial pollution, but it retained its name of The Alkali Inspectorate until 1983, when it became Her Majesty's Industrial Air Pollution Inspectorate (NSCA, 1998, p5). The approach of the Alkali Act, of allowing industry to cause pollution, but setting constraints and limits over how much pollution it can emit, has become the standard UK approach to pollution control.

9   Chlorine gas is produced by the electrolysis of brine (sodium chloride) in Castner-Kellner cells (first operated in 1886), the main purpose of which is the production of sodium hydroxide solution. Williams (1972, p98) reports that the extent to which the Castner-Kellner process was worked in Britain depended on the ability to dispose of the chlorine. In this light the production of chlorinated organic compounds can be seen as a response to the need to use chlorine. The argument that we need to produce chlorinated organic compounds to use up chlorine was indeed put to me by manufacturers of polyvinyl chloride (PVC) at a DETR-organized seminar on the lifecycle assessment of PVC in July 2001: PVC is the only product made in sufficient quantities to use up all the chlorine produced by other processes. This suggests that if a particular use of a chemical is stopped, because there is a better (less hazardous) way of achieving that purpose, it will have knock-on effects on the availability of chemicals that are co-produced

with it, unless other ways of producing those chemicals can be found. In the case of sodium hydroxide, it can be produced from brine in ways that produce a chloride salt, rather than the toxic chlorine gas.

10   The non-identical compounds include ones that have the same chemical structure and formula as ones found in nature, but which are not the same stereoisomer: the molecule (or part of it) is asymmetric, so can take two spatial forms which are mirror images of each other. Often only one of these forms is made by natural systems, but both are made by industrial synthesis. The biological effects of the two forms may be quite different (see RCEP, 2003, pp13–14).

11   Substances that are adequately covered by other legislation, such as wastes, radioactive substances, and substances used in food or as medicinal products do not have to be registered. Polymers do not have to be registered but the monomers they are made of do. Substances listed in REACH Annex IV do not have to be registered because 'sufficient information is known about these substances that they are considered to cause minimum risk because of their intrinsic properties' (Article 2(7)(a)). These include vegetable oils, water, carbon dioxide, limestone and basic biochemical molecules such as glucose, ascorbic acid and fatty acids. Annex V lists types of substances whose 'registration is deemed inappropriate or unnecessary' (Article 2 (7)(b)). These include naturally occurring substances such as minerals, ores, crude oil and coal. Also listed are 'substances occurring in nature [...] if they are not chemically modified, unless they meet the criteria for classification as dangerous according to Directive 67/548/EEC'.

12   The Stockholm Convention and the Protocol on Persistent Organic Pollutants of the UNECE 1979 Convention on Long Range Transboundary Air Pollution.

13   Substances produced in quantities of less than 10 tonnes per year include most of the chemicals used as textile dyestuffs and auxiliaries (CEC, 2003b). This illustrates the inadequacy of using tonnage thresholds as a measure of human exposure. Chemicals used to dye or treat cloth are present in our clothes and may leach from clothes through our skin into our bodies. We may also inhale the chemicals, after the skin has flaked off and become part of household dust (ENDS, 1994). Clothes are probably one of the major routes of human exposure to synthetic chemicals and the long-term effects of those chemicals should surely be investigated.

14   The 'Copenhagen Charter' was agreed by a conference of environmental NGOs in Copenhagen in October 2000. It asks for:

1   a full right to know, including what chemicals are present in products;
2   a deadline by which all chemicals on the market must have had their safety independently assessed. All uses of a chemical should be approved and should be demonstrated to be safe beyond reasonable doubt;
3   a phase-out of persistent or bioaccumulative chemicals;
4   a requirement to substitute less safe chemicals with safer alternatives; and
5   a commitment to stop all releases to the environment of hazardous substances by 2020.

15   REACH (Annex XI) recommends that a weight of evidence approach is used for deciding whether or not a chemical has a particular dangerous property. See also De Rosa et al (1996) on the use of a weight of evidence approach in the assessment of the effects of chemicals.

References

Cadbury, D. (1998) *The Feminization of Nature: Our Future at Risk*, Penguin Books, Harmondsworth

CEC (Commission of the European Communities) (2001) 'White Paper: Strategy for a future chemicals policy', Brussels, 27 February

CEC (2003a) 'Proposal for a Regulation of the European Parliament and of the Council concerning the registration, evaluation, authorization and restriction of chemicals (REACH), establishing a European Chemicals Agency and amending Directive 1999/45/EC and Regulation (EC) {on Persistent Organic Pollutants} and Proposal for a Directive of the European Parliament and of the Council amending Council Directive 67/548/EEC in order to adapt it to Regulation (EC) of the European Parliament and of the Council concerning the registration, evaluation, authorization and restriction of chemicals', Brussels, 29 October, COM (2003) 644

CEC (2003b) 'Regulation of the European Parliament and of the Council concerning the registration, evaluation, authorisation and restriction of chemicals (REACH), establishing a European Chemicals Agency and amending Directive 1999/45/EC and Regulation (EC) {on Persistent Organic Pollutants}', Extended Impact Assessment, Commission Working Paper Com (2003)644 final, Brussels, 29 October

Colborn, T., Dumanoski, D. and Myers, J. P. (1996) *Our Stolen Future*, Little Brown and Company, London

De Rosa, C. T. Johnson, B. L., Fay, M., Hansen, H. and Mumtaz, M. M. (1996) 'Public health implications of hazardous waste sites: Findings, assessment and research', *Food and Chemical Toxicology*, vol 34, pp1131–1138

DETR (Department of the Environment, Transport and the Regions) (1999) 'Sustainable production and use of chemicals, a strategic approach. The Government's chemicals strategy', Stationery Office, London

ENDS (1994) 'Dioxins from textiles pollute skin, sewage and rivers', *The ENDS Report*, no 235, pp3–4

ENDS (2002) 'A testing prospect for biocides', *The ENDS Report*, no 332, pp23–27

ENDS (2004) 'No "silver bullet" for addressing products under REACH', *The ENDS Report*, no 352, p7

ENDS (2006) 'Scientists call for research on HBCD flame retardant', *The ENDS Report*, no 378, p27

Environmental Defense Fund (1997) 'Toxic ignorance: The continuing absence of basic health testing for top-selling chemicals in the United States', www.environmentaldefense.org, accessed October 2006

European Commission (2006a) 'REACH in brief', http://ec.europa.eu/environment/chemicals, accessed December 2006

European Commission (2006b) 'Q and A on the new chemicals policy, REACH', Memo/06/488, Brussels, 13 December, http://ec.europa.eu/environment/chemicals, accessed December 2006

European Environment Agency (1998) 'Chemicals in the European environment: Low doses, high stakes?', European Enviroment Agency and United Nations Environment Programme Annual Message 2 on the State of Europe's Environment, European Environment Agency

Freemantle, M. (1987) *Chemistry in Action*, Macmillan Education Ltd, London

Geiser, K. and Tickner, J. (2003) *New Directions in European Chemicals Policies: Drivers, Scope and Status*, Lowell Center for Sustainable Production, University of Massachusetts, Lowell, MA

Langley, G. (2001) *The Way Forward: Action to End Animal Toxicity Testing*, The British Union for the Abolition of Vivisection, London

NRC (National Research Council) (1983) *Risk Assessment in the Federal Government: Managing the Process*, National Academy Press, Washington, DC

NSCA (National Society for Clean Air and Environmental Protection) (1998) *Pollution Handbook*, NSCA, Brighton

RCEP (Royal Commission on Environmental Pollution) (2003) 'Twenty-fourth report: Chemicals in products: Safeguarding the environment and human health', Stationery Office, London

Silva, E., Nissanka, R. and Kortenkamp, A. (2002) 'Something from "nothing": Eight weak estrogenic chemicals combined at concentrations below NOECs produce significant mixture effects', *Environmental Science and Technology*, vol 36, pp1751–1756

SLIM (Simple Legislation for the Internal Market) (1999) 'Final report of the SLIM Phase IV Team on Dangerous Substances (Directive 67/548/EEC)', European Commission

Steingraber, S. (1998) *Living Downstream: An Ecologist Looks at Cancer and the Environment*, Virago Press, London

The United States Mission to the European Union (2006) 'Ambassador Gray discusses EU's REACH chemicals proposal, 8 June', http://useu.usmission.gov/About_The_Ambassador/Gray/Jun0806_Gray_REACH.asp, accessed January 2007

Williams, T. I. (1972) *The Chemical Industry*, EP Publishing Ltd, Wakefield

WWF (World Wide Fund for Nature) (2006) 'WWF REACH briefing', 8 December, http://detox.panda.org/news_publications/news.cfm?uxNewsID=89961, accessed January 2007

EU directives and regulations

Council Directive 67/548/EEC on the approximation of the laws, regulations and administrative provisions relating to the classification, packaging and labelling of dangerous substances, *Official Journal*, L196, 16.8.1967, p1

Council Directive 76/769/EEC on the approximation of the laws, regulations and administrative provisions of the Member States relating to restrictions on the marketing and use of certain dangerous substances and preparations, *Official Journal*, L262, 27.9.1976, p201

Council Directive 79/831/EEC amending for the sixth time Directive 67/548/EEC on the approximation of the laws, regulations and administrative provisions relating to the classification, packaging and labelling of dangerous substances, *Official Journal*, L259, 15.10.1979, p10

Council Directive 91/414/EEC concerning the placing of plant protection products on the market, *Official Journal*, L230, 19.8.1991, p1

Council Directive 92/32/EEC amending for the seventh time Directive 67/548/EEC on the approximation of the laws, regulations and administrative provisions relating to the classification, packaging and labelling of dangerous substances, *Official Journal*, L154, 5.6.1992, p1

Commission Directive 93/67/EEC laying down the principles for assessment of risks to man and the environment of substances notified in accordance with Council Directive 67/548/EEC, *Official Journal*, L227, 8.9.1993, p9

Regulation (EEC) No 793/93 on the evaluation and control of the risks of existing substances, *Official Journal*, L84, 5.4.1993, p1

Commission Regulation (EC) No 1488/94 of 28 June 1994 laying down the principles for the assessment of risks to man and the environment of existing substances in accordance with Council Regulation (EEC) No 793/93, *Official Journal*, L161, 29.06.94, p3

Directive 98/8/EC of the European Parliament and of the Council of 16 February 1998 concerning the placing of biocidal products on the market, *Official Journal*, L123, 24.4.98, p1

Regulation (EC) No 1907/2006 of the European Parliament and of the Council of 18 December 2006, concerning the registration, evaluation, authorisation and restriction of chemicals (REACH), establishing a European Chemicals Agency, amending Directive 1999/45/EC and repealing Council Regulation (EEC) No 793/93 and Commission Regulation (EC) No 1488/94 as well as Council Directive 76/769/EEC and Commission Directives 91/155/EEC, 93/67/EEC, 93/105/EC and 2000/21/EC, *Official Journal*, L396, 30.12.2006, p1

Directive 2006/121EC of the European Parliament and of the Council of 18 December 2006, amending Council Directive 67/548/EEC on the approximation of laws, regulations and administrative provisions relating to the classification, packaging and labelling of dangerous substances in order to adapt it to Regulation (EC) No 1907/2006 of the European Parliament and of the Council of 18 December 2006, concerning the registration, evaluation, authorisation and restriction of chemicals (REACH) and establishing a European Chemicals Agency, *Official Journal*, L396, 30.12.2006, p850

6
Risk

Introduction

Chemicals, so industry and many in government insist, must be regulated on the basis of risk, specifically the risk of specifiable types of physical harm. As discussed in the last chapter, in debates about regulation this risk-based approach is contrasted with a precautionary approach.

Proponents of the risk-based approach emphasize that decisions should be made on the basis of what is known. There must be clear evidence that harm of a specified nature may be caused by a technology, harm of sufficient severity to justify the proposed restrictions on that technology. In contrast, it is less clear what a precautionary approach involves.[1] It is often presented as being the taking of restrictive action when there is a lack of clear evidence or of scientific certainty. Principle 15 of the 1992 Rio Declaration on the Environment and Development puts it as follows:

> *In order to protect the environment, the precautionary approach shall be widely applied by States according to their capability. Where there are threats of serious or irreversible damage, lack of full scientific certainty shall not be used as a reason for postponing cost-effective measures to prevent environmental degradation.* (United Nations, 1992)

In Chapter 7 I will examine how risk assessment of chemicals is carried out. In this chapter I take a closer look at the concept of risk as it is used both in technical risk assessments and in everyday life. I suggest that rather than trying to assess the *risks* of a technology we should ask how *risky* the technology is. Riskiness is a way to think about the uncertain threat that the precautionary principle refers to. I also discuss the importance of the context of the risky situation in risk evaluation and attitudes to risks.

The Meaning of Risk

Sven Ove Hansson has identified five different meanings of risk in technical contexts:

1   risk = an unwanted event which may or may not occur;
2   risk = the cause of an unwanted event which may or may not occur;

3   risk = the probability of an unwanted event which may or may not occur;
4   risk = the statistical expectation value of unwanted events which may or may not occur; and
5   risk = the fact that a decision is made under conditions of known probabilities ('decision under risk'). (Hansson, 2004)

All these meanings involve the idea of an unwanted event and/or that of probability. An unwanted event is a happening, an outcome of a situation perhaps, not a property of a thing. But when we do risk assessment of a technology we are assessing material things and activities involving them, not events. One problem for risk assessment then is the establishment of a causal connection between the technology in question and an event of a specified type that is regarded as constituting harm. The evidence for such a connection may concern the causal capacities of the technology – whether it has the appropriate capacities that, in the right conditions, may bring about the event in question – and/or an observed association between the technology and the event. Note that the relationship between the technology and the unwanted event is always contingent on the presence of other conditions needed for the event to come about. Risks can be reduced or increased by changes to those other conditions, while the technology stays the same.

The second idea embedded in the concept of risk is that of probability. Probability is a rather complex concept, of which there are two major accounts: the aleatory and the epistemic.[2] In the aleatory account, probability is a matter of frequency; in the epistemic it is a matter of the degree of belief in a proposition. Thus the probability (aleatory) of getting a six when one throws an unbiased die is 1/6, because if one threw a die an infinite number of times, it would land with the six uppermost on one sixth of those times (assuming things like a flat surface, so there is no ambiguity as to which face is uppermost). The probability (epistemic) that 1/6 is the frequency of sixes in a large number of trials of dice-throwing is close to 1: I could say that I am very certain (given an unbiased die and so forth) that this would be the frequency, or that, given the evidence (from previous experience of dice-throwing, or knowledge of dice and dice-throwing), it is very reasonable to believe that this would be the frequency.

The aleatory account of probability is suited to repeatable events such as dice-throwing, but cannot deal with one-off, unique, specific events. By definition such events happen only once, and the question of their frequency does not arise. All events can be regarded as unique and specific because they take place within time, at specific places. To ascribe probability of the frequency type we have to regard an event as an instance of a more general type of event which happens many times. The probability of an event is the frequency with which it is the outcome over a large number of instances of the preceding conditions of the event – a large enough number to give a stable frequency that does not change significantly with more instances. Events for which there are an insufficient number of instances do not have knowable probabilities. Risk in the technical sense does not exist in such situations; all we can say is that there is uncertainty (Knight, 1921).

However, there are always multiple valid descriptions of any particular event and its preceding conditions: what the risk is thought to be will depend on what description is chosen. As an example, let us suppose that I go rock climbing on a crag in the Lake District – let's call it Raven Crag – one Sunday in June after a rain shower and I fall while leading, and break my ankle when I hit the ground. This event, in all its particularities, is unique, so cannot be said to have a probability. We can only talk about the risk of it happening by describing it as an instance of a more general type of event. But a great many of those more general types happen too infrequently to have probabilities: I have never been to that crag before, nor have I fallen while leading or broken my ankle; only one other person has broken their ankle while climbing at that crag in the past ten years. To get to events with stable frequencies we probably have to consider climbing accidents in general, happening to all the climbers in the Lake District that summer, or perhaps that year, or perhaps all the climbing accidents in the UK. We can see that what group we choose – whether it is all climbing accidents or only those on certain types of rock or involving certain types of injuries – will affect the answer we get when we ask about the probability of an event happening, and thus the risk. Note that there must be some rationale for the general type of the event that we choose. We would not think that considering accidents at all crags named 'Raven Crag' (there are quite a few of these in the Lake District) would be very informative with regard to the probability of my breaking my ankle, but it would make sense to consider accidents happening to climbers on the same grade of route, or in the same weather conditions.

Epistemic probability, the degree of certainty accorded to a proposition, may be considered a matter of personal belief, about which the person holding the belief is the only authority (Ramsey, 1931; Savage, 1954), or it may be a logical matter, deducible from the evidence for that proposition in a way that can, in theory, give one unique, correct answer (Keynes, 1921; Carnap, 1950). The first seems to suggest that probabilities are 'subjective' matters that are unchallengeable by others, the second that they are 'objective', in the same sense as logic and mathematics – their truth is independent of whether they are believed to be true. However, theorists of both ideas make use of Bayes' rule, which relates the probabilities of competing hypotheses to evidence (Hacking, 2001, p70). If one requires that people are consistent between their degrees of belief in different propositions,[3] and that they revise their beliefs in the light of evidence according to Bayes' rule, then personal probabilities are not arbitrary and they are open to challenge. Though people may start with differing degrees of belief, it can be argued that these will converge as evidence increases (Hacking, 2001, p257). Objectivity – that is attention to the world and the evidence it provides – is here a virtue required of people if consensus is to be achieved, rather than a property of probabilities as such. On either account, what is important is the extent to which evidence supports a hypothesis, and thus makes it more probable.

An important question is the extent to which probabilities, in the epistemic sense, can apply to unique, singular events. At first glance it seems that they can – I can talk about the probability of falling and breaking my ankle while climbing that hypothetical Sunday in June in the sense of the degree of belief I have that it will occur, or how likely it is, given the evidence. A possible problem arises, however, when one considers what that evidence is likely to consist of. Does it consist only of data on climbing accidents under various categories? If it does, then we do not get away from treating the unique, singular event as a member of a more general class of events. An alternative type of evidence is knowledge of the causes of climbing accidents and whether they are present in the particular situation. Falls may be caused by a climber slipping on wet rock, or by a rock used as a hold coming loose. Someone leading may hit the ground, and thus be injured, because the gear they have placed to stop their fall has come out of the cracks in the rock that they put them in, or because the person belaying them was not paying sufficient attention and let out too much rope. While insurance assessors consider the first type of evidence – data on injuries while climbing – climbers assess the latter, because this is what gives guidance in the particular, unique situations they are confronted with. The cause of the fall is not understood to be a matter of observed regularities between events of certain types, rather it is the interplay of the properties, capacities and actions of things and people.

To speak of the probability of a singular event we therefore have to allow some notion of things having tendencies to behave in certain ways, or capacities to cause things, and that, contrary to the claims made by David Hume (Hume, 1748, section IV part I), we can have knowledge about these causes, not merely about the regularities between phenomena (Cartwright, 1989). It is through such knowledge that we can say what is likely to happen in a situation that has not occurred before. Thus John Stuart Mill argued that even if there had never been absolute kings we could say something about whether such a king was likely to rule oppressively from 'observations of the tendencies [in human nature] which nature has manifested in the variety of situations in which human beings have been placed' (Mill, 1844, p325). This is also how we think we can predict the probability of an event of which there is no past experience, such as an accident at a new type of industrial plant before it has been built.

The probabilities of different outcomes can thus be seen as resulting from the causal powers and capacities of the system and their arrangement. This makes probability a function of the nature of the system, not merely a statement of degrees of belief or the frequency with which an outcome occurs. We can account for the observed probability (in a frequency sense) by the interplay of capacities or causal powers, and we can estimate a probability (in the epistemic sense) if we know something about the capacities of the things that may influence the outcome.

Riskiness

Hansson notes that:

> *in non-technical contexts, the word 'risk' refers, often rather vaguely, to situations in which it is possible but not certain that some undesirable event will occur.*
> (Hansson, 2004)

People would call such situations *risky*. I suggest that the riskiness of a situation is a measure of the possibility of harm occurring in that situation. The greater the magnitude of the possible harm, or the more possible it is (here the degree of probability comes into play), the more risky the situation. Riskiness differs from risk, used in the technical sense discussed in the preceding section, because it applies directly to a situation, rather than to an outcome or an event that results from the situation, and because it is primarily a matter of possibility rather than probability. The concept of riskiness can be applied to situations and to activities in which the salient feature is the material things that are used or produced in them, in other words technologies can be said to be risky.

The riskiness of a technology cannot be reduced by certain strategies that can be used to reduce technological risks. Such strategies involve changes to the other conditions that are needed for the unwanted event to occur. Thus the risks (the frequency of unwanted events, such as cancers) from toxic synthetic chemicals in the environment could be reduced by banning practices that result in people being exposed to those chemicals, such as by banning the sale of food produced in particularly contaminated areas. Similarly, the risks from road traffic can be reduced by removing pedestrians and cyclists from the roads. In both cases risks are reduced because the frequency of adverse outcomes (diseases caused by chemicals, deaths of pedestrians and cyclists in road traffic accidents) are reduced, even though the salient features of the technology (the hazardousness of the chemical, the speed and volume of road traffic) have not been changed. The technology is just as risky. We might also say that it is just as dangerous.

Moving from probability to possibility has important implications for our treatment of knowledge and ignorance. The impossible is not merely the highly improbable. A great many events that happen every day can be regarded as highly improbable, in the sense of having a low probability. For most people it is improbable that their television will be stolen, however for me it is impossible, because I do not own one. Note that the sense of possibility in use here is 'natural possibility': what is possible given how things actually are, not how they could be without involving logical contradiction. However, the most useful sense of possibility is epistemic possibility. Epistemic possibility is a function of our knowledge: if we do not know that something is impossible, if it is possible 'for all we know', then it is an epistemic possibility regardless of whether or not it is a natural possibility. This is generally what we mean when we talk about things being possible, since we do not know how things actually are independent of our knowledge of them. If asked, my neighbour, who does not know that I do not have a television, would have to say that it was possible the burglars stole a television from my house. For her, it is an epistemic possibility.

In academic discussions of risk it has become common to distinguish between risk, uncertainty and ignorance, as proposed by Brian Wynne (Wynne, 1992). In situations where we can assign probabilities to possible harmful outcomes, we can speak of risk; where we know the possible outcomes but cannot assign probabilities to them, there is uncertainty; where we do not even know what the possible outcomes are, what domains we should be considering or what questions we should ask, we are ignorant. For there to be a risk we must have knowledge of outcomes and their probabilities. This focus on knowledge means that risk assessment procedures generally take no account of areas of ignorance: in some ways it can be said that ignorance reduces risks. However, we all know that ignorance with respect to salient features of an activity or situation makes that activity or situation more, not less risky. It is risky in that for all we know harm is possible, and the greater the extent of our ignorance, the greater the (epistemic) possibility of harm.

In this light we can see conventional risk assessment as taking 'epistemic risks' (Gärdenfors and Sahlin, 1988) in that it ignores epistemically possible probabilities because they have a low epistemic reliability. For example, where we know little about a chemical substance, it is possible both that the probability of it causing harm is very low and that it is very high. Producing the substance is equivalent to placing a bet on the tennis match discussed by Peter Gärdenfors and Nils Eric Sahlin, where we know nothing about the contestants. While, if pushed, we might say that the probability of either contestant winning was 0.5, we might refuse to bet on the match, even though we would place the same bet on a match where we had sufficient information about the contestants to know that they were evenly matched. In the latter match the reliability of the estimated probability of 0.5 is much greater than in the former. Where we have little information we have just as much reason to believe that the probability of one of the contestants winning is 0.9 or 0.1 as 0.5. In the case of chemicals about which we have little information, we tend to ignore the possible high probability of harm, and instead only take into account what we consider to be the more reliable high probability of its benefits.

Focusing on possibility also gives greater weight to small probabilities, as prospect theory suggests people do when making decisions (Tversky and Kahneman, 1981). The shift from the impossible (zero probability) to the possible, even if the probability is thought to be very low, is of much greater significance in people's decision making than an equivalent incremental increase in probability. Thus even though we think that the probability of harm being caused by a chemical is small (say 0.0001), it may be considered worthwhile to avoid using that chemical entirely in favour of an alternative where there is no possibility of harm, but we would not devote similar effort to reducing risks by that interval if the probability were to increase, say, from 0.0099 to 0.0100.

Risks in Context

The importance of context in risk evaluation

The riskiness of a situation or activity is not the only factor we take into account in our evaluations of it. The situation exists in a particular context that includes people who can act, and who may have various types of relationships to each other. A person's position in that context is very likely to affect whether they think that the risk is acceptable or not.

To describe something as a risk is already to suggest something about its context – we talk of risks as being 'taken', in exchange for benefits. A risk implies that there has been a decision, that someone has benefited and that someone has been put 'at risk'. Whether these are the same person or not makes a considerable difference to our moral evaluation of the risk. Another important factor is whether those put at risk, by themselves or by others, have any agency to affect the outcome in the risky situation. Our attitude also depends on whether we believe that those who have taken the risk will take responsibility if harm actually occurs. These three aspects, risk-taking, agency and responsibility, are discussed in the following sections.

Risk-taking: who decides, who benefits and who is put at risk

In the background of discussions about risk is the fact that risks are things that are 'taken' by someone. To take a risk is to choose to do something which may result in harm. However, this 'chance of harm' is accepted in return for an actual or possible gain:[4] '*Chi non risica non guadagna*' (who does not risk does not win) was a maxim in a 1589 publication, *Della Ragion di Stato*, by Giovanni Botero (discussed in Luhmann, 1993) and is one of the first known uses of the term. Botero distinguished taking risks from vain, foolhardy projects (Luhmann, 1993, p10). Risk-taking implies wise calculation, not recklessness. Luhmann defines risk as a decision that may be regretted if the possible loss, that one hopes to avoid, occurs (Luhmann, 1993, p12). He argues that the concept of risk has gained in importance in contemporary society because of the increasing dependence of society's future on decision making (Luhmann, 1993, xii).

The importance of taking calculated economic risks in market economies means that risk-taking is valued in cultures that value entrepreneurial activity. Thus Langdon Winner argues that in American culture risk-taking in economic activity is regarded as a badge of courage (Winner, 1986, p147). It is courageous because the entrepreneur may suffer a financial loss, in other words harm to him or herself. Similarly, in other areas of life where risk-taking is valued, the risks are of harm to the risk-takers: what they put *at risk* is their own interests, not those of others. For example, Mike Thompson argues that in Himalayan mountaineering, a proposed route is only felt to be worthwhile if there is considerable uncertainty as to its outcome (Thompson, 1980). But the ethics of mountaineering are such that the risks of a route must be understood by each individual involved, and each must make their own choice to take them. It would be unethical to take someone up a difficult route who was not fully aware of the risks, and who had not made a positive choice to take them.

With modern technological risks, those taking the decisions, those gaining the benefits and those who may suffer the resulting harm are more and more isolated from each other (Luhmann, 1993, p109). We often cannot, as individuals, decide whether or not to take a technological risk, as we can decide whether or not to climb a mountain. Such risks are thus termed 'involuntary', as opposed to the 'voluntary' risk of mountain climbing. This has led some to question whether 'risk' is the term that should be used. Barbara Adam, for example, suggests renaming Ulrich Beck's concept, of the 'risk society' (Beck, 1992), the 'hazard society', because 'business takes risks which turn into no-choice hazards for the general public' (Adam, 1998, p83). Modern environmental threats, from radiation, genetically modified organisms, hormone-disrupting chemicals, global warming, ozone depletion and acid rain are 'hazards' not 'risks' because they are uninsurable, non-calculable and exclude the element of choice (Adam, 1998, pp82–83).

Winner also argues against using the term 'risk'. He argues that using it implies a willingness to compare expected gain with possible harm and an acceptance of the assumption that the object or practice under scrutiny brings some good, and that the speaker is a recipient of at least some portion of this good. He therefore considers that debates about risk are bound to have outcomes that uphold the status quo of production and consumption in an industrial, market-oriented society. They are therefore debates that those who wish to challenge this status quo should be wary of entering (Winner, 1986, p149).

The use of the term 'risk' in chemicals regulation thus tends to imply that the production and use of a chemical brings benefits. It suggests that society as a whole has decided to take the risk that harm may be caused, in exchange for the benefits; that those who may be harmed are also those who benefit. The reality, however, is that the decisions of some (those in key positions in industry and government, both current and past generations) to produce or use risky technologies put others at risk, and the benefits are very unevenly shared, with no correlation between benefits received and the degree to which people are put at risk. For example, those most put at risk by the production and use of many persistent organic chemicals, such as the polychlorinated biphenyls (PCBs) that were used as oil in electrical transformers, have turned out to be people living in the Arctic. The highest concentration of PCBs in human tissues has been found in a population of Inuit living in Northern Canada, a population that benefited very little from the production and use of PCBs, and certainly were not involved in the decision to produce them. Ironically, the contamination was discovered because researchers were looking for a control population, remote from industrial civilization, with low levels of PCBs. It has since been realized that PCBs are volatile at temperate latitudes, so in the populated, industrial regions they evaporate and are taken by the prevailing winds to the Arctic, where they condense and accumulate in the Arctic food chain (Colborn et al, 1996, pp107 and 196; ENDS, 1996).

Decisions about technology form part of a relationship between those making the decisions and those who are being put at risk, and as such are subject to moral norms of responsibility, respect and consideration for others. That relationship is mediated by the world that those taking the decisions and those affected by them have in common, which may be the global atmosphere, or the local street, depending on what is affected by the technology in question. That world has value independent of the benefits that we as individuals gain from it, and recognition of that value leads some to protest against technologies that they regard as putting that world at risk. The protest is that some things should not be put at risk, whatever the benefits, and however low the probability of harm.[5]

Agency in risky situations

Being able to decide whether to take a risk or not is one type of agency with respect to risk. Another is whether there is any scope for how we act in the situation to affect the outcome. Situations of possible harm – risky situations – vary greatly in terms of the opportunities they afford to human action to affect the outcome. Thus driving a car, riding a bike or rock climbing are very different from breathing polluted air or eating pesticide-contaminated food. The driver, cyclist and climber all feel that they have at least some control over their fate; that they have appropriate knowledge, the capacity to judge situations correctly and the skills needed to act so as to avoid harm. Risks from synthetic chemicals are very different. Very often our senses are not even capable of detecting such chemicals, and we have little control over the response of our bodies to them.

The risk we feel we take on when we drive, cycle or climb depends in large part on how confident we are in our abilities to avoid harm (and we may err by being over or under confident), even if we acknowledge that things may happen which are beyond our control. Individual climbers judge the risks of a climb by considering the condition of the rock, the expected weather and their abilities as climbers. It is an assessment of the particular, unique situation, on the basis of available information and past experience. In contrast, the insurance risk assessor considers statistical data on rates of injury from climbing, subsuming the individual instance as a general case of a type of event that is sufficiently frequent to have a knowable probability. The individual's agency within the situation is not apparent in such risk assessments: the risks of driving, cycling and rock climbing are treated like those from breathing polluted air or eating pesticide-contaminated food, as matters of the probability of death, injury or disease associated with the situation or activity. This is because statistical analysis of data can only discover observable regularities between events of general types and their antecedent conditions. These conditions may be labelled 'risk factors'. To know whether they are also causes of undesirable outcomes we have to have some knowledge, not merely of the regularities between events, but of the causal mechanism, in terms of the capacities of objects or matter, or the actions of people, through which the 'risk factor' brings about the event.

This invisibility of individual agency in insurance risk assessment has led François Ewald to suggest that the calculation of risk by insurers (in which accidents are regarded as simply happening with a set regularity) is at odds with moral and legal ascription of responsibility (Ewald, 1991). The calculation of risk involves making predictions as to how people will behave in particular circumstances, predictions that are essentially the same as other scientific predictions: they are derived as generalizations from past observations. In contrast, moral and legal systems assume that people have choices about how they act, that they make decisions about their actions, and could have acted differently. What they do is at least in part their responsibility; it is not merely a result of the circumstances they are in.

If we recognize that people are responsible for their actions where they have some choices about how to act, then we should treat situations where those put at risk have some capacity to affect the outcome differently from those where they do not. This means, for example, that we should not weigh the risks from fires against the risks from the use of the brominated flame retardants that are used in soft furnishings, foams and electrical equipment. People have considerable agency when it comes to preventing fires – from being careful with candles and cigarettes, to unplugging electrical equipment. In contrast, there is almost nothing they can do to prevent themselves from being contaminated by widely used flame retardants. Brominated flame retardants, such as polybrominated diphenyl ethers (PBDEs) and hexabromocyclododecane (HBCD), are now widely dispersed in the environment and the levels of PBDEs in human breast milk have been increasing exponentially (doubling every five years) since the 1970s (Meironyté et al, 1999).

They may interfere with thyroid metabolism and have effects on neurological development (RCEP, 2003, p2; Covaci et al, 2006; Langley, 2004). These effects should not be weighed against the deaths and damage caused by fires, because those affected can do almost nothing to reduce them.

Where those put at risk do have some agency to affect the outcome, the risk (in the sense of the frequency of adverse outcomes) may not bear much relation to the riskiness of the situation. The presence of dangerous, fast moving traffic on a road means that pedestrians avoid that road, or learn to cross it only with great care, so accident rates are often low (Adams, 1995, p5). Changes in behaviour to avoid contaminated food – such as not eating shellfish from coastal areas near to industrial discharges of toxic chemicals – reduce people's exposure to those chemicals and thus the risk (see Chapter 7 for the role of exposure assessments in chemicals risk assessments). However, the dangerous traffic and the toxicity are still there – the riskiness of crossing the road or eating the shellfish has not been reduced. This riskiness, which is a feature of the world, is something that we should be concerned about. It is a restriction of people's freedom of action in the world caused by the actions of others.

Responsibility for the consequences

If someone takes a risk and the outcome is harm, then the risk-taker bears at least some responsibility for that harm. One can argue, perhaps, about how far *moral* responsibility extends if that harm could not have been predicted before the taking of the risk. This is an issue I will discuss in Chapter 9. For now I will point out that there are two possible strategies for dealing with this situation. The strategy embedded in technical risk assessment approaches is to aim for certainty in prediction of the risks, and to proceed only if the predicted risks are 'acceptable' or 'tolerable'. The strategy more often followed in everyday life is to maintain the ability to cope with or remedy possible harms, and to take responsibility for doing this if harm occurs, even if that harm was not expected. The first strategy aims to reduce uncertainty, the second recognizes that uncertainty is inevitable and seeks to be able to cope with what may occur. An important part of the second strategy is the avoidance of risks with possible outcomes that could not be coped with.

Research on public attitudes to controversial new technologies suggests that suspicion of such technologies is often a reaction to the denial of uncertainty, and ignorance, by the institutions promoting the technology, not a demand for 'zero risk' (Grove-White et al, 2000, p29). Because they do not recognize uncertainty, it can be expected that those institutions will not take responsibility for remedying 'surprise' harms, so the public does not trust them. This lack of trust is not necessarily a matter of the factual accuracy of what the institutions say, but rather of whether the institutions will take responsibility, or will be held responsible, when unexpected harmful effects emerge. There may also be doubts about the ability of anybody to remedy the situation created by the new technology. This lack of trust is based on past experience of the reactions of industry and regulators to the 'surprise' consequences of past novel technologies – most notably synthetic chemicals. It is a rational response to the 'organized irresponsibility' of modern society (see Chapter 9).

Attitudes to risks

It should be clear from the above discussion that risk is not a one-dimensional quantity that can be expressed in a table, such as those showing annual risk of death from various causes (see, for example, Wilson and Crouch, 1987). Not only is there the probability of the harm occurring, there is also the extent of the harm, which may mean that it is rational to want to avoid something altogether – where the possible harm is very great – even if the probability of it occurring is very low (it has been argued that this is the main reason for public opposition to nuclear power (Slovic et al, 1980)). Moreover, there are also the questions of whether the risk-taker puts themselves or others at risk, who receives the benefits, the distribution of benefits and harms, our judgement of the capacity of ourselves or others to act in the risky situation to affect the course of events, and whether we trust those who have taken the risks to accept responsibility for the consequences of their actions.

Given this complexity, it should come as no surprise that public acceptance of risk is not related in any straightforward way to the magnitude of the risk (the possible harm times the probability) or even to 'expected utility' (the combination of probable benefits and harms). It is quite rational for me to decide to take risks where I receive benefits in exchange for possible harm and where I have some capacity to act to avoid the harm occurring, but not to accept risks which are quantitatively the same in terms of probability of harm, but are imposed on me by others without my consent and where I do not receive benefits as a result of the risk being taken and cannot do anything to affect the outcome. Social research on people's attitude to risk, such as that carried out by Paul Slovic and others (collected in Slovic, 2000) suggests that these factors all run together in people's assessments of risk.

For example, the official risk discourse clearly separates risks from benefits, regarding them as separate factors that have to be balanced against each other. However, when people are asked about the benefits from things they perceive to be a risk, they consider benefits from large risks to be small (Slovic et al, 1980). This inverse relationship between perceived risks and perceived benefits seems to result from the assessment of risk already including an assessment of the benefits – what it evaluates is whether the risk is worth taking or not, not the risk in isolation. Slovic suggests that 'experts' assess risk in essentially the same way as the general public; they just have different biases and preconceptions (Slovic, 2000, p411). It may therefore be important that toxicologists' evaluation of the benefits of chemicals to society is greater than that of the general public (Kraus et al, 1992).

Much sociological discussion of risk links it to trust, or rather the lack of trust. Trust and risk are related in that trust is only needed where there is risk. Where there is certainty, and no possibility of things going badly, there is no need for trust. The contentiousness of risk assessment and risk management, particularly in the adversarial legalistic culture of the US, is considered to result from a climate of distrust between the public, industry and regulators (Slovic, 2000, p410). Industry and regulators are the takers and authorizers of modern technological risks, while it is the public who suffer harm.

It is not surprising that those elements of the public who trust institutions and authorities, perhaps because they have positions of power within them, perceive risks from technology to be much lower than do other groups in the population.[6] Like the running together of risks and benefits, what may be being reported here is the excess of risk over trust, which is low for those with trust in the authorities, but high for those who have little faith that current institutions will protect their own wellbeing or that of the world in which they live.

Conclusions

In this chapter I have explored the complexity of risk. The usual technical understanding of risk as the probability of harm can be understood in different ways depending on the account of probability that is being assumed. Risks may be understood as the statistical frequency of particular types of harm. This understanding always assumes that there is a general category of event or situation to which the particular one under consideration is considered to belong. In what category we place an event or situation affects what the risk is. Alternatively, the risk of a particular harm may be considered to be an expression of how certain we are that the harm will occur – or how certain we should be, given the evidence. Understanding the causes of the harm, not just having data on frequencies, here contributes to making us more or less certain that a particular harm will occur.

In everyday language the word 'risk' does not imply that a *probability* can be assigned. Rather, what is generally being referred to is the *possibility* that some unwanted event may occur. We think in terms of how *risky* the situation is, not just what the known risks are. I suggest that in assessments of technology we should consider this possibility of harm and I have called this the 'riskiness' of the technology. Whereas in the current approach to risk assessment ignorance about a technology results in no identified risks and the conclusion that there is no risk, assessments of riskiness would conclude that a technology about which we have little knowledge is highly risky because we do not have sufficient knowledge to rule out harm being caused by it.

Calling something a risk implies that it results from a decision to 'take' a risk, a decision made because it resulted in a benefit as well as the risk. Who has taken the risk, who benefits, and who or what is put at risk are important considerations in the evaluation of the risk. It cannot be assumed that risks from technology are ones that 'society as a whole' (in other words all who are put at risk) has decided to take.

Deciding to take a risk puts us, and perhaps others, in a risky situation. This situation may or may not afford opportunities to act so as to avoid harmful outcomes. Our attitude to a risky situation in which there are such opportunities will depend on our assessment of our abilities to avoid the harm. If people are successful at avoiding harm in risky situations, then the risks (the harm that actually results) may be low. However, the inherent riskiness of the situation has not been reduced. The fact that certain activities have been made more risky than they were, and perhaps therefore have to be avoided, is a restriction of people's freedom of action in the world. This restriction is caused by human action and is therefore of moral and political concern.

If a decision to take a risk does result in harm, the risk-taker is responsible. What is generally important in this situation is the ability to cope with or remedy the harm. Public mistrust of government and industry over new technology may be a matter of not believing that those promoting the technology can or will take responsibility and remedy the harm when unexpected harmful effects emerge. This lack of trust is a rational response to the reactions of government and industry to the 'surprise' consequences of past new technologies, most notably synthetic chemicals. I will show in Chapter 9 that those reactions are characterized by 'organized irresponsibility'.

Risk is a complex, multi-dimensional concept. Evidence from social research on attitudes to risk suggest that in assessing a risk, people (including experts) tend to run all the different factors together: the expected benefits as well as the harms; who takes the decisions; what is put at risk; whether they have any agency in the risky situation to avoid the possible harm; whether the harm is something that can be remedied or coped with.

In the next chapter I will look at how risks from chemicals are assessed. Do the current methods of assessment succeed in estimating risks as the probability of harm? I suggest that rather than trying to estimate risks we should assess how risky a chemical is.

Notes

1   For various interpretations of the precautionary principle see O'Riordan and Cameron (1994).
2   For an interesting account of why there are these two ideas of probability see Hacking (1975).
3   Consistency can be tested by the 'coherence' of betting rates: the bets one would place on contradictory propositions should not be such as to allow a loss whatever happens (Lacey, 1996, p271).
4   Gain, as well as loss or harm, is thus associated with risk. This leads some to define risk in a neutral way as 'the possibility of more than one outcome occurring' where those possible outcomes may be more as well as less desirable than the expected one (UK Treasury guidance on economic appraisal, quoted in RCEP, 1998, p51).
5   Hansson notes that 'Major policy debates on risks have in part been clashes between the "noun" and the "verb" approach to risk. Proponents of nuclear energy emphasize how small *the risks* are, whereas opponents question the very act of risking improbable but potentially calamitous accidents' (Hansson, 2004). Opponents think that what nuclear power puts at risk should not be put at risk.
6   In a US study reported by Slovic about 30 per cent of white males appear to fall into the group that trusts institutions (Slovic, 2000, pp396–402).

References

Adam, B. (1998) *Timescapes of Modernity: The Environment and Invisible Hazards*, Routledge, London

Adams, J. (1995) *Risk*, UCL Press, London

Beck, U. (1992) *Risk Society: Towards a New Modernity*, trans. Mark Ritter, Sage Publications, London

Carnap, R. (1950) *Logical Foundations of Probability*, University of Chicago Press, Chicago, IL

Cartwright, N. (1989) *Nature's Capacities and their Measurement*, Clarendon Press, Oxford

Colborn, T., Dumanoski, D. and Myers, J. P. (1996) *Our Stolen Future*, Little Brown and Company, London

Covaci, A., Gerecke, A. C., Law, R. J., Voorspoels, S., Kohler, M., Heeb, N. V., Leslie, H., Allchin, C. R. and de Boer, J. (2006) 'Hexabromocyclododecanes (HBCDs) in the environment and humans: A review', *Environmental Science and Technology*, vol 40, pp3679–3688

ENDS (1996) 'Evidence accumulates on global distillation of POPS', *The ENDS Report*, no 261, pp9–11

Ewald, F. (1991) 'Insurance and risk', in G. Burchell, C. Gordon and P. Miller (eds) *The Foucault Effect: Studies in Governmentality*, Harvester Wheatsheaf, Hemel Hempstead, pp197–210

Gärdenfors, P. and Sahlin, N. E. (1988) 'Unreliable probabilities, risk-taking and decision making', in P. Gärdenfors and N. E. Sahlin (eds) *Decision, Probability and Utility*, Cambridge University Press, Cambridge

Grove-White, R., Macnaghten, P. and Wynne, B. (2000) *Wising Up: The Public and New Technologies*, The Centre for the Study of Environmental Change, Lancaster University, Lancaster

Hacking, I. (1975) *The Emergence of Probability*, Cambridge University Press, Cambridge

Hacking, I. (2001) *An Introduction to Probability and Inductive Logic*, Cambridge University Press, Cambridge

Hansson, S. O. (2004) 'The concept of risk', *Techne: Journal of the Society for Philosophy and Technology*, vol 8

Hume, D. (1748) *An Enquiry Concerning Human Understanding*, reprinted in *Classics of Western Philosophy*, Third Edition (1990), edited by S. M. Cahn, Hackett Publishing, Indianapolis, IN, pp783–869

Keynes, J. M. (1921) *A Treatise on Probability*, Macmillan, London

Knight, F. (1921) *Risk, Uncertainty and Profit*, Houghton Mifflin, Boston, MA

Kraus, N., Malmfors, T. and Slovic, P. (1992) 'Intuitive toxicology: Expert and lay judgements of chemical risks', *Risk Analysis*, vol 12, no 2, pp215–232

Lacey, A. R. (1996) *A Dictionary of Philosophy*, Third Edition, Routledge, London

Langley, G. (2004) *Chemical Safety and Animal Testing: A Regulatory Smokescreen?*, British Union for the Abolition of Vivisection, London

Luhmann, N. (1993) *Risk: A Sociological Theory*, trans. Rhodes Barret, Walter de Gruyter, Berlin and New York

Mill, J. S. (1844) 'On the Definition of political economy; and on the method of investigation proper to it', in *Collected Works*, vol IV (1967), Toronto University Press, Toronto

Meironyté, D., Noren, K. and Bergman, A. (1999) 'Analysis of polybrominated diphenyl ethers in Swedish human milk. A time related trend study, 1972–1997', *Journal of Toxicology and Environmental Health Part A*, vol 58, no 6, pp329–341

O'Riordan, T. and Cameron, J. (eds) (1994) *Interpreting the Precautionary Principle*, Earthscan, London

Ramsey, F. P. (1931) 'Truth and probability', in R. B. Rraithwaite (ed) *The Foundations of Mathematics and Other Logical Essays*, Routledge and Kegan Paul, London

RCEP (Royal Commission on Environmental Pollution) (1998) 'Twenty-first report: Setting environmental standards, Stationery Office, London

RCEP (2003) *Twenty-fourth Report: Chemicals in Products – Safeguarding the Environment and Human Health*, TSO, London

Savage, L. J. (1954) *The Foundations of Statistics*, Wiley, New York

Slovic, P. (ed) (2000) *The Perception of Risk*, Earthscan, London

Slovic, P., Fischhoff, B. and Lichtenstein, S. (1980) 'Facts and fears: Understanding perceived risk', in R. C. Schwing and W. A. Albers Jr (eds) *Societal Risk Assessment: How Safe is Safe Enough?*, General Motors Research Laboratories, Plenum Press, New York

Thompson, M. (1980) 'The aesthetics of risk', in J. Perrin (ed) *Mirrors in the Cliffs*, Diadem Books, London

Tversky, A. and Kahneman, D. (1981) 'The framing of decisions and the psychology of choice', *Science*, vol 211, pp453–458

United Nations (1992) *Report of the United Nations Conference on Environment and Development*, Annex I, Rio Declaration on Environment and Development, A/CONF.151/26 (Vol. I), Rio de Janeiro, 3–14 June 1992, United Nations General Assembly, New York

Wilson, R. and Crouch, E. A. C. (1987) 'Risk assessment and comparisons: An introduction', *Science*, vol 236, pp267–270

Winner, L. (1986) *The Whale and the Reactor: A Search for Limits in an Age of High Technology*, MIT Press, Cambridge, MA

Wynne, B. (1992) 'Uncertainty and environmental learning: Reconceiving science and policy in the preventative paradigm', *Global Environmental Change*, vol 2, no 2, June, pp111–127

7

Assessing Risks from Chemicals

Introduction

The European system for regulating synthetic chemicals, described in Chapter 5, is predominantly 'risk-based'. This means that restrictions on the manufacture or use of chemicals must be justified by reference to evidence that there is a risk of the chemical causing a specified type of harm. REACH (Registration, Evaluation, Authorization and restriction of Chemicals) does not define the term 'risk', but the directive on risk assessment of new substances defined it as the 'incidence and severity of the adverse effects likely to occur [...] due to actual or predicted exposure to a substance' (Article 2 of Directive 93/67/EEC). In the first part of this chapter I look at how risks from chemicals are assessed. What does chemicals risk assessment in practice aim to achieve? Can it provide the reliable evidence needed for agreement by all parties on whether or not a chemical poses a risk? My answer to this second question is no: there are multiple uncertainties in chemicals risk assessment which lead to protracted debates as to whether a chemical poses a risk or not.

I argue that rather than trying to calculate risks, we should try to assess how risky a chemical is. Riskiness is a concept that I introduced in the last chapter. It is a matter of the possibility that the thing in question causes harm. Assessing riskiness puts the focus on attributes of chemicals that make them more or less risky, rather than on whether or not harm actually results. It widens the scope of assessments to include consideration of the extent of our ignorance – as we do not know how things are independent of our knowledge about them, what we have to consider as being possible depends on our state of knowledge. In this sense of possibility (epistemic possibility) the less we know, the more things are possible, as less is ruled out by our knowledge. So if we know little about a chemical, for example because it is novel, we would have to conclude that it is risky, even if we have no evidence that it causes any specific harm. In contrast, current risk assessment practice would conclude that there were no risks from a chemical we knew little about, because the harm it may cause cannot be identified. This is contrary to everyday judgements, where unfamiliarity and novelty generally increase a thing's riskiness.

In the second part of this chapter I discuss attributes of chemicals that contribute to their riskiness. In Chapter 10 I address how such assessments of riskiness could be used in regulation.

Chemicals Risk Assessment in Practice

Models of risk assessment

There are two basic models of risk assessment: in the actuarial model data is collected on the frequency of events of a certain type in order to calculate insurance premiums, so that the premiums paid cover losses incurred; in the engineering model the probability is calculated of various modes of failure of a complex system such as an aircraft or power station, on the basis of knowledge of the component parts of the system and how they fit together and interact. Engineering risk assessments use data on the rates of failure of critical components of the system – data on the whole system generally not being available as the assessment is carried out before the system is built – with the aim of modifying the design of the system to reduce the probability of it failing. The actuarial model can only be applied to familiar events, which happen with a stable frequency, not to novel situations, such as those created by the production of a new synthetic chemical. The risk assessment of chemicals has therefore grown out of the engineering model of risk assessment, which was developed to estimate the probability of future events of which there was no past experience.

The hardest part of engineering risk assessment has turned out to be the prediction of the modes of failure. Serious accidents at nuclear installations, such as those at Three Mile Island or at Chernobyl, have been caused by modes of failure that had not been analysed at all. For example, the report of the President's Commission on the Accident at Three Mile Island (President's Commission, 1979, p9) highlighted that the concentration of the assessment process on more obvious 'large break' scenarios meant that the eventual mode of failure, which was a result of a chain of a number of more minor events, was not even considered. Despite the use of significant resources in the design process, the risk assessment had been unable to characterize the complex system adequately, a system that was totally human-made and defined. In particular, the risk assessment process had not been able to identify modes of failure caused by humans involved in the operations of the reactor behaving in unexpected ways.

Chemicals risk assessment attempts to characterize the system – of a chemical in the environment or in the human body – and then estimate the risk of the chemical causing harm. A key question is whether the system can be adequately characterized to reliably estimate the probability of harm, or even to identify what harm the chemical may cause. Just as engineering systems have caused harm because they failed in ways that were not predicted, the most serious hazards of synthetic chemicals have often been unexpected, and not considered in risk assessments.

The three stages of assessment

Chemicals risk assessment generally consists of three stages: (1) hazard assessment, (2) exposure assessment and (3) risk characterization. However, REACH divides the first stage into four: human health hazard assessment, physicochemical hazard assessment, environmental hazard assessment, and persistent, bioaccumulative and toxic (PBT) and very persistent and very bioaccumulative (vPvB) assessment (Article 14(3)). When assessing hazards to human health and the environment the aim, if possible, is to derive 'no-effect levels'[1] from tests for specific types of 'end points', such as death or tumour formation – the hazards that are being tested for. No-effect levels are the doses or environmental concentrations below which the substance does not have an adverse effect. The second stage estimates exposure, of particular groups of people (workers, consumers and 'exposure of humans via the environment') or within particular environmental compartments (air, water, soil and so forth). The output is a predicted dose or environmental concentration. The third stage compares this with the no-effect level. If the predicted dose or concentration in the environment is significantly lower than the no-effect level, the risk assessment concludes that there is no significant risk, or, in the terminology of REACH, that the risks are 'adequately controlled'.

Risk assessment of chemicals does not, in practice, estimate 'the incidence and severity of the adverse effects likely to occur in the human population or environmental compartment due to actual or predicted exposure to a substance' – the definition of risk characterization in Article 2 of Directive 93/67/EEC. The assessment process hinges on being able to say that there is a threshold below which the chemical has no adverse effects, in other words on being able to derive a no-effect level. Recent debates, discussed later, challenge the idea that there normally is such a threshold.

In the following two sections I discuss the many sources of uncertainty in the exposure assessment and hazard assessment stages.

Exposure assessment

The assessment of exposure of humans or the environment to a particular chemical is primarily done by modelling of the sources of the chemical and its pathways through the environment. This modelling uses basic data on the physicochemical properties of the chemical. There is no requirement to carry out monitoring of the actual concentration or dose. Annex I of REACH simply states that 'where adequately measured representative exposure data are available, special consideration shall be given to them when conducting the exposure assessment' (paragraph 5.2.5).

The exposure assessment attempts to model a very complex system, that of a chemical substance in the environment, an environment which is not static but is a continuously shifting mosaic of elements – soil, water, air, plants, animals, people and so on. The quantities of the chemical in any particular environment depend on the amount released into that environment during production, processing, transport, storage, use and disposal, and how much is dispersed there from other, perhaps very distant, locations. The latter depends on how the chemical partitions between soil, water and air under different climatic conditions and its rate of degradation or other chemical transformations. The exposure of an organism to a chemical, by ingestion, inhalation or absorption through the skin, then depends not only on the concentrations of the chemical in the relevant medium, but also on the behaviour of the organism.

It is obviously impossible to have all the information needed to predict exposures with accuracy and certainty. Some aspects, such as those that depend on the behaviour of humans, or on complex processes such as weather systems, are inherently indeterminable. Other information is not available for legal or commercial reasons: for example, manufacturers often consider detailed information on uses to be commercially confidential (CEC, 2001, p6). REACH tries to get around some of these problems by basing the estimates of exposure in chemical safety assessments (CSAs) on 'exposure scenarios'. An exposure scenario is:

> *the set of conditions that describe how the substance is manufactured or used during its life-cycle and how the manufacturer or importer controls, or recommends downstream users to control, exposures of humans and the environment. These sets of conditions contain a description of both the risk management measures and operational conditions which the manufacturer or importer has implemented or recommends to be implemented by downstream users.* (Regulation (EC) 1907/2006, Annex I, paragraph 0.7)

Exposure scenarios specify the conditions in which the chemical is to be used (including the protective equipment to be used, working practices, products it is incorporated into, how consumers use those products and how these are disposed), limiting the range of the conditions that must be considered in the exposure assessment. The exposure scenario is annexed to the chemical safety data sheet that is passed to downstream users of the chemical. Those downstream users are required to pass information back to their suppliers about their use of the substance, the exposure to the substance involved in that use and the practicality of specified risk reduction measures. If a use is significantly different from those identified in the CSA, the user must report this to the European Chemicals Agency and prepare its own CSA, or ask the manufacturer to revise the CSA to include that use.

The development of exposure scenarios is an iterative process: if, using the initial assumptions, the estimated exposure is greater than the no-effect level, the exposure scenario should be amended by altering the conditions in which the chemical is to be used. The hazard assessment may also be refined, for example by generation of more data on the hazards (Regulation (EC) 1907/2006, Annex I, paragraph 5.1.1). The aim of the CSA is not to decide whether there is a risk or not, but to describe, in the exposure scenario, how the chemical can be used so that risks are adequately controlled.

A key question here is whether the actual conditions of use will be those that are specified in the exposure scenario. For industrial uses of chemicals, where people have access to safety data sheets and are governed by health and safety and pollution control legislation, there is some hope that people will use the chemical in the way that the exposure scenario envisages. Even here, however, there are bound to be departures from the exposure scenario conditions: people will not always wear protective equipment, or follow instructions, and accidents are bound to happen. Consumers, on the other hand, will usually not even know what chemicals a product contains, let alone have access to the details of the exposure scenario. Even if they had, there is no way that their following it and acting in the way it envisages could be enforced. There are therefore major uncertainties as to whether the exposure estimates derived from the exposure scenarios really represent the actual exposure of people and the environment to a chemical.

Hazard assessment

The hazard assessment identifies the adverse effects that a chemical may cause and investigates the relationship between their magnitude and the dose to which an organism is exposed. A major source of uncertainty is the use of data from tests on laboratory animals (or plants) to investigate toxicity to other species (including humans). There are at least four reasons why there is uncertainty in the application of test data to exposures of humans and wild animals (RCEP, 2003, pp21–22; Rodricks, 1992, pp158–179):

1   the extrapolation across species – tests are carried out on small, often homogeneous populations of laboratory animals, using high doses and over short time scales, but the results are to be applied to large heterogeneous human or wildlife populations;
2   the extrapolation from the high doses used in animal tests to the low doses to which humans and wildlife are generally exposed;
3   the inability to detect very long-term effects – because the lifetime of laboratory animals is much shorter than that of humans, tests cannot mimic a human being's lifetime of exposure; and
4   the effects of mixtures – tests are usually carried out on a single chemical, whereas exposure in the environment is to multiple substances.

Because of the first of these uncertainties (the extrapolation across species), assessments of risks to human health apply an 'uncertainty' or 'safety' factor of 100 to the experimentally derived no observed adverse effect concentration (NOAEC), in other words the NOAEC is divided by 100 to derive a no-effect level for human toxicity. This factor has been used since 1961, when it was chosen on an essentially arbitrary basis (RCEP, 2003, p22). In the assessment of risks to the environment, 'application factors' of 10, 50, 100 or 1000 are applied to the results of tests carried out on specific species,[2] depending on the species used and whether the tests were long term or short term. Evidence to the Royal Commission on Environmental Pollution (RCEP) for their report 'Chemicals in products' indicated that these are merely extrapolation factors – they express the statistical variability of test results but do not effectively take into account inter-species variability, the vulnerability of threatened species, lifetime exposures or the complexity of biological systems (RCEP, 2003, p25).

The second source of uncertainty, the extrapolation from high to low doses, has been the subject of much recent controversy among toxicologists. The standard toxicological model has assumed that, with the exception of carcinogens which act by damaging the genetic material of the cell, there is a threshold concentration, or dose, below which the chemical has no adverse effects. However, it has been argued (Calabrese and Baldwin, 2003) that the dose–response relationship, for carcinogens as well as other toxins, is most often a 'U' or 'J' shape: as concentrations increase, harmful effects initially decline with increasing concentration, but then increase. This bi-phasic response, known as hormesis, could be a result of a chemical interacting with the biochemistry of an organism in a number of different ways, some of which increase and others of which decrease the measured effect. Any non-linearity between the magnitude of these interactions and the concentration of the chemical will result in differing, to the extent of opposing, relationships between concentration and effect over different concentration ranges.

Edward Calabrese and Linda Baldwin give examples of instances where the effects of low doses are beneficial. Low doses of some substances have, for example, been found to reduce the number of tumours compared to controls, when at higher doses the number of tumours per animal increases with increasing dose.[3] They then go on to argue that this means we do not need to be so concerned about the risks of low doses of chemicals. This only follows, however, if it is assumed that low doses are beneficial compared to zero doses. The more general claim of hormesis, that the dose–response relationship is different over different dose ranges, simply abolishes the idea that we can be sure that there is a threshold concentration below which a chemical does not have adverse effects. Rather than implying that low doses are safe, U-shaped dose–response curves may mean that low doses are more potent than slightly higher ones. This is what is claimed for many synthetic chemicals thought to disrupt the endocrine system: some studies have found that the low concentrations found in the environment have a greater effect than the higher concentrations used previously in animal tests to determine acceptable daily intake levels (ENDS, 2003).

Another reason for scepticism with regard to the existence of threshold concentrations is that for some substances, and some effects, different chemicals act together so that the total effect depends on the sum of their concentrations. This has been found to be the case for a number of oestrogenic substances (Silva et al, 2002, and see Note 3 for Chapter 5). The apparent no-effect level of such chemicals crucially depends on which other chemicals are present. In other words, laboratory tests in which animals are exposed to individual substances may have little relevance to the 'real world' situation in which we are exposed to hundreds of different chemicals.

Problems with chemicals risk assessment

The multiple uncertainties in chemicals risk assessment mean that it is possible for its conclusions to be attacked from both sides: the use of the results from the most sensitive species tested, the application of uncertainty factors and the use of worst-case assumptions about exposure all may mean that risks are currently overestimated; it is also possible to argue that, because of the many uncertainties, current methods of risk assessment grossly underestimate risks. Thus even in the comparatively rare cases where there are lots of data on a chemical, there may be little consensus as to what the risks of that chemical actually are. Trichloroethylene, for example, is a widely used industrial solvent which has been tested for carcinogenicity in both animal studies and several large epidemiological studies. Christina Rudén reports that 29 different expert groups have assessed the risks of cancer posed by trichloroethylene. Thirteen of these concluded that trichloroethylene may pose a carcinogenic risk to humans while 16 thought it probably does not. Furthermore, different groups often interpret the results from the same study in different ways. Rudén observes that 'the way that scientific uncertainty is handled seems to be an important factor determining the overall outcome of the risk assessment' (Rudén, 2000). The extent of uncertainty is so great that the evidence can reasonably be interpreted either way.

The effect of all this uncertainty is generally the continued production and use of possibly harmful chemicals. The chemicals are, in effect, given the benefit of the doubt because regulation requires that for restrictions to be imposed there be at least a degree of scientific consensus that there is a risk of harm of an identified type. The uncertainties in the assessment process mean that there is plenty of scope for challenging evidence of harm – for arguing that it does not show that risks from a particular chemical are sufficient to warrant restrictions. In North America these debates have sometimes resulted in legal proceedings, such as in the case of the pesticide Alachor (see Leiss and Chociolko, 1994, pp16–23). In the European Union (EU) the scope for debate resulted in very slow progress in assessing risks under the 'existing substances' regime (see Chapter 5).

Attempts to reduce the uncertainty of particular aspects of the risk assessment process do not succeed in decreasing the uncertainty attached to the overall assessment. For example, great efforts are put into standardizing methods of testing, so that a test will produce the same result time after time, from laboratory to laboratory.[4] This increases the certainty as to whether a chemical has a particular hazardous property or not and enables the concentration at which it has an adverse effect to be precisely defined. However, precision and certainty are only achieved because the property is defined in relation to the very particular conditions under which the test is carried out; it is doubtful that these conditions are representative of the situations that are of concern, in which heterogeneous wild animal or human populations are exposed to chemicals. We may be sure of the result of the test, but very uncertain as to its relevance with respect to the risks we are trying to assess.

While uncertainty about the probability of a chemical having a particular adverse effect is an obvious problem in chemicals risk assessment, perhaps a more serious one is ignorance of the effects that a chemical may have. The history of the production and use of synthetic chemicals is littered with examples of chemicals with serious effects that were not even imagined at the time the chemical was introduced, only to be discovered after decades of use. The classic example is the effect of chlorofluorocarbons (CFCs) on the ozone layer,[5] but one could also include the chronic health effects of organochlorines and the endocrine disrupting properties of a wide range of chemicals. Assessing the risk of identified adverse effects, as risk assessment of chemicals currently does, cannot hope to deal with this problem of ignorance, since if the nature of the harm cannot be identified, the assessment process concludes that there is no risk.

Assessing the Riskiness of Chemicals

Implications of moving from risks to riskiness

In Chapter 6 I suggested that when assessing technologies we should ask how risky they are, where the riskiness of a technology is the possibility of it causing harm.

Asking how risky a chemical is would make the task of assessment less demanding in terms of precision, but more demanding in scope. The need for precision is decreased because the attempt to calculate, or estimate, probabilities (which in the case of synthetic chemicals is not successful in any case) is abandoned. The scope is widened because we clearly have to take into account possible outcomes to which we cannot assign probabilities (they are 'uncertainties', rather than 'risks', to use the terminology of Wynne, 1992), and we have to consider the possibility of harm even when we cannot specify the nature of that harm. The latter is often the case in novel situations, where our knowledge is limited so we cannot identify what the potential harm is, but the possibility of harm is not ruled out by what we know. Conventional risk assessment would conclude that there are no risks in such situations. A more common sense view is that such situations are risky: they are risky because we are ignorant. Ignorance increases riskiness, though in conventional risk assessment it results in a lack of identified risks and the conclusion that there are no risks.

In assessing the riskiness of a chemical it would not be important to estimate exposures to the chemical, since unlike risks (the probability of harm being caused by it), how risky a chemical is does not depend on the amount people are exposed to. Risks can be reduced by strategies that reduce exposure (such as not eating food from contaminated environments), but these do not change the capacity of the chemical to cause harm, and thus its riskiness.

In the following I make suggestions for how we should assess this capacity to cause harm. I then discuss three other features of synthetic chemicals – novelty, persistence and mobility – that have a bearing on how reliable we should consider our knowledge about a chemical to be and the degree of reliability that we should seek. In Chapter 10 I discuss how assessments of riskiness could function in regimes for regulation of chemicals.

The capacity to cause harm

The capacity of a chemical to cause harm is what the 'hazard identification' stage of risk assessment is intended to identify – the hazards of a chemical are 'the adverse effects [harm] which [it] has an inherent capacity to cause' (Article 2 of Directive 93/67/EEC). The identification of adverse effects on the health of humans and wildlife relies heavily on tests on laboratory animals. I have already discussed some of the many uncertainties that result from the use of animal tests. A key question is whether there are viable alternatives. Before proposing an alternative testing strategy I first consider animal tests as scientific experiments and ask whether they are good experiments, given what we want to find out.

In animal tests various doses of a chemical are administered to a population of laboratory animals in one of a number of ways (for example orally, by application to the skin or by inhalation) in single or repeated doses. During or at the end of the test the animals are examined for the 'end point' of the test. This is the type of harm that the test is designed to investigate, such as effects on the skin, the appearance of tumours, indications of damage to the nervous system, effects on reproduction or death. A positive result in such tests is considered to be evidence that the chemical causes harm, but what it actually shows is only that it causes harm under the conditions of the test. Those conditions have to be closely controlled and standardized to ensure that the test gives a consistent result when performed in different laboratories; they are far from representative of the conditions that are of concern, in other words those in which human beings or organisms in natural ecosystems are exposed to the chemical.

This criticism suggests that the test should create a situation that is as near as possible to the 'real' situation – that it should aim to represent the world outside the laboratory, be carried out on the species that are of concern, and so on. However, this is obviously not possible because of ethical and practical difficulties, not the least of which would be the very large number of tests required. Moreover, this response fails to understand how science actually works. Good scientific experiments do not attempt to replicate the complex, messy world outside the laboratory; rather they are designed to provide the conditions in which particular capacities that things have to behave in certain ways are revealed. Such 'ideal' conditions are ones in which the capacities we are interested in give rise to the behaviour that characterizes them without interference from other causes (Cartwright, 1999, p84).

That animal tests attempt to reveal the capacities of chemicals, rather than to replicate 'real world' conditions, is demonstrated by the use of high doses in animal tests. However, the capacities of interest in the hazard identification stage of chemicals risk assessment are those that cause adverse effects on the health of humans or populations of wild organisms. Tests on laboratory animals do not provide the 'ideal conditions' needed to reveal these capacities because the effects of a chemical can vary greatly from species to species.[6] The toxicity of a chemical is a result of interaction between the chemical and the biochemical molecules that constitute the organism. A chemical causes a toxic effect through initiating changes at the molecular level, but those changes will not lead to a toxic effect if the organism's biochemical defence mechanisms are successful at counteracting those changes and maintaining the health of the organism. Despite the fact that basic biochemical processes are the same in all living organisms, there are significant differences between species, and often between individuals of the same species, in the metabolism and/or excretion of many chemicals and in whether the organism can block changes initiated by a chemical or counteract those changes. These differences mean that the resulting effects on the health of the organism may differ substantially from one species or individual to another.

Instead of trying directly to investigate the capacity of a chemical to cause harm in a whole organism, I suggest that we should investigate more basic capacities of chemicals, those that mean it can initiate changes at the molecular level that can lead to adverse effects on the health of an organism. This testing strategy would use *in vitro* tests on cell cultures rather than live animals and would aim to elucidate the mechanisms by which chemicals have adverse effects. When it is the capacity to harm humans we are concerned about, the cell cultures can be of *human* cells, from particular tissues of concern, avoiding the problem of extrapolation from laboratory animals to humans and allowing the identification of toxicity to particular cell types. Such tests are also much faster and cheaper than tests on animals. The European Coalition to End Animal Experiments (see Langley, 2001), who advocate such a testing strategy, suggest that these *in vitro* tests should be supplemented by computer modelling techniques. These are of two types: one type simulates the absorption, metabolism, distribution and excretion of chemicals to calculate the predicted concentration of a chemical in different organs of the body; the other predicts the likely behaviour of a chemical on the basis of a comparison of its structure and properties with those of other chemicals whose behaviour is known (Langley, 2001, pp15 and 22).

These methods do not, of course, provide certainty with regard to the probability that a particular level of exposure to a chemical will cause harm, but neither do the current animal test methods. What they do provide is information on more limited questions, questions about the capacity of the chemical to initiate changes which have the potential to cause harm to the organism. This information is, I suggest, more relevant to chemicals regulation than that provided by animal experiments, because it is of more general applicability. It is less likely to give the false reassurance of non-hazardousness that is provided by an animal test where the animal tested happens not to be susceptible to the chemical, while the species we are concerned about is.

One limitation of non-animal test methods might be that we need to have some knowledge of the possible mechanisms by which a chemical may have an effect: we need to know, for example, what type of cell we ought to use in the *in vitro* tests.[7] This limitation means there may be a place for some testing on animals: where *in vitro* tests have suggested that a chemical is not biologically active, tests on live animals may be justified to check that there are no effects on whole organisms (I am not considering here whether such tests are acceptable on ethical grounds). However, as with all technologies, we cannot rely on laboratory testing strategies to be sure what the effects of synthetic chemicals are: the results of laboratory tests have to be checked against and supplemented by the results of research into the effects of chemicals in the real world. As the RCEP points out, there is a need to do far more monitoring of chemicals in the environment and to look for changes to the health of humans and wildlife that may be caused by exposure to chemicals (RCEP, 2003, pp116–122).

So far, systematic monitoring for synthetic chemicals has been virtually non-existent. For example, no routine monitoring of human blood or breast milk is carried out. In the UK an environmental non-governmental organization (NGO), rather than a government department, has tested samples of human blood for synthetic chemicals. In 2003 the World Wide Fund for Nature (WWF) took blood samples from 155 individuals and analysed them for around 80 specific synthetic chemicals. Between 20 and 40 different chemicals were found in each person.[8] There has been an exponential increase in the concentration of polybrominated diphenyl ethers (PBDEs) in human breast milk since the 1970s, but this was only discovered in the late 1990s, when stored samples of breast milk were analysed (Meironyté et al, 1999). Ongoing monitoring for these substances, which are widely used as flame retardants, should have been put in place as soon as they were introduced, and their appearance in breast milk should have signalled their removal, or at least led to the urgent instigation of further studies to assess their toxicity (Langley, 2004).

Despite the woeful inadequacy of systematic monitoring, it is research into the causes of diseases in humans, damage to wildlife or other environmental changes, rather than systematic risk assessment, that has been the main impetus to the restrictions that have been placed on synthetic chemicals.[9] The banning of CFCs came about because they were discovered to be widespread in the atmosphere and causing depletion of stratospheric ozone over the Antarctic (Farman, 2001); restrictions on many organochlorine pesticides were introduced after research into declining populations of birds of prey found the cause to be egg-shell thinning caused by such pesticides (Smith, 1992, pp290–293); the use of tributyl tin in anti-fouling paint on ships was restricted after French fishermen noticed that the failure of oyster beds in the Bay of Arcachon correlated with areas where large numbers of boats were being treated with tributyl tin-containing paint (Langley, 2004, p24). The British Union for the Abolition of Vivisection (BUAV) argues that the considerable efforts put into devising valid animal tests for new end points, such as endocrine disruption, have been a distraction from the routine monitoring of humans and wildlife for synthetic chemicals (Langley, 2004). Such pro-active monitoring, with results correlated with environmental changes or incidents of human diseases, could do much to reveal the capacity of chemicals to cause harm.

When deciding how risky a chemical is, this information on the capacity to cause harm needs to be considered along with other relevant aspects of the chemical, not in isolation. How we could regulate on the basis of riskiness is a matter I discuss in Chapter 10.

Novelty

One factor that affects how risky we consider something to be is how much we know about it and how certain we can be of that knowledge. Knowledge is affected by how novel something is, novelty being a matter of the degree to which something is different in kind to what has gone before, as well as how new it is. Novelty is associated with lack of knowledge, because for novel things we do not have the experience of how they behave and how we should behave towards them that we have for familiar things. Novelty therefore increases the riskiness of a chemical because, in the epistemic sense of possibility, it is possible for a novel chemical to cause harm: we have insufficient knowledge to rule out this possibility.

It might be countered here that we actually know much more about the effects of novel synthetic chemicals than we do about natural ones because the former have been subject to much more scientific investigation (see, for example, Ames and Gold, 1990). However, even if we cannot identify which natural chemicals have what effects, we do know that the effects of natural chemicals are ones we have already encountered[10] – they are already with us and we have learned to avoid or cope with them, at least to some extent. We know that certain plants or parts of plants are toxic; we light fires in fire places with chimneys so we do not live in rooms full of smoke; and we know that we should wear a dust mask if we are doing work that generates fine dust. Harm caused by our current exposures to natural substances is already with us, and we generally know about how to deal with these effects, although we can always, of course, learn more, and science has a very important contribution to make to such learning.

In many cases it is not just the effects of the chemical that we are able to cope with, but exposure to the chemical itself. This is not done by scientific or any other sort of knowledge, but by what may be regarded as analogous to such knowledge at the population or species level: adaptation achieved through evolution, whereby a population becomes biochemically adapted to novel toxic chemicals in its environment.[11] The time scale over which this occurs will be much faster for species that reproduce quickly and prolifically than for species such as humans where it takes decades for a generation to grow to maturity and to reproduce. Thus during the past 50 or so years in which novel, non-naturally occurring chemicals have been produced in significant quantities by humans, many bacteria have become adapted so they can metabolize them[12] or resistant to chemicals that previously killed them, insects have become resistant to pesticides, and many plants to herbicides. But the effects of these and other synthetic chemicals on humans are probably only now, after one or two generations have been exposed from conception, just beginning to become apparent. All non-nature-identical synthetic chemicals should therefore be considered to be novel as far as human beings are concerned.

It is important to note that novelty is a relative, not an absolute, property. A thing may be more or less novel in two ways: it may be more or less different in kind from what has gone before; or it may be more or less new. Novelty also relates to a particular feature or aspect, so something may be novel in one respect but not in others. It may, for example, have a novel design, but use traditional materials, or it may be a traditional design made with novel materials. Most novel artefacts are novel with regard to the form that they take: they are novel with respect to the human-constructed world. In contrast, a novel chemical, because it is new matter, is novel with respect to the earth, which previously provided all the material with which humans constructed their world.[13] This new matter now takes part in the processes of the earth: it enters our bodies, soil, water and air, where it interacts with the natural chemicals it encounters, transforming them and itself. In effect, it starts new processes in nature (Arendt, 1968, p58).

Making a novel chemical is different, therefore, from making a novel artefact out of natural materials. The latter, because it introduces something novel into the human-constructed world, may have repercussions for the human society that shares that world. In contrast, a novel chemical may have repercussions for the earth – the natural environment. It may not just represent a danger to the lives of individuals, as do many toxic natural chemicals, but may interfere with basic biological and perhaps geochemical processes, causing disruption to ecosystems. The new processes started by novel chemicals cannot be stopped once they have been started, and thus they create uncertainty of a new type: natural phenomena can no longer be relied upon to have the same effects as they did in the past. For example, the sunlight at the earth's surface now has a greater capacity to cause skin cancer because CFCs have destroyed stratospheric ozone; fish from the Arctic used simply to be a nutritious food, but now the chemicals in them may harm our health; human breast milk is not of the unalloyed benefit to the human infant that it once was, because it now contains chemicals that may harm the infant's development, as well as the nutrients it needs.

The importance of the processes set in motion by a novel chemical suggests that when assessing how risky a particular novel chemical is we should think about how it will degrade, interact with other molecules, and fit into natural processes and cycles. Chemicals that are transformed into substances that are common in natural systems are likely to be much less risky than ones that are not. For example, one could argue that a pure metal, such as aluminium, is as novel as many non-naturally-occurring organic substances: it did not exist until humans learned to produce it, relatively recently, from bauxite ore (hydrated aluminium oxide). However, when exposed to the air, the pure aluminium that we produce from the ore is rapidly oxidized back to aluminium oxide. Thus the creation of metallic aluminium, like the creation of other metals from their ores, can be seen as a minor diversion from the natural cycles in which the metallic element takes part.

One response to the argument that we are ignorant about the effects of producing novel chemicals is to point out that ignorance with regard to the future course of events is a fundamental feature of human life. In our dealings with each other we know that what we and others do is inherently unpredictable. What we do is not determined by factors outside of ourselves, but at least in part by our own deliberations and decisions: we act, rather than merely behave in predictable ways. And such actions start processes: chains of events in which others act in response to our actions. The results of such a process cannot be predicted, because the process never comes to an end and because each person who contributes to it has the freedom to act otherwise than they did. To limit the unpredictability of human action we make promises to each other and take on responsibilities. We can also curtail the boundlessness of the processes started by people's actions by forgiving them – releasing them from the consequences of what they have done and breaking the process of action and reaction they have started (Arendt, 1958, pp236–247). In contrast, the boundlessness and unpredictability of the processes started by the human action of introducing a novel chemical into the environment cannot be limited by forgiveness and promising.

I should point out that the argument being made here is not that nature is always benign, or that non-natural substances are always harmful. There are, after all, plenty of natural substances that are toxic to us. However, such substances pose little risk to the biological and geochemical systems in which they occur. Indeed they may play an important role in such systems. The toxicity of natural chemicals is integral to the interactions between organisms, and between organisms and the non-living aspects of their environment, and these interactions are fundamental to the functioning of ecological systems. On the other hand, the introduction of novel chemicals may cause change in such systems, change that from our perspective may well constitute harm.

Saying that non-nature-identical chemicals are more risky than nature-identical ones perhaps involves an assumption that nature is satisfactory: while there are dangers and threats in nature, it can provide what is needed for human life collectively to flourish, provided we are skilful and make use of what our environment affords (though this does not of course mean that all individuals will flourish). Nature is not so hostile to us that most changes would be an improvement, or so limited in the materials it provides that we would have a miserable, unfulfilling existence without non-nature-identical chemicals. While some may challenge this assumption, I think it is a reasonable one to make given that we are natural beings, dependent on the living systems of the earth for our existence, and flourished without non-naturally-occurring synthetic chemicals for tens of thousands of years. And given that we are unable to sustain ourselves without functioning natural systems, we should not put the functioning of those systems at risk. Where serious harm to such systems is an epistemic possibility (where, that is, it is not contradicted by what we know, even if we have no positive evidence for it), we take an epistemic risk if we ignore that possibility (Gärdenfors and Sahlin, 1988). The 'maximin' decision rule recommended by Gärdenfors and Sahlin states that one should choose the course of action with the 'largest minimal expected utility'. This rules out actions which may have serious negative consequences if alternatives with better worst possible outcomes are available (Gärdenfors and Sahlin, 1988, p324). As long as the worst possible outcome from not producing a novel chemical is better than the worst possible outcome from producing it, the maximin rule suggests we should not produce it.

One might argue, of course, that this is an extremely risk averse, pessimistic approach, and that we ought to be more adventurous. But this is to misapply our positive evaluation of individual risk-taking behaviour, where the one who decides to take the risk (which they do in exchange for a benefit of some kind) is the one who may suffer harm. We do not applaud risk-taking where it is not the risk-taker, but someone else, who is put at risk, that person having had no say in the decision. And the production and use of synthetic chemicals is clearly an action of this type: the decision is made by a small number of people in government and industry, but everyone, including members of future generations and other species, may be affected.

The onus of proof should therefore be on those who think they can improve on nature, by producing novel substances, to demonstrate that such substances really are improvements, not only in the narrow frame of their intended function, but in the wider frame that includes their effects on the whole biosphere.

Persistence

Persistence and the related property of bioaccumulation were not previously considered in risk assessments under EU legislation, but do have to be considered in CSAs carried out under REACH. Persistence and bioaccumulation do not in themselves denote adverse effects, so a chemical cannot be said to pose a risk simply by virtue of it having these properties. However, persistence and bioaccumulation of organic chemicals render those chemicals more risky in that they increase the magnitude of harmful effects, if any are caused.

Organic chemicals are usually broken down into simple molecules, such as carbon dioxide and water, by the action of living organisms. Organic chemicals that are not easily broken down (generally because they do not occur naturally, so living organisms have not evolved to metabolize them) persist in the environment and may accumulate in living organisms. The processes of bioaccumulation result in concentrations in animals, particularly those higher up the food chain, being much higher than would be expected given the concentrations in the animals' environment. Standard methods of estimating exposure are not appropriate as it makes little sense to think of the dose as the amount received by the organism from external sources over a set period of time. The biochemically important dose is the available concentration of the chemical in particular tissues or body fluids. Internal sources (such as from stored fat) may make just as important a contribution to this dose as recent external ones.

If persistent chemicals do have the capacity to cause harm (in other words they are hazardous), the effects they have are likely to be much greater in magnitude than the effects of non-persistent chemicals of equal hazardousness, because the time span over which exposure will occur is much longer and doses likely to be higher. This exposure cannot be stopped by the cessation of production and use of a chemical, as is possible with non-persistent chemicals. Once released into the environment the presence of persistent chemicals is effectively irreversible on a human time scale – though they may be transported from one place to another and so decrease in some environments while increasing in others. This appears to be the case with many persistent semi-volatile organic compounds. Some such chemicals used in the tropics are found in temperate latitudes but not in tropical soils. Others, such as polychlorinated biphenyls (PCBs), which were used extensively in temperate regions, are volatilized at temperate latitudes, where their concentrations are now declining, following bans on their use, but they appear to be accumulating in Arctic ecosystems (ENDS, 1996).

Persistence and bioaccumulation thus increase the risks posed by a hazardous chemical (in other words the probability of a particular level of harm of the type caused by the chemical), while if a chemical is not hazardous there are no risks to be increased. The problem here, however, is knowing whether or not a chemical is hazardous. If we accept that we may be wrong, and think a chemical is not hazardous when it is, then our attitude to the supposedly non-hazardous persistent chemical will be different from our attitude to the supposedly non-hazardous non-persistent one. The persistent chemical can thus be said to be more risky because once we have introduced it into the environment we are not able to remove it, so if we are wrong about its non-hazardousness, we will not be able to stop the harm it will cause. This inability to stop harm continuing goes against the everyday strategy for dealing with risky situations, in which the aim is not certainty of prediction but maintenance of the ability to cope with or remedy possible harm.

Mobility

A substance that is mobile, in the sense of being easily dispersed in the environment, is clearly more risky than one that is not. This is because the harm it causes, if it does have a capacity to cause harm, is likely to be spatially dispersed, perhaps affecting places remote from the site of use of the chemical. This dispersal makes it more difficult to obtain evidence for causal links between the chemical and effects on human health and the environment. It also makes retrieval of the chemical, if it is persistent, more difficult than for a persistent, non-mobile chemical. As with persistence, mobility is a property that affects how we should regard our knowledge about the substance's capacity to cause harm. If we are wrong – thinking that a substance does not have such a capacity when it does – the harm caused is likely to be greater and less reversible the greater the mobility of the chemical.

The mobility of a chemical depends on properties such as its melting and boiling points (and thus how it partitions between the solid, liquid and gaseous states at ambient temperatures) and solubility (in water and fats). The extent to which a chemical is actually dispersed in the environment depends on how it is used. Some uses, such as in pesticides, involve dispersal. In other uses the chemical is contained, for example by the reaction vessel of an industrial chemical process. However, even in such situations, more mobile chemicals are more inherently risky than non-mobile ones: if the containment is breached, a non-mobile chemical will not become widely dispersed, whereas a mobile one will.

Conclusions

Risk-based systems of regulation, such as that for synthetic chemicals, are dependent on the availability of reliable evidence as to whether or not what is being regulated causes an identified type of harm. Such reliable evidence, which commands the agreement of all parties, is generally not available for the effects of synthetic chemicals; nor can it be obtained using the methods currently available to investigate those effects. The search for agreement on what effects a chemical has, and therefore whether it poses a risk, leads to efforts to increase certainty and precision, for example through the standardization of test methods. These tests give repeatable results but do not represent the conditions under which people and wildlife are exposed to synthetic chemicals, so are frequently of questionable relevance.

A more fundamental problem is that risks can only be assessed where the possible harm has been identified. But the major types of harm caused by synthetic chemicals were unexpected: no risk assessment of them could have been carried out. Insisting that regulation is 'risk-based' will not help to prevent such future surprises.

Instead of assessing risk, I suggest that we should try to assess riskiness in the everyday sense of this term, where it refers to the epistemic possibility of harm, not merely probabilities of identified types of harm. Whereas risk relates to outcomes, riskiness is a property of a thing, situation or activity and is relative to our knowledge about it. I suggest that what are normally termed precautionary approaches are concerned with riskiness, rather than just risk: they are concerned with whether, for all we know, there is a possibility of harm, not just with the probabilities of known, specifiable types of harm.

The degree of risk depends on our exposure to a chemical, which may be affected by our behaviour, but riskiness just depends on the nature of the chemical and what we know about it. The hazardousness of a chemical (its capacity to cause harm) is one thing that contributes to its riskiness, but a chemical is also more risky if it is novel and we do not have a full understanding of how it fits into natural processes and cycles and if it is persistent or mobile.

In Chapter 10 I consider how assessments of chemicals for their riskiness could fit into a regulatory system. But first I turn to the ethical and political presuppositions of risk-based regulatory systems. Why is there such an insistence that regulation be risk-based?

Notes

1   REACH uses the terms 'derived no-effects level' (DNEL) for hazards to human health and 'predicted no-effect concentration' (PNEC) for hazards to the environment.

2   When assessing risks to the aquatic environment, for example, tests are normally done on an algal species, the freshwater shrimp (*Daphnia magna*) and a species of fish. From tests on this very limited number species, conclusions are drawn about the risks of a chemical to the aquatic environment in general.

3   Other examples they give include that modest consumption of alcohol reduces total mortality in humans, while high levels of consumption increases it; that low levels of cadmium, dioxin, saccharin, various polycyclic aromatic hydrocarbons and X-rays (which are all considered carcinogenic) reduce tumours in some species; that various drugs which are harmful at one dose are beneficial at another (which may be lower or higher than the harmful dose) (Calabrese and Baldwin, 2003).

4   The standardization of test methods so that they give repeatable results is a long and complicated process. It involves identifying the other factors, besides the concentration of the chemical being tested, which influence the end point of the test and deciding at what they should be held constant. For example, the results of tests on the freshwater shrimp, *Daphnia*, one of the tests for ecotoxicity specified by EU legislation, are affected by the species of *Daphnia* used, the particular genotype within the species and how it has been cultured. For some substances, the offspring of mothers that have been poorly fed are less sensitive than those that have been well fed. Deciding a protocol that specified all the relevant variables – setting out exactly how the test was to be performed, so that different people performing the test in different laboratories would get the same result with the same chemical – involved one pilot and two full ring tests (where many different laboratories perform the test on the same substance and results are compared), three international workshops and a research programme. It took over ten years (Calow, 1998).

5   When CFCs were invented in the 1930s, no one imagined that they could destroy ozone in the stratosphere, the importance of which was barely understood. Reviewing the history of our understanding of the effects of CFCs on the ozone layer, Joe Farman considers that a conventional risk assessment in the 1960s would have concluded that there were 'no known grounds for concern' (Farman, 2001).

6   Perhaps the most dramatic case of this is the acute toxicity of dioxins. At very low doses dioxins are lethal to guinea pigs, but they have only mild acute effects in humans (for a discussion of the resulting controversies around dioxins see Powell and Leiss, 1997, pp41–76).

7   Though it can be argued that *in vitro* tests are less end point specific than *in vivo* tests, Langley suggests that high-throughput tests on human cell cultures that look for chemical-induced changes in patterns of gene activity or production of metabolites can scan for changes that underlie a number of different toxicities (Langley, 2004, p23).

8   The chemicals tested were either organochlorine pesticides, polychlorinated biphenyls (PCBs) or polybrominated diphenyl ethers (PBDEs) (the latter are used as flame retardants) (www.wwf.org.uk/chemicals, accessed November 2006).

9   Of the 22 amendments to the EU Marketing and Use Directive (76/769/EEC), only two have come about as a result of formal risk assessment under the new or existing chemicals regimes (RCEP, 2003, p53).

10 The caveat on this is so long as we are not exposed to them in a completely new way, or they are not distributed to spheres where they have not been present before.

11 It can also fail to adapt and either be weakened in health and vigour, and therefore made vulnerable to being made extinct by other factors, such as disease or predation, or be made extinct by the novel chemicals themselves. The mass extinction of a high percentage of the life forms on the planet by oxygen, when this was first produced by photosynthesizing bacteria, is an example of the latter.

12 If bacteria can metabolize a chemical, this will mean that the chemical will not persist in an environment where those bacteria are present. Thus it can be expected that some currently persistent chemicals will become less persistent over time. However, such bacteria are likely to evolve only where the persistent chemical is present at particularly high concentrations. There is no reason to think that bacteria able to degrade a chemical will be available to do so wherever that chemical is present at concentrations sufficient for it to affect biological organisms.

13 See the discussion of the world/earth distinction in Chapter 3.

References

Ames, B. and Gold, L. S. (1990) 'Chemical carcinogenesis: Too many rodent carcinogens', *Proceedings of the National Academy of Sciences of the United States of America*, vol 87, pp7772–7776

Arendt, H. (1958) *The Human Condition*, University of Chicago Press, Chicago, IL

Arendt, H. (1968) *Between Past and Future*, Viking Compass Edition with additional text, New York

Calabrese, E. J. and Baldwin, L. A. (2003) 'Toxicology rethinks its central belief: Hormesis demands a reappraisal of the way risks are assessed', *Nature*, vol 421, pp691–692

Calow, P. (1998) 'Standards, science and the politics of chemical risk', in R. Bal and W. Halffman (eds) *The Politics of Chemical Risk*, Kluwer Academic Publishers, Dordrecht, pp251–263

Cartwright, N. (1999) *The Dappled World: A Study of the Boundaries of Science*, Cambridge University Press, Cambridge

CEC (Commission of the European Communities) (2001) 'White Paper: Strategy for a future chemicals policy', Brussels, 27 February

ENDS (1996) 'Evidence accumulates on global distillation of POPS', *The ENDS Report*, no 261, pp9–11

ENDS (2003) 'Growing problems: Endocrine disruptors under the spotlight', *The ENDS Report*, no 336, pp20–23

Farman, J. (2001) 'Halocarbons, the ozone layer and the precautionary principle', in European Environment Agency *Late Lessons from Early Warnings: The Precautionary Principle 1896–2000*, Office for the Official Publications of the European Communities, Luxembourg, pp76–83

Gärdenfors, P. and Sahlin, N. E. (1988) 'Unreliable probabilities, risk-taking and decision making', in P. Gärdenfors and N. E. Sahlin (eds) *Decision, Probability and Utility*, Cambridge University Press, Cambridge

Langley, G. (2001) *The Way Forward: Action to End Animal Toxicity Testing*, British Union for the Abolition of Vivisection, London

Langley, G. (2004) *Chemical Safety and Animal Testing: A Regulatory Smokescreen?*, British Union for the Abolition of Vivisection, London

Leiss, W. and Chociolko, C. (1994) *Risk and Responsibility*, McGill-Queen's University Press, Montreal

Meironyté, D., Noren, K. and Bergman, A. (1999) 'Analysis of polybrominated diphenyl ethers in Swedish human milk. A time related trend study, 1972–1997', *Journal of Toxicology and Environmental Health Part A*, vol 58, no 6, pp329–341

Powell, D. and Leiss, W. (1997) *Mad Cows and Mother's Milk*, McGill-Queen's University Press, Montreal

President's Commission (1979) *The Need for Change, the Legacy of TMI: Report of the President's Commission on the Accident at Three Mile Island*, President's Commission on the Accident at Three Mile Island, Washington, DC, available at www.threemileisland.org

RCEP (Royal Commission on Environmental Pollution) (2003) 'Twenty-fourth report: Chemicals in products: Safeguarding the environment and human health', Stationery Office, London

Rodricks, J. V. (1992) *Calculated Risks: The Toxicity and Human Health Risks of Chemicals in our Environment*, Cambridge University Press, Cambridge

Rudén, C. (2000) 'Risk assessment and scientific uncertainty – The trichloroethylene example', *Philosophy of Risk Newsletter*, vol 1, no 4

Silva, E., Nissanka, R. and Kortenkamp, A. (2002) 'Something from "nothing": Eight weak estrogenic chemicals combined at concentrations below NOECs produce significant mixture effects', *Environmental Science and Technology*, vol 36, pp1751–1756

Smith, S. (1992) 'Ecological and health effects of chemical pollution', in R. M. Harrison (ed) *Understanding our Environment: An Introduction to Environmental Chemistry and Pollution*, Second Edition, The Royal Society of Chemistry, Cambridge, pp245–318

Wynne, Brian (1992) 'Uncertainty and environmental learning: Reconceiving science and policy in the preventative paradigm', *Global Environmental Change*, vol. 2, no 2, June, pp111–127

EU directives and regulations

Council Directive 76/769/EEC of 27 July 1976 on the approximation of the laws, regulations and administrative provisions of the Member States relating to restrictions on the marketing and use of certain dangerous substances and preparations, *Official Journal*, L262, 27.09.1976

Commission Directive 93/67/EEC laying down the principles for assessment of risks to man and the environment of substances notified in accordance with Council Directive 67/548/EEC, *Official Journal*, L227, 8.9.1993, p9

Regulation (EC) No 1907/2006 of the European Parliament and of the Council of 18 December 2006, concerning the registration, evaluation, authorisation and restriction of chemicals (REACH), establishing a European Chemicals Agency, amending Directive 1999/45/EC and repealing Council Regulation (EEC) No 793/93 and Commission Regulation (EC) No 1488/94 as well as Council Directive 76/769/EEC and Commission Directives 91/155/EEC, 93/67/EEC, 93/105/EC and 2000/21/EC, *Official Journal*, L 396, 30.12.2006, p1

8

The Ethical and Political Framework of Regulation

Introduction

Previous chapters have shown how UK government and European Union (EU) policy conceives the regulation of chemicals as a matter of reducing the risks from chemicals while maintaining the economic and other benefits of their production and use. Regulation is seen as a matter of striking the right balance between protecting human health and the environment and preserving existing economic activities that produce and use chemicals. To assess whether the right balance has been struck regulations are subject to 'socio-economic analysis', in which costs are compared to benefits.

Socio-economic analysis assumes that the introduction of a new regulation, such as REACH (Registration, Evaluation, Authorization and restriction of Chemicals) itself, or one that restricts the use or production of a particular chemical, has effects on the economy that can be counted as costs or benefits. The costs and benefits are assumed to be reducible to the interests of individuals (or institutions such as companies that are 'legal persons') and can be quantified by assessment against some common measure (money), or at least aggregated and compared so that one can say whether the regulation has a net positive or negative effect of large or small magnitude.

The ethical theory underlying this approach is that of utilitarianism: what is important are the consequences of an action, consequences which are to be judged good or bad by aggregating the wellbeing of individuals and comparing the total wellbeing before and after the action. In this first part of this chapter I take issue with the use of this utilitarian framework to assess a new regulatory regime such as REACH. Drawing on Nancy Cartwright's concept of nomological machines (1999), I argue that regulations are part of an ordered framework in which the causes of economic activities have effects. Rather than asking what the costs and benefits of a regulation will be, we should ask how the regulation will change the effects that the causes of economic activity have. We can also judge the regulation directly, not in terms of its consequences, but according to whether it implements principles of justice, fairness, openness and so forth.

This framework, in which causes have effects and people's actions have consequences, is the world that we build by our technology as well as by law-making. As I argued in Chapter 3, the world should be a home for human life on earth and we should judge changes to the world in terms of whether they make the world better or worse as a home. Here I show that this cannot be done by the method that utilitarian thinking suggests, by aggregation of individual interests.

The other important influence on the regulatory framework, apart from utilitarianism, is the 'harm principle', one of the key tenants of the political philosophy of liberalism. As formulated by John Stuart Mill in his essay *On Liberty* (first published in 1859), this states that 'the only purpose for which power can be rightfully exercised over any member of a civilized community, against his will, is to prevent harm to others' (Mill, 1859, p135). Unlike many modern liberals, Mill was committed to a form of utilitarianism, so the harm principle was for him a necessary but not a sufficient condition for restricting the liberty of an individual: not only must an action cause harm to others, but the measures taken to stop or prevent that action must not cause greater harm. This reasoning is present in chemicals regulation: socio-economic analysis is carried out where there is evidence that a chemical causes harm, with the aim of ensuring that restrictions on the chemical do not cause greater harm than that caused by the chemical. Normally the onus of proof is on the regulator to show that the costs of restrictions are outweighed by the benefits of restrictions (the prevention of harm caused by the chemical). However, under REACH this burden of proof is reversed for chemicals subject to authorization: applications by industry for uses of such substances have to show that the socio-economic benefits of their use outweigh the risks associated with them.

In the field of technology, the harm principle is effectively a reverse precautionary principle: it puts the onus on the regulator to show that a technology causes harm, working against a precautionary approach to the novel. Here I examine the two lines of argument for the harm principle within liberalism: that the state should be neutral between different conceptions of good and not favour certain ways of life over others, and that people should make their own decisions about their lives because this autonomy of the individual is of overriding value in human life. I argue that what is missing in both these arguments is a recognition that there is a shared public world. That world, which lies *between* people, is the legitimate concern of politics. In that decisions about technology are decisions about the world, they are matters for public decision. Government can legitimately prevent individuals from causing harm to the world, not just to other individuals. I also argue that, with respect to the manufacture and use of synthetic chemicals, the arguments for the harm principle do not apply because it is organizations, not human individuals, whose actions need to be restricted.

Finally, I argue for a broadly republican position that recognizes the existence of a public realm and is concerned with promoting the virtues of independence of thought, accountability and responsibility that individuals must have if the world is to be preserved as a fit home for human life on earth.

Problems with the Utilitarian Framework for Assessing Regulations

Socio-economic analysis in chemicals regulation

Under European chemicals legislation, proposals to restrict the production or use of chemicals, or to authorize the use of a chemical subject to the authorization procedures of REACH, are subject to a socio-economic analysis. The socio-economic analysis should include the following: consideration of the commercial impacts on manufacturers, importers and downstream users; the impacts on consumers; the social impacts, such as effects on job security and employment; the availability, suitability, technical and economic feasibility of alternative substances and/or technologies; implications for trade, competition and economic development; and the benefits for human health and the environment and the economic and social benefits of restrictions or refusal of authorizations (Regulation (EC) 1907/2006, Annex XVI).

REACH itself was assessed in this way. The 'extended impact assessment', published with the proposals in October 2003 (CEC, 2003), described the EU chemicals industry, the expected economic impacts of REACH, and the potential health and environmental benefits. The economic costs of REACH were considered to consist of the following: the costs of testing, which would fall on manufacturers and importers of chemicals; the costs of running the European Chemicals Agency, paid for in the most part by industry through fees charged for registration; and the costs to downstream users arising from having to reformulate products when chemical substances are withdrawn. The report also considered the possible effects on innovation and the competitiveness of the European chemicals industry with respect to companies based elsewhere. This section of the report is defensive, arguing that costs are not high in relation to the turnover of the chemicals industry and highlighting changes that were made to the proposals, following consultation, to reduce costs and encourage innovation. Total costs to industry are estimated at between 2.8 and 5.2 billion euros, and the report claims that costs of this scale are unlikely to have any more than a very limited effect on the size of the economy (CEC, 2003, p20) and will not put European companies at a competitive disadvantage internationally (CEC, 2003, p22).

In contrast to the estimates of the costs of REACH, no financial estimates of the health and environmental benefits of REACH were made by the impact assessment: the report pointed out that the lack of knowledge about exposure to and the effects of chemicals – a knowledge gap that REACH is intended to fill – makes quantitative assessment of them impossible. But the report does say that 'the evidence available supports the assessment that the health burden related to chemicals is considerable' (CEC, 2003, p25) and that 'it seems that the impacts of chemicals on the environment are potentially large' (CEC, 2003, p26). However, a calculation of the monetary value of possible health benefits was made as an 'illustration': assuming 1 per cent of disease is attributable to chemicals, and that this would be reduced by 10 per cent following the implementation of REACH, 45,000 disability adjusted life years (DALYs) of disease would be avoided every year. This is equivalent to 4500 lives per year, assuming 10 DALYs is equivalent to one mortality. A value of 1 million euros per statistical life then results in health benefits from REACH of 50 billion euros over 30 years. The report emphasizes that this is not an estimate, but an illustration of the potential scale of the benefits of REACH.

The notion of balance implies that a quantitative assessment should be made of the consequences of proposed regulations, but the extended impact assessment of REACH demonstrates the difficulties, if not impossibility, of doing this. Our ignorance of the effects of synthetic chemicals is one side of the problem, but it is also difficult to assess what the effects of more controls on the use of chemicals will be. In many ways these depend on how businesses respond and whether the changes they make are beneficial in terms of their business interests and the economy as a whole. The idea that environmental regulations and restrictions always increase the costs to industry assumes that current practices are maximally efficient. Yet there is little evidence that this is generally the case. On the contrary, there are many instances where the need to meet pollution control standards has led to industry examining its processes and thereby reducing wastes and costs.[1] This is the 'ecological modernization' argument, used to explain the success of industries in northern European areas with strong environmental protection legislation, such as Germany, The Netherlands and Scandinavia: strict environmental legislation makes industry less wasteful because in response to such legislation industry improves its 'housekeeping' – operating its current technology so that it wastes less material – and invests in new, more efficient technology. It thus makes it more competitive relative to industry elsewhere, as well as spawning new industries to provide clean technology and pollution control equipment. These new industries are also then in a strong position to export to other countries when the latter bring in stricter pollution control legislation.[2]

Although undoubtedly imposing costs on existing manufacturers of chemicals – they will now have to test and register their chemicals – it is thus difficult to say whether the impact of REACH on the profitability of companies that make up the economy, or on the amount of economic activity, will be positive or negative. The requirement for testing, for example, itself generates new economic activity. The money spent on it will not be lost to the European economy overall provided the testing is carried out in Europe, as will probably be the case.[3] REACH may simply result in changes to the types of synthetic chemicals produced, or it may encourage a shift to products and processes that do not use synthetic chemicals, perhaps reducing costs or stimulating industries that provide alternatives. The overall impact on employment could be positive, rather than negative. The socio-economic analysis of REACH seems to assume that the benefits of chemicals are represented by the size of the market for them and how many people are employed in industries associated with them. These perhaps represent the extent of the changes required were the manufacture and use of chemicals to be restricted but do not indicate whether after such changes the resulting situation would be worse or better than before.

Socio-economic analysis assumes that a new regulatory regime such as REACH is something that gives rise to economic costs and benefits, as a cause has effects. This, I think, is its fundamental error. A regulatory regime such as REACH is not a cause that can increase or decrease overall economic activity or profitability (though it may do this locally, for particular businesses, if they are unable to change their activities in response to the new regulations); rather it is part of the legal framework – the relatively ordered structure in which economic activity takes place.[4] It is only in this ordered structure that the causes of economic activity – human needs, wants and desires – have reliable effects. Changes to that framework change the effects that those causes have. The framework can be judged in terms of what effects the causes have in that framework: whether the world created through economic activity is a fit home for human life, and the effects of economic activities on the earth. It can also be judged directly, as to whether it makes visible the connections between causes and their effects, enables those responsible for harms to be held to account, and is just and fair.

Nomological machines and the socio-economic system

The above argument – that we should distinguish between the framework in which economic activities take place, which includes regulatory regimes such as REACH, and the causes and effects of that economic activity – is informed by Cartwright's concept of the 'nomological machine'. In *The Dappled World* (Cartwight, 1999) Cartwright defines a nomological machine as follows:

> *a fixed (enough) arrangement of components, or factors, with stable (enough) capacities that in the right sort of stable (enough) environment will, with repeated operation, give rise to the kind of regular behaviour that we represent in our scientific laws.* (Cartwright, 1999, p50)

What we call the 'laws of nature' – the observed regularities between sets of properties (Cartwright, 1999, p49) – are manifest only in the context of such machines: they provide the stable, ordered conditions needed for the interplay between the capacities of the things present to result in a predictable outcome. The solar system is a natural nomological machine, but most nomological machines are built by humans. The computer (with the appropriate software as well as hardware, its supply of electricity and so on) is a nomological machine in which pressing the keys on the keyboard causes the corresponding characters to appear on the screen. Scientific experiments build nomological machines, either by the arrangement of matter or by the construction of conceptual models, in order to investigate the capacities, or 'natures', of things. Things do not behave in the ways that they do because they are constrained by the laws of nature to behave in that way, rather they behave according to how it is in their nature to behave. When conditions are just right, so that the arrangement of things and the connections between them are ordered and stable, the result is the regularities between causes and effects that we call laws.

The system of ordered interconnections of a nomological machine means that events of a particular type (inputs) are converted in a regular, predictable fashion into other events (outputs). In the context of the machine, the inputs cause the outputs: there is a regular, law-like association between them. The machine itself, however, does not cause the effects, rather it is responsible for the causal laws: the relationship between causes and effects (Cartwright, 1999, p130). For example, the rise in the age at which women have their first child is often said to be one of the causes of the increase in breast cancer in Western countries, as epidemiological studies show a correlation between later childbirth and breast cancer. However, an explanation of this correlation is that changes to the breast cells that occur during the latter part of a woman's first pregnancy make the cells less vulnerable to damage by carcinogens (Steingraber, 1998, p264): given this explanation, is it true to say that delayed childbirth causes breast cancer? Is it not rather that carcinogens cause cancer more easily in women who have not had children than in those who have? What delayed childbirth causes is not cancer, but a difference in the 'nomological machine' of the woman's body in which carcinogens cause cancer.

This is not, of course, to claim that the human body is a machine; rather it is to say that it has a sufficient degree of order and stability (because it is a living organism, this is a dynamic stability) with respect to the natures of its components and their arrangement, so that causes give rise to effects in a regular(ish) and thus predictable (to some extent) manner. It also suggests that we can gain understanding of how it works – how particular causes regularly lead to particular effects – by studying the natures and capacities of individual mechanisms and components which we then piece together. Not that this method is foolproof: we generally need to check the results against observations of whole organisms.

Cartwright argues that economics proceeds in the same way: it investigates the natures and capacities of particular aspects of the economy by constructing models which separate out those aspects of the economy from others, the models being the nomological machines which generate laws (Cartwright, 1999, Chapter 6). The reverse also holds in that we can only make predictions about what the effects of causes will be when the socio-economic system, or parts of it, has at least some of the order and stability of a nomological machine. There are no universal, necessary connections between causes and effects in economic systems: changing the structure of the system is to change the machine, and therefore what effects causes will have. To understand how a different system will work, knowledge of the regularities between economic variables in the existing system will be of little help; rather we need to understand the natures and capacities of the components of the system. We may then be able to build a socio-economic system in which the causes of economic activity have good, rather than bad, effects (Cartwright, 1999, p124).

This suggests that socio-economic analysis could help in the assessment of regulations: an understanding of the relevant components of the socio-economic system could suggest how the structure of the economy (the nature of economic activities carried out, the technology they use and so on) may change as a result of such regulations. These changes could be evaluated in terms of how they change the effects caused by human needs, wants and desires – the causes of economic activity. Do those changes mean that economic activity produces a world that is better or worse as a home for human life on earth? For chemicals, a key question would be whether a regulation resulted in a decline in the production or use of risky chemicals. This would be rather different from the attempt at cost–benefit analysis currently carried out.

The world and its interests

The socio-economic system is part of the world: the relatively ordered structure in which human life, including the economy, takes place, consisting of laws and institutions as well as technology. A key feature of socio-economic impact analysis as it is currently carried out is that it assesses changes to the world in terms of their resulting costs and benefits to individuals (or to institutions such as companies that in relevant respects are considered by the law to be individuals). These costs or benefits are aggregated and together considered to be the costs or benefits of, for example, REACH. This practice of aggregating costs and benefits to individuals and weighing them against each other, even though the costs and benefits accrue to different individuals, is the general approach of utilitarianism. It assumes that the public good is simply the aggregate of the goods of individuals.

A key question here is whether this is how decisions about the public world should be made. Is the public good simply the sum of individual goods? Against this idea, Hannah Arendt argued that the world has interests which may conflict with those of directly concerned individuals. The example she gave is of a building in need of renovation to make it fit for human habitation. That this be done was, she argued, in the interest of the world, but not in the self-interest of either the landlord, whose interest is in high profits, or of the tenant, who wants a low rent. The profit and rent are matters of today and tomorrow, whereas the deterioration of the building is a matter of years. For the self – who may shortly die, move out or sell the building – the short-term interest is never outweighed by long-term interests, which are not of the self but of a world that survives its inhabitants (Arendt, 1970, p78). Arendt's view perhaps seems rather too bleak here: landlords do renovate buildings, and people are often willing to sacrifice some short-term gain for a long-term improvement, even one that they themselves will not enjoy. In reply she would perhaps say that when they do this it is for the sake of the world – because they recognize that the public world, which they share with others, has some claim on them, not because of an 'enlightened' self-interest.

Aggregating the interests of individuals to decide what is in the interests of the world implies that individuals are constituent parts of the world. This is a fundamental error. The relationship between individuals and the world is not one of constituent parts to a whole, but of particulars to context. The world is one of the conditions of human life, in which the individual life is lived and has its meaning. Aside from mere biological survival, which may be comfortably achieved in a prison, much of the content of individual interests is a function of the world in which the individual lives. Individuals would have no interest in possessing the pieces of paper that are bank notes if they could not be exchanged for other things, nor in having cars if there was no fuel for them nor somewhere to drive. Without a world human life would have no human meaning, nor would the individual have interests.

In making private decisions we have to take the world as it is and try to satisfy the interests that we have. But this is not the way to make public decisions. If these are made on the basis of trying to satisfy existing individual interests, the result is a conservative continuation of current trends, leading to unbalanced and unsustainable growth of what meets the particular interest considered. This is most clearly seen in the case of traffic and road-building. A key 'benefit' of the latter in UK cost–benefit analysis procedures has been the aggregate of time saved by the faster, less congested proposed new road. This obviously meets the interests of the individual driver in getting to their destination more quickly, but because it lowers the time and financial costs of travel by car it in turn results in more people choosing to drive further and more often, hence the continual increase in traffic (see Bowers, 1997, p168, on the argument, long resisted by the UK government, that road-building generates traffic).

The question we should ask is how changes to the world will change what the interests of individuals are; what is in the interests of the world cannot be derived from consideration of the interests of individuals. This question is a wider version of one I suggested earlier: how will changes to regulatory regimes change the effects economic activity have? Economic interests are the particular form that human desires, needs and wants (that cause economic activity) have in the world as it is. Changing the world in a way that changes those interests will thus change what the effects of economic activity are. Technology, and the regulatory regimes that govern it, are part of the world, and changes to them may be judged in terms of whether they result in individual interests that threaten or preserve the ability of the earth to support life, or the world as a home for human life, but also, more directly, as to whether they are just and fair.

One objection to Arendt's claim that the world has 'interests' might be to argue, as Joel Feinberg does, that something can only have interests if it has a 'conative' life – wishes, desires, goals and tendencies (Feinberg, 1974) – and the world is not the sort of thing that can have a conative life. But Arendt perhaps used the term because of the idea that politics is about negotiation between different interests; if this is what is generally accepted to be the case, then the public world – which is at the heart of politics – must be granted interests of its own. However, to say that the world has interests which are not the aggregation of individual private interests is not to claim that the world has a life independent of human affairs and that it is not to be judged by reference to human wellbeing in some sense. The interest of the world is the interest of the human body politic – the diverse individuals who together form a political unit that lasts for much longer than the individual human life span – in there being a fit home for human life on earth: a world which is stable, has a place for each individual and affords the possibility of action.

The distinction between persons

The practice of aggregating costs and benefits to individuals and weighing them against each other, even though the costs and benefits accrue to different individuals, is the aspect of utilitarianism that was criticized by John Rawls in *A Theory of Justice* (Rawls, 1971, pp19–24). Rawls argued that the most natural justification for utilitarianism appeals to the rationality of individuals balancing their losses against their gains, or forgoing a benefit now for the sake of a greater one later, with the aim of maximizing net benefit. Utilitarianism applies this thinking to society as a whole by assuming the existence of a sympathetic impartial spectator who can organize the desires of different individuals into one coherent system, as the individual must organize their own desires for different goods. This is to conflate all persons into one and to 'not take seriously the distinction between persons' (Rawls, 1971, p24).

This conflation can be seen in the use of the term 'risk' in regulation. As I pointed out in Chapter 6, risk implies the existence of a risk-taker, who in return for possible benefits decides to put themselves in a position where they may suffer harm. To consider that 'society' is the recipient of the potential harm and benefits, and makes the decision, is to treat society as a single person. Pointing out the non-identity of those making the decision, those receiving the benefits and those who are harmed by chemicals raises issues of justice that utilitarianism is ill equipped to address.

Rawls' criticism is close to a point made repeatedly by Arendt. The members of a political community do not have a single interest and one opinion. Rather, they are a plurality of individuals, all alike in that they are members of the same species, but different in their perspective on the world and in their opinions. The domination of one interest and one opinion, and the assumption that it is shared by everyone, is in effect equivalent to one-person rule – it is a form of tyranny (Arendt, 1958, p40).

Liberalism and the Harm Principle

The reason for risk-based regulation

At the end of Chapter 7 I asked why government insists that regulation be 'risk-based'. Why must there be evidence that an identified type of harm is, or is likely to be, caused by a technology before legal restrictions can be placed on that technology? The answer, I suggest, lies in the political philosophy of liberalism, which has had a profound effect on the constitutions of Western democratic states.

Liberalism is concerned first and foremost with the preservation of the freedom of the individual. Freedom is understood as the absence of constraints on individual action and is exercised in the private sphere. The role of government is to protect this private sphere and its rights and freedoms, so government should not interfere in the actions of individuals unless such interference is warranted by the need to protect the rights and freedoms of others, in other words where the individual's actions cause harm to others: this is the harm principle.

Insisting that regulation be risk-based implies that the production and use of particular technologies (such as synthetic chemicals) are actions that should not be forcibly restricted unless they cause harm to others, because to do so would be an infringement by the government on the rights and freedoms of individuals. Whether the rights and freedoms of individuals really would be infringed by such restrictions is an issue I turn to later. First, in the next two sections I examine the two principle arguments put forward by liberals for restricting the scope of government action to that justified by the harm principle: the neutrality argument and the autonomy argument. These two arguments represent different versions of liberalism. I will argue that the main problem with both is that they implicitly leave out the public world.

The neutrality argument for the harm principle

One line of argument for why government action should be limited to what is justified by the harm principle is that government should not impose particular ways of life on individuals as this would infringe their freedom to live their own lives in the way that they see fit. However, this freedom can also be infringed by others, harming being such an infringement. Thus the argument against government interference in the lives of individuals supports such interference in particular instances.

An extension to the first premise in this line of argument is that the state should not merely refrain from imposing particular ways of life but should not favour one way of life over others: it should be neutral.[5] In recognition of the fact that public policy decisions almost inevitably favour some ways of life over others, what is generally sought is neutrality of justification rather than of outcomes.[6] The justification of state decisions must not involve reference to the relative merits of different ways of life, though it can involve reference to rights – the right to life, to privacy, to own property, for example. Rawls puts it in terms of the right being *prior* to the good: the principles of right (of justice) take priority over what is considered to be good. They restrict what a person can reasonably conceive their good to be and thus the ways of life that can legitimately be pursued (Rawls, 1971, p35).

However, Rawls recognizes that the principles of right are themselves based on ideas of goodness. In *A Theory of Justice* he calls this a 'thin' theory of goodness: it should be as limited an account of goodness as possible, its purpose being to 'explain the rational preference for primary goods and to explicate the notion of rationality underlying the choice of principles in the original position' (Rawls, 1971, p397).[7] In a later paper he outlines five ideas of the good found in his theory of justice as fairness: goodness as rationality; primary goods; permissible comprehensive conceptions of the good; the political virtues; and the good of a well-ordered (political) society (Rawls, 1988, p251). These ideas of goodness do not, however, constitute a comprehensive religious, philosophical or moral doctrine (comprehensive in the sense of applying to the whole of life in the way that classical utilitarianism purports to be relevant to the decisions of individuals as well as those of government). Rather, they apply only to a particular subject, the 'basic structure' of constitutional democratic regimes: 'a society's main political, social and economic institutions, and how they fit together into one unified system of social cooperation' (Rawls, 1985, p225). This is because if political power is to respect its citizens as free and equal, its exercise must be publicly justifiable to them, but in modern societies people have many different comprehensive conceptions of the good (beliefs about how one should live and what makes life worthwhile). To be justifiable to all, the basic structure of society must therefore rely only on what people could agree on were they behind a 'veil of ignorance' as to what their particular conception of the good is. The principles of justice as fairness that Rawls put forward in *A Theory of Justice* (Rawls, 1971) are, he claims, principles that would be agreed on in this hypothetical situation and which can be agreed to by people in modern liberal democracies, with their different conceptions of the good. They can therefore provide the basis for a stable constitutional regime (Rawls, 1987, pp4–5).

Rawls' basic structure to which his ideas of goodness apply (the political and economic institutions of a country) is part of the public world. However, Rawls' theory is not directly concerned with this public world, but with how rights, liberties and goods should be distributed between individuals (Rawls, 1971, p61).

This may be because Rawls' theory is a theory of justice, and issues of distribution have always been at the heart of justice. However, he also claims that it is a political theory: one of the ideas of the good that Rawls says it contains is that of a well-ordered political society (Rawls, 1985). But the content of that good seems to relate only to the nature of the relationship between the state and individuals and to the distribution of goods between individuals – the common aim of citizens is simply political justice: 'the aim of ensuring that political and social institutions are just, and of giving justice to persons generally' (Rawls, 1987, p10). This, it seems to me, is a very 'thin' conception of the world, one that leaves out innumerable issues that are of common concern to citizens, that make the world a better or a worse place to live, and that structure and give meaning to people's lives.

Rawls considers communities to be associations 'whose unity rests on a comprehensive conception of the good' (Rawls, 1987, p10). He considers such associations to be essentially different from the basic structure because they are voluntary (Mulhall and Swift, 1992, p200). However, in any group of people that consider themselves to be a community, what you will find, I suggest, is not a single comprehensive conception of the good that informs all aspects of the lives of the members, but a divergence of beliefs and opinions. What defines the community and holds it together is not a unity of belief but a common interest in something external to each individual. Communities form around things of the world: tangible objects, institutions or the pursuit of excellence in a particular practice. Thus the local community is constituted by the people who share the local neighbourhood and scientific communities are based on their shared pursuit of science. The worldly thing gives the community, and thus the individuals *qua* members of that community, its meaning and purpose, which is the thing itself. These things are collective goods: they are common in the sense of shared by the community, so are *ours*, rather than *mine* or *yours*; they are not instrumental to or constructed out of private interests, but are sources of value to individuals as members of the community whose collective interest they are (Postema, 1987). In often ignoring collective goods liberalism shares with utilitarianism a tendency to regard the individual as the sole locus of what is of value.[8]

This concept of what makes for a community suggests that the political community is not so different from other communities. It too is based on shared worldly things: the shared land as well as shared political, social and economic institutions, and technology. Decisions about the worldly thing that a community shares must be based on some idea of what would make it a good thing of that type. For example, good football clubs should have well-maintained pitches, skilful players and enthusiastic supporters, whether they are in the local junior Sunday afternoon league or the Premiership. Communities, including the political community, can come to agreement on how to change their shared world to make it a better place, despite the diversity of comprehensive conceptions of the good among the members of that community. The process whereby those agreements are made is not one in which individuals make claims for themselves, which need justification, but one where there is an exchange of different opinions – different because offered from different perspectives – on what would be for the good of this shared world. Forming an opinion on this matter on the basis of one's individual interests, rather than from a 'dis-interested' view of how the world should be, is a form of corruption.

The role of government is to put into effect the agreements of the political community with regard to the world shared by that community. And this sometimes means protecting that world from harm by individuals, so it is legitimate for government to use coercion to prevent individuals from harming the common world, as well as from harming other individuals. It also places on government a duty to create and preserve a world that is a collective good for its citizens. One aspect of what that world is like is the riskiness of technologies. This suggests that government action to restrict the production and use of risky chemicals can be justified by its responsibilities for the world, rather than by its role in preventing the actions of some people from causing harm to others. In Chapter 9 I argue that action by government is necessary: action by individuals, although important, is not sufficient to ensure that the technology we produce and use constitutes a world that is a home for human life on earth.

The autonomy argument for the harm principle

Some liberals (notably John Stuart Mill and, in modern times, Joseph Raz) do not argue that the state should be neutral between different ways of life. Instead, these 'perfectionist liberals', are explicit in their support for some ways of life, or the development of certain traits of character, over others. Mill's argument for the harm principle in *On Liberty* is that people should be allowed to make their own decisions about what affects only them because it is only through making such choices that we use and can thus develop the faculties of 'perception, judgement, discriminative feeling, mental activity and moral preference' which are the distinctive endowments of human beings (Mill, 1859, p187). However, Mill, influenced by the Romantics, also thought that individuals have capacities that are peculiar to themselves and that need to be discovered and then developed by the individual if the life of that individual is to be fulfilled. We will thus not all choose the same, but choice will lead to a divergence of different ways of life, of 'experiments in living'. These are valuable for society as a whole because they test the worth of those ways of life and challenge that of alternative ways of life in a similar way to how differing opinions challenge the prevailing opinion and may reveal it to be only part of the truth, or wholly false. In modern liberalism the term generally used for what Mill is valuing here is 'autonomy' – the ability of the individual to make their own choices, direct their own lives, create their own selves.

Why is autonomy of value? The answer given by liberals generally concerns the value of autonomy to the individual: autonomy is valuable because an autonomous life is more valuable to the individual whose life it is than the same life would be without autonomy (Raz, 1986). In support of this view is the fact that some ways of life are only valuable at all if they have been chosen by the individual: life in an enclosed monastery or convent can be a rich and fulfilling one for the monk or nun who has chosen it, whereas a person who is forced to live in such a way is living in a prison. This does not commit liberals to the obviously erroneous view that a way of life is good because it has been chosen. Rather, the value of autonomy derives from the idea that even things that are good according to some objective criteria are not of value to the individual unless that individual endorses them as such (Dworkin, 1983).

Another line of argument – that made by Mill – is that autonomy results in better people. Here what is important about choice is that through making choices and making mistakes we develop the capacity to think, judge and choose wisely, which are the characteristic capacities of human beings. This is clearly an Aristotlean view, in that it sees the goal of human life as being the actualization of potentials that are unique to human beings, and that happiness, or flourishing, for the individuals consists in this actualization, which is the possession and exercise of virtues. This argument is therefore linked to the previous one: the virtues of the autonomous person are constituents of that person's flourishing, so autonomy is of value to the individual. But it is of value because it increases their capacities, and thus their range of activity, not because of the intrinsic value of what the autonomous person chooses.

A third line of argument for autonomy is that society as a whole needs people who can and do think and act for themselves, and who take responsibility for their actions, as only such people will challenge prevailing norms, beliefs and practices that are morally or intellectually suspect. This argument is independent of the previous two: it does not rely on an autonomous life being better for the individual than a life lacking in autonomy, indeed under some conditions it may in many respects be much worse. It is similar to the argument that Mill makes for freedom of speech in *On Liberty*: freedom of thought and discussion are essential for the pursuit of truth because the prevailing opinion may be wrong, or only a partial truth, in which case other opinions are needed to supply the remainder of the truth. Even if the prevailing opinion is the whole truth, it is necessary for it to be continually contested if it is to be held as a well-grounded conviction rather than as a prejudice.

Under some forms of government such continual testing of opinions is not allowed. Arendt's account of totalitarianism suggests that the result is not merely that false beliefs and opinions are unchallenged, but that people's capacity to think and to form convictions is destroyed (Arendt, 1966, p468). When she attended the trial of the Nazi war criminal Adolf Eichmann, Arendt was struck by the fact that Eichmann did not lack a sense of moral obligation. On the contrary, he was keen to do the right thing, but no one around him thought that the final solution was wrong so neither did he. Doing his duty meant doing what others thought he should do, even though this involved the mass killing of Jews and other 'undesirables' (Arendt, 1963). What he lacked was the ability to think: this is not to say that he was stupid, or lacking in knowledge, but that he was thoughtless. He did not recognize the claim that the world around us has on our thinking attention (Arendt, 1978, p4). Ordinary morality (which for Arendt is simply the mores or customs of a community) failed to prevent the rise of Nazism. The following of rules of conduct accustoms people, first and foremost, to following rules, rather than rules of any particular content. If people do not think for themselves, it is all too easy to simply change the content of those rules (Arendt, 1978, p177). In *The Origins of Totalitarianism* Arendt identifies the isolation of the individual, caused by the breakdown of society in 1920s Germany, as an important precondition for the rise of a totalitarian movement. As well as being isolated from each other, and therefore not able to take effective political action, mass unemployment meant that individuals were not able to contribute something to the world through work. They were in the desperate situation of not belonging to the world at all, and joined totalitarian movements because this was the only form of belonging available to them (Arendt, 1966, pp474–478).

This third argument for autonomy thus claims that without sufficient numbers of autonomous people, the public world is liable to become a world in which individual autonomy is not possible. This argument raises questions as to how we should think of autonomy, or whether autonomy (government of the self by the self) is really the appropriate term for what it is that is being valued. The liberal ideal is essentially that of self-creation: autonomy consists in the individual choosing for themselves how they are to live their own lives. But if such choices are private, hidden from public view, they can have no effect on prevailing norms, beliefs and values. To have an effect the individual must engage publicly, either through debate or through the publicity of their lifestyle choices,[9] about how it is best for *us*, not simply *me*, to live. This is recognized by Mill in his discussion of 'experiments in living' and of freedom of speech, but receives little attention from modern liberals.

Much criticism of liberalism has focused on its implicit conception of the self. The liberal ideal of self-creation seems to suppose that there is a self that exists independent of particular beliefs and values and the society of which the self is a part, one that is able to choose what to value and what goals to take up to give its life meaning (Mulhall and Swift, 1992, pp10–18). This, it is argued, is the conception of the self implicit in Rawls' view that a fair distribution of goods in society is that to which people would agree if they were in an 'original position', behind a 'veil of ignorance' as to the position in society they occupy, the abilities that they have and what their conception of the good is (Rawls, 1971). In contrast, the communitarian tradition considers that the self is at least partly constituted by the community of which it is a part (Sandel, 1982; Taylor, 1990), while eco-feminists argue that the self is relational – it cannot be understood in isolation from its relationships with others (Plumwood, 1993). In response to these criticisms there is greater recognition by liberals that individuals live in communities and that the wellbeing of individuals depends in large part on the wellbeing of the community of which they are a part (Dworkin, 1989; Feinberg 1988; Raz, 1986). Raz goes further in arguing that a precondition for individual autonomy is the existence of an adequate range of 'social forms' – a term that encompasses not just behaviour and attitudes to it, but 'shared beliefs, folklore, high culture, collectively shared metaphors and imagination, and so on' (Raz, 1986, p311) – on which personal comprehensive goals that give meaning to an individual's life are based. As Raz is a perfectionist liberal who thinks government should protect and promote autonomy, he argues that government should be concerned with the social forms of society. This gives a much wider justification for government action than that provided by the harm principle.

However, even with this recognition of the importance of social context to the possibilities of individual self-creation, the liberal model of autonomy still at heart seems to be about the individual making choices about his or her own life. For Raz social forms determine the range of options open to the individual, but he does not discuss whether one of the other conditions that he thinks necessary for autonomy, the ability of the individual to make choices (Raz, 1986, p373), is also socially constituted. The importance of others to our ability to reason, evaluate options and make decisions for ourselves is apparent when we consider how it is that we come to have those abilities – they are not abilities of newborn infants, neither are they constants in the lives of adults. They can be impaired by crises and traumas in our emotional and mental life as well as by physical degeneration. The infant, as it grows up, learns to reason and to make good choices through the loving care of its parents and teachers, from their examples and by reasoning with them. When, as adults, our reasoning and choosing abilities are paralysed, the wise thing to do is to seek the help of others, not necessarily to choose for us, but to reason with us and thus help us to come to a decision. Reasoning with others is thus prior to individual choice and the quality of that reasoning will affect whether the individual is able to make good choices: choices that result in his or her flourishing.

These arguments for the social nature of our ability to reason – that it depends on the existence of others with whom to reason – draw attention to what is often forgotten in the Western philosophical tradition: that we do not come into the world as independent, reasoning adults but as helpless infants, totally dependent on the care of others, and that throughout our lives, during shorter or longer periods of sickness, disability or frailty, we may need to be taken care of by others. Those able to do everyday tasks for themselves still need others to correct their moral and intellectual errors and to prevent them from becoming victims of their own fantasies.

In *Dependent Rational Animals*, Alasdair MacIntyre (1999) takes these facts about human life as the starting point for an exploration of what a flourishing community is. He concludes that to provide the care individuals need, such communities must consist of networks of relationships in which there is unconditional giving and receiving – unconditional in the sense of not being conditional on the qualities and aptitudes of the receiving person, or on what they have contributed in the past, but only on their needs. Such networks foster and are sustained by people who are 'independent practical reasoners'.

MacIntyre argues that the ability to reason depends on the engagement of the individual in reasoning with others: 'practical reasoning is by its nature [...] reasoning together with others, generally within some determinate set of social relationships' (MacIntyre, 1999, p107). He defines independence as:

> *the ability and the willingness to evaluate the reasons for action advanced to one by others, so that one makes oneself accountable for one's endorsement of the practical conclusions of others as well as for one's own conclusions.* (MacIntyre, 1999, p105)

Becoming an independent practical reasoner involves moving from merely having reasons for acting (as animals and babies do) to being able to evaluate those reasons as good or bad, and so to be able to change our reasons and thus our actions. To do this we need to be able to stand back from our present desires and our evaluation needs to be informed by an imagined future. The care, admonishment and advice of others are needed both to develop and to maintain our ability to reason independently (MacIntyre, 1999, p95).

While the hallmark of the autonomous person is self-creation through choice-making, that of the independent practical reasoner is accountability – for conclusions and their practical consequences. This accountability follows from the fact that the individual evaluates the reasons for such conclusions and is prepared to give an account of them to others: to answer for them and their practical consequences. The individual *acts*: she recognizes herself, rather than her circumstances, as the cause of her actions, and therefore can be held responsible for them. Accountability implies there are others to be accountable to: in acting as well as in reasoning the individual is always embedded in a network of relationships with others.

What is of value here – what is generally called freedom – is thus not a matter of unconstrained choice. Rather it is an achieved ability to be who one is within a network of relationships, a network that affords opportunities to, even while it constrains, the individual. Such networks are located in the world of things; indeed, as I argued above, they are often formed around such things. Arendt talks of the 'web of human relationships' as being bound to the objective world of things (Arendt, 1958, p183). Without this bond, human relationships lack solidity and are liable to wither away. To preserve networks of relationships that foster and sustain people as independent practical reasoners, the world must be a place for such networks. The creation and preservation of such a world in turn needs people who are independent practical reasoners – people who think and act for themselves and who take responsibility for their actions.

At the end of the previous section I argued that the duty of the government to preserve the public world as a common good for its citizenry justifies its restriction of actions by individuals that harm the world, not only those that harm individuals. Making the world more risky by the use of risky technology may be one such type of harm. Neutral liberalism fails to recognize this justification of government action because it does not recognize the existence of a public world, but sees only individuals and the distribution of rights, liberties and goods between them. The argument of this section suggests that if what perfectionist liberals value about human life is conceived of as independent practical reasoning, rather than as autonomous self-creation, there must be a shared public world that provides the place for networks of relationships that foster independent practical reasoning. Valuing the capacity for independent practical reasoning entails supporting the construction and protection of a world that supports such networks. This in turn provides a justification for government concern with the nature of the world and for government action to control technology according to what type of world it brings into being, not merely according to whether it is likely to cause harm.

Individual liberties and the regulation of chemicals

It should be noted that the classic formulation of the harm principle by Mill refers to actions of *individuals* and that it is with the individual that both liberal justifications for the harm principle are concerned. The principle is justified by the need to protect the rights of individuals to live according to their own beliefs, or with the promotion of the autonomy of the individual. Individuals in society are to be respected as free and equal citizens.

To regard the harm principle as relevant to the regulation of chemicals is thus to see the production and use of chemicals as actions of individuals with which the government should not forcibly interfere without good reason, the only acceptable good reason being that those actions cause physical harm to others. However, the relevant actors in the chemicals industry are not individuals but institutions. These are complex organizations that for some purposes are recognized as 'legal persons', but which differ in key respects from human individuals: they are not 'free and equal citizens' and cannot become 'independent practical reasoners'.

In response it might be argued that restrictions on the actions of companies should be regarded as restrictions on the actions of the real human persons who own or run them, and that therefore the harm principle can appropriately be applied. However, it is questionable whether a company *is* the human individuals who own it or run it, and thus that the freedom of these individuals is restricted by restrictions on the company. A case for the identity of a company with particular human individuals can probably be made with respect to small, private companies. In such companies one or a small number of individuals is clearly responsible for what the company does and can be said to be the company. But this case is less easily made for large corporations, owned by anonymous shareholders, where it is difficult to hold to account any particular individuals for the actions of the company.[10] In such companies all the key individual human beings may change while the company remains the same company.

Such companies are large, complex organizations. They have considerable financial, technical and administrative resources at their disposal, can in principle be immortal, and have a very much greater effect on society and the environment than an individual person. These factors mean that there is a fundamental asymmetry between complex organizations and natural individuals, with the power on the side of the organization. Only by joining together with others to form big groups to act in unison (for example trade unions, political parties and consumer organizations, which to have any long-term stability must themselves become complex organizations) is it possible for the individual to deal with a complex organization of this type on any sort of equal footing (Bovens, 1998, pp15–19).

Where, as in the case of chemicals regulation, those whose actions are being restricted are complex organizations, the arguments for the harm principle are not relevant. Controls on chemicals would not infringe the right of any individual to live according to their own beliefs, nor affect the autonomy of any individual, but only the autonomy of a company. The significant inherent inequality between large organizations and individuals means that they should not be given equal rights. Indeed, preserving the freedoms of the individual may require that those of large complex organizations be restricted.

Republican Technology Assessment and the Importance of Responsibility

I suggested above that it is the duty of a government to use its powers to ensure that the public world is a good for its citizens, and that the world provides a place for networks that foster the development of individuals as independent practical reasoners. The ethical and political theories that dominate current thinking on public policy do not acknowledge the existence of such a public world distinct from the individuals within it.

Because technology in part constitutes the public world, government must discharge those duties partly through the decisions it makes about technology. Such decisions must be made on the basis of whether the world will be made a better place, not on the basis of whether private interests will be advanced, even when those private interests happen to be those that a majority of citizens have, since what is generally referred to as the public interest is not the aggregation of individual private interests. We can think of it as being the interest of the world: it is the interest of those who have a world in common in that world being a fit home for human life on earth. Those who have a world in common may be quite diverse as individuals, but they together form a political unit, a 'body politic'. Because the world endures for longer than the life span of the human individual, so does the political unit: its interest in the world is a long-term interest, extending from the past into the future.

A technology assessment process that is first and foremost concerned with the nature of the public world the technology brings into being may be conceived as a republican one, for the republican tradition is concerned with the preservation of a *res publica* – a public realm which is not reducible to matters of individual interest. The *res publica* does not arise because of a 'consensus of common interests and political principles' but is the world shared by the public in question, about which there may well be conflicts and lack of consensus (Bellamy, 2002, p273). Conflict is an unavoidable feature of human life. What republicanism proposes is that conflict can be managed and resolved while maintaining equality between the conflicting parties. This is as likely to be achieved by the making of compromises as by the reaching of consensus, or by making decisions through means that do not require that everyone agrees, such as voting (Canovan, 1983). Conflicts and lack of consensus do not necessitate the setting up of one single authority to make decisions.

Republicanism shares with liberalism a concern for individual liberty, but that liberty is rather differently conceived: as non-domination rather than as non-interference (Pettit, 2001, pp138–144; Skinner, 1998), or as having a status as an independent person not subject to the arbitrary will of anyone else (Skinner, 2003). It is not, as in liberalism, primarily a matter of being able to exercise one's individual rights and liberties without interference. One may have individual rights and liberties but not be a free, independent person if those rights and liberties may arbitrarily be taken away. Conversely, one's status as an independent person is not compromised by restrictions to one's particular rights and liberties if one has freely consented to those restrictions. Free, independent persons are citizens of the republic and together share responsibility for the public realm, there being no higher authority over them that bears this responsibility.

In classical republicanism only a small proportion of the population were considered to have the independence required to be citizens. The economic independence that went with the ownership of land was often a key criterion. Ownership of a certain amount of land is now untenable as a criterion for citizenship; rather, we give political rights and responsibilities to those who have the capacity to be independent in the sense of being independent practical reasoners (so children are excluded). However, it is not enough merely that citizens have the capacity to be independent practical reasoners, they have to *be* independent practical reasoners. This is not something for which there can be an objective test, and any attempt to carry out such a test would be contrary to the need to show respect for fellow citizens.[11]

What the world inhabited by citizens is like is an important influence on whether citizens are independent practical reasoners and are able and willing to discharge their responsibilities for the world. To have political power, and therefore the ability to change the world, citizens must be able to act together. This is more likely in a world built so that people have to meet and interact with each other than in one where it is possible for the individual to be isolated from others. As I will explain in the next chapter, power is a precondition of responsibility: if citizens feel that they have no power to change the world, they will not feel that they have any responsibility for it.

A sense of responsibility for the world is one of the most important of the virtues of citizenship that, along with concern for the world, have traditionally been emphasized by republicanism. In the following chapter I examine this virtue, along with other meanings that responsibility can have. I also look at how decisions about technology are made, by government and by individuals. To what extent are they responsible decisions, informed by a sense of responsibility for the world?

Notes

1   The *ENDS Report*, published monthly in the UK, contains numerous examples.
2   For an overview of ecological modernization see Young (2000).
3   This makes the key issue whether European-produced chemicals, which have to be tested, are substituted by chemicals produced elsewhere that are not tested. Imported chemicals are covered by REACH, but those chemicals that are already incorporated into articles when they are imported are only covered in limited circumstances (see Chapter 5).
4   Andrew Feenberg makes a similar point when he says that 'regulation defines the cultural framework *of* the economy; it is not an act *in* the economy' (Feenberg, 1999, p97, emphasis in original).
5   Liberal theorists who argue for neutrality include Robert Nozick (Nozick, 1974), Richard Dworkin (Dworkin, 1985), John Rawls (Rawls, 1971 and 1988) and Richard Rorty (Rorty, 1989).
6   Rawls claims that his 'political liberalism' is neutral in aim but not in effect. It is procedurally neutral in that it seeks common (or neutral) ground between the plurality of comprehensive moral, religious or philosophical doctrines, but not in that it is based on substantive principles of justice, rather than just on procedural values such as impartiality (Rawls, 1988, pp261–263).

7   The 'original position' in Rawls' theory is the hypothetical situation in which people deciding on the distribution of goods are behind a veil of ignorance as to their place in society and their particular conception of the good.

8   This is not always the case. Joseph Raz, for example, who is a perfectionist liberal, argues that rights are collective goods in a similar way to beautiful, economically prosperous, socially tolerant and cultured towns that are good to live in. The government has a duty to promote and preserve such places, that duty deriving from what is in the public good, not from the rights or interests of any individual (Raz, 1986, pp201–203 and 245–263).

9   For example, Dave Horton notes how the lifestyles of green activists challenge conventional norms of behaviour and can thus be seen as a form of political action, not merely an expression of private preference (Horton, 2002).

10 On the problems of holding to account complex organizations see Mark Bovens (1998).

11 Arendt argues that respect for others is a 'regard for the person from the distance which the space of the world puts between us' that is 'independent of qualities which we may admire or of achievements which we may highly esteem'. It is the equivalent in the public sphere of love in the private sphere (Arendt, 1958, p243).

References

Arendt, H. (1958) *The Human Condition*, University of Chicago Press, Chicago, IL

Arendt, H. (1963) *Eichmann in Jerusalem: A Report on the Banality of Evil*, Faber and Faber, London

Arendt, H. (1966) *The Origins of Totalitarianism*, Second Edition, Harcourt, Inc, New York

Arendt, H. (1970) *On Violence*, Harcourt and Brace & World, New York

Arendt, H. (1978) *The Life of the Mind: Part One, Thinking*, Secker & Warburg, London

Bellamy, R. (2002) 'Being liberal with republicanism's radical heritage', *Res Publica*, vol 8, no 3, pp269–274

Bovens, M. (1998) *The Quest for Responsibility: Accountability and Citizenship in Complex Organisations*, Cambridge University Press, Cambridge

Bowers, J. (1997) *Sustainability and Environmental Economics*, Addison Wesley Longman, Harlow

Canovan, M. (1983) 'A case of distorted communication: A note on Habermas and Arendt', *Political Theory*, vol 11, pp105–116

Cartwright, N. (1999) *The Dappled World: A Study of the Boundaries of Science*, Cambridge University Press, Cambridge

CEC (Commission of the European Communities) (2003) 'Regulation of the European Parliament and of the Council concerning the registration, evaluation, authorisation and restriction of chemicals (REACH), establishing a European Chemicals Agency and amending Directive 1999/45/EC and Regulation (EC) {on Persistent Organic Pollutants}', Extended Impact Assessment, Commission Working Paper Com (2003)644 final, Brussels, 29 October

Dworkin, R. (1983) 'In defence of equality', *Social Philosophy and Policy*, vol 1, pp24–40

Dworkin, R. (1985) *A Matter of Principle*, Oxford University Press, Oxford

Dworkin, R. (1989) 'Liberal community', *California Law Review*, vol 77, no 3, pp479–520

Feenberg, A. (1999) *Questioning Technology*, Routledge, London

Feinberg, J. (1974) 'The rights of animals and unborn generations', in W. T. Blackstone (ed) *Philosophy and Environmental Crisis*, University of Georgia Press, Athens, pp43–68

Feinberg, J. (1988) *Harmless Wrongdoing. The Moral Limits of the Criminal Law, Volume 4*, Oxford University Press, New York

Horton, D. (2002) 'Searching for sustainability: An ethnography of everyday life among environmental activists', PhD Thesis, Lancaster University, Lancaster

MacIntyre, A. (1999) *Dependent Rational Animals: Why Human Beings Need the Virtues*, Duckworth, London

Mill, J. S. (1859) *On Liberty*, in M. Warnock (ed) *Utilitarianism*, Collins/Fontana (1962), London

Mulhall, S. and Swift, A. (1992) *Liberals and Communitarians*, Second Edition, Blackwell, Oxford

Nozick, R. (1974) *Anarchy, State and Utopia*, Blackwell, Oxford
Pettit, P. (2001) *A Theory of Freedom: From the Psychology to the Politics of Agency*, Polity Press, Cambridge
Plumwood, V. (1993) *Feminism and the Mastery of Nature*, Routledge, London
Postema, G. J. (1987) 'Collective evils, harms and the law', *Ethics*, vol 97, pp414–440
Rawls, J. (1971) *A Theory of Justice*, Harvard University Press, Cambridge, MA
Rawls, J. (1985) 'Justice as fairness: Political not metaphysical', *Philosophy and Public Affairs*, vol 14, no 3, pp223–251
Rawls, J. (1987) 'The idea of an overlapping consensus', *Oxford Journal of Legal Studies*, vol 7, no 1, pp1–25
Rawls, J. (1988) 'The priority of right and ideas of the good', *Philosophy and Public Affairs*, vol 17, no 4, pp251–276
Raz, J. (1986) *The Morality of Freedom*, Oxford University Press, Oxford
Rorty, R. (1989) *Contingency, Irony and Solidarity*, Cambridge University Press, Cambridge
Sandel, M. (1982) *Liberalism and the Limits of Justice*, Cambridge University Press, Cambridge
Skinner, Q. (1998) *Liberty Before Liberalism*, Cambridge University Press, Cambridge
Skinner, Q. (2003) 'Freedom, representation and revolution, 1603–1651', Ford's Lectures in British History, Oxford University
Steingraber, S. (1998) *Living Downstream: An Ecologist Looks at Cancer and the Environment*, Virago Press, London
Taylor, C. (1990) *Sources of the Self*, Cambridge University Press, Cambridge
Young, S. C. (ed) (2000) *Emergence of Ecological Modernisation: Integrating the Environment and Economy*, Routledge, London

EU regulations

Regulation (EC) No 1907/2006 of the European Parliament and of the Council of 18 December 2006, concerning the registration, evaluation, authorisation and restriction of chemicals (REACH), establishing a European Chemicals Agency, amending Directive 1999/45/EC and repealing Council Regulation (EEC) No 793/93 and Commission Regulation (EC) No 1488/94 as well as Council Directive 76/769/EEC and Commission Directives 91/155/EEC, 93/67/EEC, 93/105/EC and 2000/21/EC, *Official Journal*, L 396, 30.12.2006, p1

9

Responsibility

The Need for Responsibility

In the previous chapter I concluded that decisions about technology should be informed by a sense of responsibility for the public world, and that the public world should foster such a sense of responsibility in its citizens. What does having a sense of responsibility involve? What factors affect whether or not people have such a sense of responsibility?

To help answer these questions I start this chapter with an examination of the various meanings of responsibility and discuss the nature of our responsibilities *for* things. I then examine how decisions about technology are currently made and point out the ways in which this leads to 'organized irresponsibility', particularly in the case of synthetic chemicals. Finally, I consider the limitations of risk assessment as a conception of responsible decision making.

The Meanings of Responsibility

In his study of the problems of responsibility in complex organizations, Mark Bovens distinguished the following five ways in which the word 'responsibility' can be used (Bovens, 1998, pp24–26):

1   as *cause*: a person, situation or thing is responsible for an event if they caused it;
2   as *accountability*: people are responsible for things if they can be asked to account for them and held to be liable for them (and thus can be required to pay compensation or suffer punishment);
3   as *capacity*: to be responsible in a situation one must have certain causal powers (to effect the course of events) and intellectual abilities (to reason, or to foresee the consequences);
4   as *task*: things that one is responsible *for*, which are then one's responsibilities; and
5   as *virtue*: the excellence of character that means one takes one's responsibilities seriously, acts only after careful deliberation and considers oneself answerable to others for the consequences of one's actions.

Thus one is responsible *for* one's deeds and may be responsible *to* persons, organizations or ideals who may hold one to account (or by comparison with which one holds oneself to account). In a different sense of responsibility one is responsible *for* other persons or things and, arising from this, one may have a responsibility *to do* certain things and not others. Finally, one can *take on* responsibilities, by taking on a particular task or role and can *take* responsibility by taking control in a situation and recognizing that one may be held to account for what happens, or by making oneself accountable for something that has happened (and thus liable to pay compensation or suffer punishment) even if what happened was not within one's control.

Hans Jonas put responsibility at the centre of his 'ethics for the technological age' (Jonas, 1984). His main concern was responsibility *for* things (number 4 above), the archetypal case of which is that of the parent for the child. This responsibility arises from the claim that the thing has by virtue of it being 'worthy of being and in need of my acting' (Jonas, 1984, p85). For something to have a claim on me it must have some actual or potential good in itself that is threatened or vulnerable, and I must have some power to act to protect or nurture that good. Responsibility is thus a non-reciprocal relationship:[1] persons who are responsible have power to act and the capacity to act responsibly (the third meaning of responsibility listed above); what they are responsible for is vulnerable and is in need of that action (Jonas, 1984, p94). The precariousness of the *res publica* – the fact that the public realm can all too easily be taken over by private interests, or made a place in which there is no freedom but only terror and oppression and therefore little possibility of responsible action – means that it is something for which the citizen is responsible, to the extent that he or she has the power to preserve and enhance the public realm as a place where responsibility is possible (Jonas, 1984, p104). In addition to this traditional responsibility of the citizen, the increase in human technological powers brings with it a new responsibility: for the continued existence of humanity. This is something which is a precondition for responsibility existing at all, but which previously was not threatened, nor was in our power to affect, so was not an object of responsibility for us (Jonas, 1984, p118). This responsibility for the continued existence of humanity as a species is in effect a responsibility for the earth: the continued existence and functioning of the natural systems that sustain human life on this planet.

Jonas recognizes that as well as 'natural' responsibilities that arise because of the claims of things which are good in themselves and therefore ought to be, we may have 'contractual responsibilities'. These are the result of agreements we have made, roles or tasks we have taken on. He argues that these only have a moral claim in so far as their ultimate object is a good in itself. Thus tax officials have a contractual responsibility to collect taxes which does not depend on the merits of the tax system. However, they also have a 'natural' responsibility to uphold loyalty relations in society, relations which are good in themselves but which may be destroyed by disloyalty. To the extent that this good is the ultimate object of the tax official's contractual responsibilities, then those responsibilities have a moral claim (Jonas, 1984, p95).

If I am receptive to the claim of what is good but vulnerable that I have some power to affect, then it produces in me a 'feeling of responsibility'. This feeling is what motivates responsible actions – actions that take care of, protect or enhance the good of the thing. The doing of these actions, motivated by the feeling of responsibility, constitutes the virtue of responsibility (the fifth meaning of responsibility listed above). Concern for an external other, not for one's moral self, is thus central to responsibility as virtue, a position that Jonas contrasts with the modern existentialist ethic of the 'self-committing freedom of the self' and with Kantian ethics, in which the feeling that motivates moral action is directed at the moral law itself, not at an object of concern (Jonas, 1984, p88). Responding to the claims of vulnerable others may of course be done grudgingly as well as willingly, but only in the latter case is the virtue of responsibility fully developed. Then the good of what we are responsible for becomes part of our own good: furthering it is not in conflict with the needs of the self but is one of the ways in which those needs are met. The responsibilities that we have for others give meaning and purpose to our lives.

Bovens gives five criteria for deciding whether conduct is responsible: first, there must be an adequate perception of the situation – of what the dangers are, of what is threatened and of how important the threatened things are relative to other things; second, the consequences must be considered; third, the agent must have a degree of autonomy; fourth, 'conduct must be based on a verifiable and consistent code'; and last, role obligations must be taken seriously (Bovens, 1998, pp34–36). The importance of the nature of the object for which we are responsible, and whether it really is a good in itself, places key limitations on the last of these criteria. If what we are responsible for in that role is something that is a bad rather than a good, then carrying out our role obligations may be morally irresponsible. The autonomy criterion requires both that the agent has some room for manoeuvre in the situation (so that the possibility of acting otherwise was reasonably open) and that the agent – though he or she may listen to the advice and commands of others – makes his or her own evaluations and judgements and acts on them, not simply on the commands of others. In other words, the agent is an independent practical reasoner (see Chapter 8). Independent practical reasoners acknowledge that they, rather than others or their circumstances, are the cause of their actions, so are willing to take responsibility for them in the sense of answering for them to others. The need to do such answering – to account for what has been done – is behind the fourth of Boven's criteria: conduct that is based on a 'verifiable and consistent code' can be explained to others, understood by them and relied on; it is not a matter of whim (Bovens, 1998, pp36–37).

There is thus a close connection between responsibility as virtue and responsibility as accountability. One aspect of responsibility as virtue is that we are willing and able to account for our actions, and giving such accounts helps us to develop the virtue of responsibility. Knowing that we likely to have to give such accounts makes us more likely to take our responsibilities seriously and to feel responsible. Bovens thus argues that if people are to act responsibly, there must be mechanisms for holding them to account for what they have done (Bovens, 1998, p39).

Holding people to account for their actions does not then simply serve the purpose of justice – of ensuring that people make good wrongs they have done or that they suffer punishment for them. It should also foster the virtue of responsibility.

To do this effectively requires careful attention to how people are to be held to account. If the emphasis is on the attribution of blame and whether people should pay compensation or suffer punishment, those called to account are less likely to be open and candid than if the emphasis is on learning from mistakes and fixing what has gone wrong. Bovens points out that in many instances simply having to appear before a forum and account for what one has done is daunting enough, without the threat of sanctions, but also that through giving an account to others something may be brought to an end and a new beginning made (Bovens, 1998, pp39–40).

The Organized Irresponsibility of Modern Technology

Organized irresponsibility as a key aspect of contemporary modernity

The concept of 'organized irresponsibility' is one of the core ideas of Ulrich Beck's theory of modernity, 'risk society'. Risk societies, he says are:

> *characterized by the paradox of more and more environmental degradation – perceived and potential – coupled with an expansion of environmental law and regulation. Yet at the same time, no individual or institution seems to be held specifically accountable for anything.* (Beck, 2000, p224)

Nobody takes responsibility for the unexpected 'side-effects' of technology: no one has to account for their actions, pay compensation or suffer punishment when it is suddenly discovered that refrigerants have caused a hole in the ozone layer or that fire retardants are present in human breast milk and may be affecting the development of our children. There is a lack of responsibility as accountability.

Jonas points out that only someone who *has* responsibilities can be irresponsible: irresponsibility is the exercise of power with disregard to the responsibilities that we have *for* vulnerable things in our care, responsibilities that mean we have positive duties. Further, we may be irresponsible either because of a positive act or because of inattentiveness or neglect (Jonas, 1984, pp93–94). Our decisions about technology may therefore be irresponsible in the sense that they neglect a responsibility that we have *for* something, as well as because no one *takes* responsibility for the consequences of those decisions.

In the next section I look at how technological choices are made and the extent to which responsibility for the public world is neglected through failure to have regard for the effects of those choices on the nature of the world that we live in. I then consider why, for synthetic chemicals, nobody is held to account for the consequences of technological decisions.

The making of technological choices

In the last 50 years one new technology after another has found its way into everyday life without, it seems, there ever having been a conscious, deliberated choice to adopt them. Technological choices *become* made, rather than *are* made.

Technological development *seems* to be autonomous, something that just happens, beyond the control of government or citizens.

Close inspection, however, reveals a whole series of decisions, made by different actors in society, that together add up to the un-deliberated societal 'choice'. These positive decisions, which mean that certain technologies are developed or taken up, are made at three levels:

1   government, research councils and industry make decisions about the funding of scientific research. These decisions currently favour sciences where it is thought that research will lead to new technologies (see Chapter 4);
2   government and business make decisions to invest in the development of certain technologies and the provision of infrastructure for them; and
3   individuals, businesses and other institutions decide what products to buy.

The negative decisions, which reject particular technologies, are made through regulatory processes, such as the system of chemicals regulation described in Chapter 5. They are generally based on risk assessment. In addition, for many product types there are various systems of statutory or voluntary standards that must be met, standards that may take into account other criteria along with safety and risk considerations. The UK building regulations function in this way for built development: they require, for example, that buildings are well insulated as well as structurally sound, damp proofed and equipped with adequate means of escape in the event of a fire. Negative decisions feed back on the positive decisions: it is unlikely that a positive decision will be made to invest in a technology that will be rejected by regulators. But in that restrictions leave a range of possible options open, they do not determine technological choices. As I have already considered a regulatory system at some length, the remainder of this section will address the way positive decisions about technology are made.

I argued in Chapter 4 that the primary concern of government should be whether a new technology will result in a better world, and that of industry should be to make a good product that contributes to making the world a better place. A prosperous economy and profits should only indirectly be of concern: they have to be achieved but this can happen in a variety of different ways, and the choice of which way (by the development of *which* type of technology, by making *which* products) must be made with reference to the world. However, government policy does not even acknowledge that there is such a choice. Rather, technological innovation in itself is regarded as important for the international competitiveness of the UK economy, and thus for the nation's prosperity, so is promoted indiscriminately. Decisions to back particular technologies are not made after consideration of what the world they would bring into being would be like – a consideration that would have to draw on a wide variety of types of knowledge and experience – but on the basis of judgements as to the potential markets for the technology and whether they will result in 'competitive advantage'.[2] In not considering the effects of its actions on what it has responsibility for (the public world), government acts irresponsibly.

Of course there is only a market for something if people or organizations buy it. A liberal view may be that it is not up to government to decide what technology should be available, but up to individuals and organizations as consumers. They may also argue that, because of the role this gives to individual choice, this is the democratic way to make such decisions. There are two responses to this point of view. The first starts from the distinction between individuals as consumers and as citizens; the second questions whether individuals have a real choice not to have technological items possessed by most other people with whom they share a world.

There are many different variations of the distinction between citizens and consumers.[3] The distinction that I propose is that as citizens we have opinions on what the public world should be like and may try to change it, whereas as consumers we take that world as it is and make decisions simply on the basis of the expected contribution of what we buy to our own wellbeing. This suggests that when, in the role of consumers, we buy things, it is unreasonable to expect us to take into account whether what we buy and how we use or consume it makes the world a better place. However, many people do take such considerations into account: they buy Fairtrade goods because they think that the producers of tea, coffee or cocoa should get a reasonable price for their products, or organic food because they think that organic agriculture is better for the environment. They may also boycott the products of certain companies or countries as a protest against what they are doing (for example the irresponsible promotion of infant milk formula by Nestlé, Esso's stance on climate change or apartheid in South Africa). Such purchasing decisions are political acts, directed at changing the world: the consumer here acts, at least in part, as a citizen.[4] A key question then is how far the responsibility of the individual to act as a citizen, and not simply as a consumer, extends. One way to answer this is to ask what power individuals have to bring about a good public world through what they buy, since, as discussed above, we only have responsibilities for the good of vulnerable things to the extent that it is in our power to act to protect or promote that good.

On one level it might appear that the individual in contemporary Western societies has very little power to change the world. Sheer numbers mean that what any one of us does is insignificant in terms of its effects. In the case of 'green' consumerism (the choosing of products with the aim, in the terms of the analysis of Chapter 3, of reducing the destructive impact that the construction of the world has on the earth) there is, additionally, the problem of knowing what the impacts of a product are and which 'green' claims one should believe. Certain people's persistence in nonetheless trying to conform their purchases as consumers to their views as citizens has been interpreted as a sign that such behaviour is really concerned with affirming their identity as a particular kind of person, belonging to a particular social group, rather than with affecting change in the world (Szerszynski, 1997). Ethical consumerism, it may be argued, is concerned with the self, rather than with the world, and is therefore non-political.

However, I do not think it really matters what someone's actual motivation is. What is important is whether their decisions are justified by reference to public rather than private criteria.[5] The developing of such justifications requires some sort of public space in which to reason with others. This is provided in local networks of activists (see Horton, 2002) and in more dispersed communities, such as the readership of the magazine *Ethical Consumer* or the membership of non-governmental organizations (NGOs) such as Friends of the Earth. This public space needs to be made broader and more central, so that whether particular technologies make for a better world or not becomes the focus of mainstream political discussion. Ethical consumerism is political because it is action with others: successful boycotts are *organized*; they are collective action, not individual, and are intended to change the actions of others. The ineliminable presence of others – those whom one is acting with and those whose actions one is hoping to change – is what renders ethical consumerism political action.[6]

Thus the power of the consumer, like all political power, depends on the ability of individuals to act in concert with others (Arendt, 1970, p44). This is not a matter, as the liberal argument for the democracy of markets may imply, of individual purchases being unreasoned expressions of individual preferences. Rather it relies on public discussion about things of the world, discussion whose outcomes are made real by the purchasing of one thing rather than another. Although the ability to have the discussion and act on its outcomes is a mark of political freedom in the society in which it occurs, that freedom is not increased by a wider range of choices of things that do not make for a better world. For though it is a condition of individual autonomy that the individual has choice, the options available to choose from must be good ones; autonomy is not increased by the availability of unacceptable, immoral choices. As Joseph Raz puts it, 'Autonomy requires a choice of goods. A choice between good and evil is not enough.' (Raz, 1986, p379)

Our current situation is one in which government does not take responsibility for the world, so does not restrict the choices that individuals have to what is in the interests of that world. Simone Weil said that in this situation, where the rules that govern our life together allow choices that injure the common interest, people:

> *either seek refuge in irresponsibility, puerility and indifference – a refuge where the most they can find is boredom – or feel themselves weighed down by responsibility at all times for fear of causing harm to others. Under such circumstances, men, believing wrongly, that they are in possession of liberty, and feeling that they get no enjoyment out of it, end up by thinking that liberty is not a good thing.* (Weil, 1952, p13)

The destructiveness of so many of the technological choices available to the modern individual is perhaps too much for the individual to bear. It is far easier to think that because the effects of our individual actions are so small compared to the whole, what we do does not matter. Because we cannot do very much, we think we do not have an obligation to do what we can, so we act irresponsibly.

The second response to the idea that it is democratic if choices about technology are made by individual consumers in markets, rather than through a political process, is to point out how difficult it is for the individual consumer not to have a technology that most other people have. This is most obviously the case with technologies of communication and transport: not having a technology with which others communicate means not being able to communicate with them, which results in social isolation. Thus while ten years ago I just needed a phone, now I need an answer machine and a computer with e-mail and internet access. Unusually, though, I do not need a car or a mobile phone because many of the people I know do not have these things, nor do they expect me to have them, and public infrastructure allows me to communicate by phone while away from home (while there are still public phone boxes) and to travel where I need to go without a car. Thus whether one really has a choice *not* to have a technology critically depends on others: on what those we live among have chosen to have and on what those in governments and business have decided should be present as public infrastructure.

This illustrates how technology – even when the technological items are privately owned – is part of the shared, public world. It means that the number of mobile phones, computers or cars that people have cannot be regarded as 'votes' for a world with such things. Many who possess them might prefer it if the world were without these things, but while they are part of the world the rational choice for the individual is most often to have them if others do.

Note that the point I am making here is in many ways the obverse of the point about positional goods made by Fred Hirsch (Hirsch, 1977). Hirsch argues that the satisfaction derived from the possession of many goods depends on the conditions in which they can be used, and that those conditions deteriorate once too many other people also have those goods. The widespread possession and use of the goods results in 'social congestion', of which traffic congestion is only a particular case. Congestion means that the benefits the good provides when only a few people possess that good (better job prospects for educational goods, the quiet rural retreat for the country cottage, the ability to travel for the car) are reduced by more and more other people acquiring it: 'if everyone stands on tiptoe, no one sees better' (Hirsch, 1977, p5). The solution, for Hirsch, is to recognize that what is available to the individual as a result of getting ahead of others is not available to all. Rather than continuing with economic growth based on isolated individual striving, people need to coordinate their objectives: 'only a collective approach to the problem can offer individuals the guidance necessary to achieve a solution they themselves would prefer' (Hirsch, 1977, p10).

For Hirsch cars are luxury items, signifying social status and bringing benefits of increased mobility. Once everyone has a car the benefits are greatly reduced, not only by the fact that they no longer signify enhanced status relative to others, but because the resulting traffic congestion restricts the mobility they once brought. If benefits are reduced, surely the value of the car to the individual would be reduced. However, my point is that this is not the case, rather the car becomes *invaluable* – a need rather than a luxury. Furthermore, technological items such as cars and phones, whose use requires a supporting infrastructure, are frequently not valuable at all if no one else has them, as then the infrastructure needed to use them is not present.

The forms taken by our needs therefore depend on the world that we share with others. This is the same point that I made in Chapter 8: the content of individual interests is a function of the world in which the individual lives. To change the world we have to act with others. This action is political action and must be justified by arguments that are concerned with what the public world should be like. Such arguments should be at the centre of mainstream political discussion, and the role of government is to put their conclusions into effect.

In contrast, the UK government's current approach to promoting technological development does not discriminate between technologies according to whether or not they will make the world a better place. Rather, the aim is to promote technological development for the sake of the economy. This is irresponsible because it neglects the responsibility that the government has for the public world.

The lack of accountability

One part of organized irresponsibility is the neglect of responsibility for the public world constituted by technology when making decisions about technology. The other is the fact that rarely is anyone held to account for that neglect.

Responsibility as accountability requires mechanisms (formal or informal) by which people can be asked to account for what they have done and be held responsible for the consequences of their actions. This responsibility means that one has obligations to remedy or mitigate the negative effects of one's actions, even if those effects were not intended. However, there are three conditions that must be met before someone can be held accountable for damage (Bovens, 1998, pp28–31).

1 *transgression of a norm:* there must be some human conduct (as opposed to an object, a natural process or the weather) that has led to the damage and that conduct must have contravened a norm;
2 *causal connection:* there must be a causal connection between the conduct in question and the damage done; and
3 *blameworthiness:* the person being held to account for their conduct must have been able to determine their own conduct – they must have had the capacities necessary for responsibility, such as mature and healthy mental faculties, and other options must have reasonably been open to them. We do not hold someone to blame if they were forced to act as they did because of the circumstances they were in.

Nobody is held to account for the damage caused by modern technology because of the many difficulties in meeting these conditions. First, the direct cause of the damage is often innumerable actions taken by individuals who are considered blameless because, given the system they are in, they had little option but to do what they did. Thus the farmers whose use of intensive methods of production results in chemical contamination of food and water supplies can claim that they are 'forced' to farm in this way by the European Common Agricultural Policy: it is not the farmers acting but 'the system' acting through them (Beck, 1992, p33). Those who devised the system are not held to account because of the difficulties of deciding who is responsible for the system being such that it results in damage, such systems being the outcome of negotiations and discussion between many parties. Also, there are only very tenuous causal connections between the conduct of those who devise the system and the damage caused.

Second, the demonstration that particular damage was caused by particular conduct is often very difficult. This is particularly the case with synthetic chemicals. Though it probably is the case that significant human ill-health, disease and death is caused by synthetic chemicals, it is almost always impossible to attribute an individual case of ill-health to exposure to chemicals, let alone particular types of chemicals. The only exceptions are acute effects, where illness follows on quickly after exposure, and where there are long-term occupational exposures to high levels of a chemical. In the latter case it is possible to correlate the higher than normal exposures to higher than normal incidents of particular diseases, normality being what is found in a control population who are as similar as possible to the exposed population, except for the exposure. Thus we know that many synthetic chemicals mimic the female hormone oestrogen, and that oestrogenic chemicals have the capacity to cause breast cancer (that is they cause changes in breast cells which in certain circumstances lead to those cells becoming cancerous). But if we take a particular woman who has breast cancer it is very unlikely that we would be able to demonstrate a causal connection between her breast cancer and exposure to chemicals, let alone to a particular chemical. Benzene causes leukaemia, but how do we know that any given case of leukaemia was caused by benzene rather than by something else?

This is the problem of multiple causation: most diseases caused by chemicals can also be caused by something else, so particular incidents of the disease cannot generally be attributed to chemicals. It means that if I have an identifiable exposure to chemicals that cause long-term health effects (as I did recently when visiting a former tip where old chemical waste was being removed) and in the future I contract a disease which these chemicals may play a part in causing, I will not be able to know whether my having that disease was caused by that exposure. Given the lack of knowledge about the effects of chemicals, any claims that the chemicals responsible for the obvious odours present no risks to health are vacuous because they cannot be verified by future monitoring. Verification is not possible because the exposure is not large enough to make the group of people exposed significantly different from the rest of the population. We are *all* exposed, long term, to low levels of synthetic chemicals from a wide variety of sources, so there is no unexposed control group to compare us with.

If, unusually, we can demonstrate a connection between a particular chemical and an incident of disease, how do we know which particular exposure to that chemical, and thus which particular source, was responsible? This is the problem of multiple sources: for any one particular chemical there are usually many sources of exposure, but only by identifying the source that has caused my disease can I identify the human conduct that has caused it, and which therefore is responsible for it.

Third, even where it is clear that a particular type of chemical has caused a particular incident of damage, and we can identify who was causally responsible for the existence of that chemical (if not necessarily its presence in a particular location), the first condition, that the conduct transgressed a norm, is often not met. This is because those norms require only that foreseeable consequences are taken into account: one is not responsible for consequences that could not have been foreseen. Thus Du Pont, the main manufacturer of chlorofluorocarbons (CFCs) – non-toxic and non-flammable chemicals that were used as a refrigerant and aerosol propellant for many decades – have not been held to account for the hole in the ozone layer caused by those chemicals because at the time the key decisions to manufacture them were made, in the 1930s, these effects could not have been predicted (Colborn et al, 1996, pp243–245).

A further problem with holding to account a company such as Du Pont is that it is an organization, not an individual.[7] If, when the effect of CFCs on the ozone layer came to light in the 1970s, Du Pont had been held responsible and required to do what was possible to remedy the situation (such as to collect and destroy all the CFCs that had not yet been lost to the atmosphere from fridges, air-conditioning systems and aerosols), the company would probably have gone bankrupt. It certainly would have been put out of business if it had been required to pay compensation for the damage caused.[8] Though not providing an effective remedy, it might be thought that this would be a suitable punishment for having caused the damage. However, in punishing the company real people would be punished, and those real people would have been the 1970s Du Pont employees and shareholders, not the ones who 40 years before had made the decision to invest in the production of CFCs. If we want to hold these responsible individuals to account it will probably be too late – they are now retired, if not dead and gone.

The complexity of causes and effects, that they are often widely separated in time and place, and the fact that the actors involved are most often corporations, not individuals, all mean that there is a severe lack of accountability for the consequences of technological choices. Seeking retribution in the form of the punishment of those responsible is likely to be futile and, as Beck points out, the 'polluter pays principle' is inoperable where the polluter either cannot be found or cannot be made to pay. Insisting that the polluter must pay means that the polluter must be identified before any action is taken. Where this cannot be done, the pollution is allowed to continue (Beck, 1992, p63). The only hope for remedy is collective, by government action: the government, as the executive of the political community, will continue to exist as long as that community exists, and bears responsibility for not having legislated against damage-causing conduct. The punishment of governments has similar limitations to that of companies, but governments can sometimes provide remedies and can prevent the continuation of damage-causing activities.

The other important outcome of processes of holding to account is that people learn from what has been done in the past and change how they act so that they do not cause damage in the future. This applies even if it is not those whose actions are under investigation that will learn, but their successors. Given the severely limited possibilities for punishing or obtaining compensation from those responsible for damage caused by synthetic chemicals and other complex modern technologies, it is this outcome of processes of holding to account that we should seek to achieve: that we learn from the past and act more responsibly in the future.

Responsibility and Risk

One possible conception of responsible conduct in the arena of technological choice is that we act responsibly when decisions are preceded and informed by a risk assessment. Risk assessment fulfils the second of Bovens' criteria for responsible conduct: it is a consideration of the consequences (Bovens, 1998, p35). However, considering known risks, and weighing such risks against benefits or the costs of reducing risks, is unlikely to be enough. The first of Bovens' criteria is that 'we have an adequate perception of threatened violations of the norm', and within this he includes an awareness of possible threats and dangers, as well as the ability to give the right relative weight to conflicting norms and interests. An awareness of possible threats and dangers means being open to the possibility that what we currently believe may be wrong. That possibility is all the stronger if there are large areas of uncertainty or ignorance in relevant domains of knowledge, something that is almost inevitable if a technology is novel.

Giving the right relative weight to conflicting norms and interests means having the right perception of the context of the situation: what is of importance, what we have responsibility for and what obligations flow from those responsibilities. When we have more knowledge, power and control than others in a situation it is particularly important that we consider the consequences for them: the utilitarian calculation of overall expected utility is not enough, and in fact may be condemned as highly irresponsible behaviour.[9] One can be held to be irresponsibly negligent if one could have avoided imposing risks on others and did not do so, even if the risks imposed are not particularly significant compared to the risks of alternatives.

For example, Jonathan Wolff (Wolff, 2002) argues that the public outcry following the Ladbroke Grove train accident in 2000 was not a matter of the acceptability or otherwise of the risks of rail travel. Even after the incident the railways were perceived as a very safe form of travel: few people stopped travelling by train for safety reasons. But there was nevertheless a public demand for vast sums of money to be spent on safety improvements. Wolff argues that these demands were not related to assessments of risks by the public, but derived from the view that the companies running the railways had been culpably negligent in their failure, on grounds of cost, to introduce systems that would have prevented the accident. He suggests that the public thought the rail companies were acting in a morally irresponsible way, similar to the societal attitude towards 'unscrupulous' landlords who, to save the costs of 'simple safety checks', put at risk the lives of their tenants, who are often 'vulnerable young people' (Wolff, 2002, pp38–39). The context of a railway run by private, profit-making companies was important in this judgement. Such arguments can also be used to support the principle of substitution of risky for less risky chemicals or other methods: even if the risks are low it is morally irresponsible to use a chemical which is more risky than the alternative if it is others who are put at risk and the substitution can reasonably be made.

Thus if our decisions about technology are to be responsible decisions, assessments of risks must be supplemented by at least two other considerations: the completeness of our knowledge of risks (that is the extent to which we are in fact uncertain or ignorant about what the consequences will be), and who or what is being put at risk.

In Chapters 6 and 7 I suggested that it is riskiness, rather than simply risk, that should be assessed, because how risky a course of action is depends on the extent to which we are uncertain and ignorant about what the consequences of following it will be. Asking about the riskiness of a course of action, rather than the risks of a particular state of affairs, encourages a questioning of the adequacy of existing knowledge. How certain can we be of any predictions we make? Are there relevant phenomena or domains that we know little about? Can we be certain that we know what the relevant phenomena are? A course of action is also more risky if its effects are irreversible, and its consequences ones that we may not be able to deal with or remedy.

Our ability to deal with consequences, and to remedy harms caused, depends on what is harmed. Responsible action is informed by consideration of the consequences for what one has responsibility *for.* We saw in Chapter 6 that when risk-taking is positively valued it is in contexts where what the risk-taker puts at risk is considered to be only their own selves or interests. Taking such risks may then be courageous, particularly if done for the sake of others (such as risking one's life to save someone else's). Taking risks that put others at risk is irresponsible if those risks could reasonably have been avoided.

When it comes to decisions about technology we should distinguish between the following: risks to individual human beings who can decide whether or not to expose themselves to the risk; risks to individuals who have no power to choose not to be exposed to the risk; risks to the stability and durability of the human-constructed world; and risks to the earth (the totality of natural systems and processes that support and constitute life on this planet). If we consider possible harms caused by chemicals, risks from smoking, alcohol and recreational drugs are in the first category, those from air pollution by chemicals harmful to human health (such as carbon monoxide) in the second, risks of damage to buildings and structures in the third (through explosions or fire, and by pollution-accelerated weathering), and those to the ability of the earth to sustain life in the fourth.

The first type of risk is primarily the responsibility of the individual: they have power to take the risk or not and it is their health that is put at risk (leaving aside the issue of passive smoking). Government responsibility is indirect: for ensuring that the public world enables and encourages individuals to be responsible for their own health. For the other types of risk responsibility falls on those who cause the pollution or who have the power to stop it. Because they put others at risk, and often because there are many who cause the pollution whose actions need to be coordinated, action by government is legitimate and often necessary: governments have a responsibility to reduce these risks.

Going from the individual, to the world to the earth, the scope and extent of what is put at risk is widened.[10] In the same way as putting others at risk is more irresponsible of the individual than putting oneself at risk, it seems more irresponsible of humanity to put the earth at risk than to put at risk its own world or the life of human individuals. Jonas gives a reason why this is the case: in putting at risk the ability of the earth to sustain life we threaten the continued existence of human life and thus the future existence of the possibility of responsibility (Jonas, 1984). Putting the earth at risk is, I suggest, what we do when we produce novel chemicals, synthetic chemicals that are not identical to ones found in nature and that may interfere with biological or geochemical processes.

Conclusions

The irresponsibility that characterizes modern technology has two aspects. One is that decisions about technology are irresponsible, the other that there is a lack of accountability for damage caused as a result of those decisions.

Decisions about technology are irresponsible when in making them we do not do the following: acknowledge the importance of the things that we are responsible for and our duties to protect and not to harm what is good for or about them; give proper consideration to the effects of the technology on all the different things we are responsible for; or take proper account of the limitedness and fallibility of our knowledge. Technological choices result from decisions made by government, businesses and individuals. These decisions are generally irresponsible in that they neglect the responsibility for the world that citizens and governments have.

However, rarely is anyone held to account for damage that results from technological choices. This is because it is generally difficult to show a clear causal link between that damage and identified human conduct. Often the conduct is that of large, complex organizations, rather than of individuals. In cases where damage has been very considerable, it makes little sense to seek redress from such organizations or from individuals.

These two aspects of irresponsibility are linked: because there is little prospect of being held to account for damage caused as a result of decisions we make about technology, those decisions are made irresponsibly. If we want to increase the responsibility of decision making, we could try to make it easier for people to be held to account for such decisions. However, there are real problems in doing this, particularly if the result we seek is the punishment of guilty parties.

I suggest that we ought to devise methods of publicly holding to account those in industry, government and regulatory authorities for key decisions made in the past that affected the technological choices that were made. The primary aim of such processes should be to confront those who made the decisions with their effects and enable those who currently make such decisions to learn from the failings and successes of their predecessors, not the identification of wrong doing and the punishment of the guilty. Such processes should affect how such decisions are made now, if those making them know they may have to publicly account for them in the future. We should also change the framework in which public decisions about technology are made so that what is assessed is not merely the risk of physical harm, but whether the technology will result in a better world. And we should make it easier for individuals to make responsible decisions about technology.

In the final chapter I elaborate on how these aims could be achieved. I propose a new framework for making decisions about technology that has at its core a concern for the world.

Notes

1   Though it should be noted that responsibility *to* others (those to whom we may have to give an account) is not necessarily non-reciprocal. These others may be our equals, superiors or those under our care and they may also have responsibilities to us to account for what they have done.

2   See the speech by Lord Sainsbury at the information day on 26 April 2004 for the UK Department of Trade and Industry's 'Technology Programme' (available on www.dti.gov.uk). The programme is to be overseen by a board that comprises 'mainly senior business representatives' to ensure that 'the technology priorities within the technology programme are market focused'.

The programme is intended to support research and development in technology areas 'critical to the growth of the UK economy'.

3   The distinction is one of the bases for criticism of contingent valuation methods, used in environmental economics to calculate monetary values for environmental goods. Mark Sagoff claimed that these methods make a category mistake in that they treat values of citizens as though they are consumer preferences (Sagoff, 1988). Other authors have since given different versions of this category mistake: what are ethical judgements are being treated as if they are judgements about expected contributions to the wellbeing of the people making them (Keat, 1997); public goods are being treated as if they are private goods (Jacobs, 1997).

4   I say in part because, after taking into account the needs of world, ruling out some products on the basis of political judgements, there are still many choices left to be made simply on the basis of the preferences of the consumer. Citizens act as consumers when they make political decisions about how the public world should be simply on the basis of whether their own interests will be furthered. This should be regarded as corruption.

5   This is perhaps a general Kantian point: 'all actions affecting the rights of other human beings are wrong if their maxim is not compatible with their being made public' (Kant, 1793). But contrary to many interpretations of Immanuel Kant, that maxim does not have to be what motivates the action. Private criteria might, for example, be concerned with the purity of the self, such as religious injunctions against eating certain kinds of foods. These can be translated into public criteria by arguing that one has the right to keep oneself pure, to not be contaminated against one's will (for example the right not to eat genetically modified (GM) food). Such arguments are public in that rights are a matter of what the public sphere should be like – it should have space for a variety of different religious beliefs and systems of values. But they are only indirectly arguments against the technology itself: the right not to eat GM food simply means segregation of GM and labelling, and implies that there should be a right to eat GM food (though as nobody is demanding that right, and because there are practical difficulties with keeping non-GM crops uncontaminated if both GM and non-GM are grown in the same area, the right to be GM free happens to be an argument against GM crops as such). In contrast, arguments that GM crops threaten ecological systems or will result in a dependence of farmers on large multinational companies are direct arguments about the merits of GM crops being part of the world.

6   The purchasing decisions of organizations are, of course, just as important as those of individuals. Many organizations are starting to take into account factors other than price and the value of the product to them. Public sector organizations, which have a clear mandate to pursue multiple objectives, are in particular developing procurement policies that require, for example, the purchasing of recycled paper and electricity from renewable sources, the use of non-peat based composts and (where trade rules allow) the use of local labour. Such decisions, even more than those of private consumers, have to be based on publicly-defendable criteria. However, the development of such criteria benefits from the debate among private consumers, and the latter are able to be more innovative in the development of norms of ethical purchasing than organizations, so the criteria of organizations often lag behind those adopted by private individuals.

7   See Chapter 5 of Bovens (1998) on the problems of holding organizations to account.

8   Unless, of course, the costs could be paid by insurance. This might be feasible for some effects, but not for really large scale ones: the whole insurance industry would be put out of business.

9   Thus Ford were condemned in the 1960s for calculating that the costs in terms of deaths and injuries caused by a faulty model were less than the costs of rectifying the fault (the fuel tanks exploded in crashes at over 25 miles per hour) (Dowie, 1977).

10   It may be countered here that damage to buildings and structures (the world) is not as serious a matter as the deaths of human individuals. If, however, we consider events such as the destruction of Dresden by bombing in the 1940s, we can see that the significance of that destruction is not accounted for only by the number of human lives lost. The destruction of Dresden was a loss of a cultural heritage – the work of previous generations, which attested to their experience and told their stories – which should have been preserved and enhanced as a legacy for the future. The destruction of Dresden did not only kill many of its then inhabitants, it destroyed their world, thereby wronging both past and future inhabitants.

References

Arendt, H. (1970) *On Violence*, Harcourt and Brace & World, New York

Beck, U. (1992) *Risk Society: Towards a New Modernity*, trans. M. Ritter, Sage Publications, London

Beck, U. (2000) 'Risk society revisited: Theory, politics and research programmes', in B. Adam, U. Beck and J. Van Loon (eds) *The Risk Society and Beyond: Critical Issues for Social Theory*, Sage Publications, London

Bovens, M. (1998) *The Quest for Responsibility: Accountability and Citizenship in Complex Organisations*, Cambridge University Press, Cambridge

Colborn, T., Dumanoski, D. and Myers, J. P. (1996) *Our Stolen Future*, Little Brown and Company, London

Dowie, M. (1977) 'Pinto madness', *Mother Jones*, September/October, pp18–32

Hirsch, F. (1977) *Social Limits to Growth*, Routledge and Kegan Paul, London

Horton, D. (2002) 'Searching for sustainability: An ethnography of everyday life among environmental activists', PhD Thesis, Lancaster University, Lancaster

Jacobs, M. (1997) 'Valuation, democracy and decision making', in J. Foster (ed) *Valuing Nature*, Routledge, London

Jonas, H. (1984) *The Imperative of Responsibility: In Search of an Ethics for the Technological Age*, The University of Chicago Press, Chicago and London

Kant, I. (1793) *Perpetual Peace*, in H. Reiss (ed) *Political Writings* (1991), Cambridge University Press, Cambridge, pp93–130

Keat, R. (1997) 'Values and preferences in neo-classical environmental economics', in J. Foster (ed) *Valuing Nature*, Routledge, London, pp32–47

Raz, J. (1986) *The Morality of Freedom*, Oxford University Press, Oxford

Sagoff, M. (1988) *The Economy of the Earth*, Cambridge University Press, Cambridge

Szerszynski, B. (1997) 'The varieties of ecological piety', *Worldviews: Environment, Culture, Religion*, vol 1, pp37–55

Weil, S. (1952) *The Need for Roots: Prelude to a Declaration of Duties towards Mankind*, Routledge, London

Wolff, J. (2002) 'Railway safety and the ethics of tolerability of risk', study commissioned by the Rail Safety and Standards Board, www.rssb.co.uk, accessed October 2006

10

Making Decisions about Technology

Introduction

I have suggested that technology is 'world-building': it is how we add things to the world and the things that we have added to the world that we use. The world is a product of human work – that of past generations and our own – and is one of the conditions of human life, forming the context of our life with others. It conditions who we are, though not absolutely. Human life has specifically human meaning only in the context of a world shared with others.

However, that there is such a shared world distinct from the individuals within it is not something that is acknowledged by the ethical and political theories that dominate public policy in Western democracies: utilitarianism and liberalism. Hence public decisions about technology and its regulation generally consider only costs, benefits and harms to individuals (or to companies that legally are treated as if they are persons). Effects on the world that those individuals share, if considered at all, are treated as effects on the interests of individuals: as effects whose scale depends on the number of individuals affected and the severity of the effect on each. The importance that liberalism places on the freedom of the individual, conceived as non-interference by the state, means that regulatory systems assume that a technology does not cause harm unless there are clear indications otherwise. Hence in the regulation of synthetic chemicals, regulators have to have good reasons to think that a chemical causes harm before action can be taken.

Because chemicals regulation is risk-based there must be evidence that an identified type of harm is likely to result from use of a particular chemical (in other words that the chemical poses a significant risk) before action can be taken to restrict its production or use. However, if we consider how risk assessment of chemicals is carried out, it is apparent that current methods are not able to provide evidence that commands agreement on whether there is a risk from a chemical or not. Partly as a consequence of this, risk assessment processes have been characterized by procrastination and delay. During this delay the production and use of potentially harmful chemicals is allowed to continue.

Instead of regulating on the basis of risks, I have suggested that we should regulate on the basis of riskiness. While risk is a matter of a particular type of outcome, riskiness is a matter of objective properties of the thing or situation, and of our knowledge. Riskiness is a feature of the world: it is one of the things that should be considered by procedures for assessing technology that are concerned with the world that a technology brings into being.

Such a technology assessment process could be called republican. Like classical republicanism it would be concerned with the preservation of the public world and with promoting the virtues of citizenship. The most important of those virtues in our current context is responsibility. The approach to technology in contemporary society is characterized by 'organized irresponsibility': in how they make decisions about technology citizens and governments neglect the responsibilities they have for the public world, and nobody is accountable for the consequences of the technological choices that are made.

How could this situation be changed? In this final chapter I suggest a new framework for making public decisions about technology in general and synthetic chemicals in particular. I also consider ways in which the responsibility of individuals and organizations for the decisions they make to purchase or use particular technological products could be enabled and encouraged.

The idea that technology is 'world-building', and that buildings rather than machines are the paradigm technological products (see Chapter 3), suggests that we should look to how we make decisions about built development for a possible model for how we could make decisions about technology in general. I therefore first outline the control of built development in the UK and argue that considerations about the public world and what it should be like are the basis for the controls. Using this system as a model I then suggest how we could make decisions about technology.

UK Controls over Built Development

The planning system

There are two types of controls over built development in the UK: planning, discussed here, and building regulations, discussed in the next section. The planning system is concerned with 'the development and use of land in the public interest' (ODPM, 2005, paragraph 11). Through the planning system, government (local and national) decides what can be built and what activities can take place where. These decisions are not made on the basis of what will result in the greatest overall economic growth, or simply on whether harm will be caused, but on what sort of world there should be. Thus because it is better if town and city centres are vibrant, rather than derelict places, development of shops and offices must generally be in town centre, rather than in out-of-town locations (PPS6: 'Town centres and retail development'); because we want to preserve the countryside and have compact urban areas, most new housing must now be built on previously used land within urban areas, not on greenfield sites in the countryside (PPS3: 'Housing').[1]

Planning decisions are not a matter of negotiation between different private interests but of public debate, where what counts are the arguments made and reasons given.[2] The type of arguments that can be made are set out in legislation and in planning policies at national, regional and local levels: these effectively set out what are 'material considerations'. Reasons based on private interests, such as the financial value of neighbouring properties, or the impact on the viability of a business, are not material. It is recognized that it can be difficult to distinguish between public and private interests, and that the two can coincide (ODPM, 2005, paragraph 29). That buildings are of a good standard and fit to live or work in is thought to be a matter of public interest. This is often represented by the idea of 'amenity', something that is an objective matter of the internal and external environment of a building and which can be harmed, for example by adjacent developments that block out light or generate noise of a type that one could reasonably expect not to find in that location. The view from a property, though it may be what the property owners value most, is not a material consideration, though how the property affects more general views, particularly from public land, is material.

Legislation specifies the types of developments that require planning permission and those that may be done under 'permitted development rights'. This permission is granted or refused by local planning authorities (district or unitary councils) or, in the case of very major developments, national government. Planning policies are subject to public consultation and planning applications must be publicly advertised (by being listed in local papers, the putting up of notices at the site of development, and letters to affected local households and businesses). Anyone has the right to make representations objecting to or supporting planning applications and these representations must be taken into account in the planning process.

It is recognized in planning that many arguments are matters of opinion. Decisions have to be based on all the material considerations, but frequently there is scope for discretion in the interpretation of policy and what relative weight should be given to the different considerations. Thus while many decisions on applications for planning permission are clear cut, a significant minority are not. Such decisions are made by committees of locally-elected politicians (local councillors), advised by professional planning officers, whose recommendation the committee can nonetheless go against, provided the decision they make is reasonable. As a remedy against unreasonable decisions applicants have the right of appeal against refusal to an inspector appointed by national government.

UK planning policy seeks to reduce the impact that how we live has on the environment and to create places that people want to do business in and live in: places in which there is a sense of community. It does what some 'civic environmentalists' in the US (Light, 2003; Dagger, 2003) would like to see done there: it sets minimum densities for new housing development (PPS3: 'Housing'); it sets boundaries to the expansion of urban areas (PPG2: 'Greenbelts'); it promotes high quality urban design and local distinctiveness (PPS1: 'Delivering sustainable development'); and increasingly it is a process that promotes public participation in decision making (PPS1). Planning theorists argue that, if made more inclusive of different knowledges and perspectives, local planning could be a means for building the capacity for collaboration among people from diverse cultures who share a common local environment. Discussions about the future of what people in our fragmented society do share – the spaces and places of their local environments, their common world – have the potential to create a political community (Healey, 1997).

Building regulations

The planning system's control over built development is complemented by that of building regulations, which are made nationally but enforced locally. These set out technical standards for the construction of buildings, so that they are well built, structurally sound, safe, well insulated and appropriately accessible to those with disabilities. They cover features that can be easily quantified and measured, about which there is limited scope for judgement and discretion, and which are of public concern. It might be countered that the matters covered by building regulations are not of public concern, rather the regulations are the state intervening on behalf of the 'consumer' (the person or organization who is going to buy or live in the building) in the relationship between the consumer and the builder, which is unequal because the consumer does not have the knowledge of the builder as to what makes a building structurally sound, for example. However, this is inadequate as an account of why building regulations are justified, since they apply just as much to a building built by a builder for his or her own use as to one that is sold to someone else. Rather, the quality of buildings is a matter of public concern because, even if privately owned, they form part of the public world. Not only are they visible from the public space around them, but they outlast their occupants. Thus building regulations apply to features that determine whether the building does last and to those that affect other concerns of public policy, such as safety and the use of energy.

Local authority building regulations inspectors can require that new buildings that do not satisfy the building regulations are rebuilt so that they do (old buildings do not have to be made to conform to current building regulations). Builders can show that they satisfy the regulations either by using products and methods that conform to the appropriate British Standard (see discussion below), or by providing their own calculations (of structural soundness, for example). The latter route means that it is possible to use novel methods of construction for which there is no standard, such as building with straw bales.

The Organization of Decision Making about Technology

Introduction

An important difference between buildings and what is normally considered as technology is that the latter lacks the fixedness to a particular location that buildings have. Decision making by local committees would therefore not be appropriate: in the current economic and political system, decisions about technology have to be made at the national, or in some cases the international, level. However, there is still scope for a system modelled on that for built development.

Like the public controls over built development, I suggest that public controls over technology should consist of two types of systems: technical standards, equivalent to building regulations, and a system equivalent to the planning system that can take into account matters that are not easily quantified and measured. The former should be overseen in some way by elected politicians. In the latter, major decisions should be made by elected politicians, following public consultation and

debate. The decisions in both systems must be guided by policies that, like planning policies, set out what should be taken into account in coming to those decisions. The principles that I concluded with in Chapter 3 should form the basis
of those policies. In this section I outline possible institutional arrangements for
both systems, in the UK context.

Technical standards

Systems of standards currently exist in many areas of technology. In the UK the
main standards-setting organization is the British Standards Institute (BSI).[3] As
well as setting British Standards (the use of which is not confined to Britain), the
BSI represents UK interests in European and international standards organizations, such as the International Organization for Standardization (ISO). The BSI
is not a branch of the elected government but an independent body with a Royal
Charter[4] that defines its purpose (principally to set standards and to promote their
adoption) and a membership composed primarily of companies and organizations. It sets standards for a great many things, from the size of structural steel
sections (the first set of standards, introduced in 1901), paper (it introduced the
'A' series of paper sizes in 1957), children's toys and the sizes of cassette tapes to
management systems. The BSI defines a standard as follows:

> *a document, established by consensus and approved by a recognized body, that*
> *provides rules, guidelines or characteristics for activities or their results, aimed at*
> *the achievement of the optimum degree of order in a given context.* (BSI, 2005,
> Part 1, paragraph 3.21)

There can be standards both for things and for how to do things. They may be
specifications (that set out requirements to be fulfilled), codes of practice, guides
or classifications (BSI, 2005, Part 2, section 3). There are some 25,000 current
British Standards and 2000 new ones may be published in a year. The BSI regards
a standard as a document that it sells, and the BSI group engages in substantial
commercial activities, such as product testing, training, inspection and accreditation services, now on a global scale. However, it also receives funding from the UK
government as well as official recognition for its standard-setting work.

Standards are set by committees composed of a balanced mix of representatives of 'interested parties' – mainly those who produce or use the relevant product or service, but also regulators, professional organizations and, for consumer
products, a consumer representative (who is funded by the UK government). For
both buyer and seller of a product those setting the standard do the job of working out what are the essential features that type of product needs to have if it is to
be able to do the job it is intended for. That a product meets a standard assures
the buyer that it is 'fit for purpose' and thus makes it easier for the seller to sell
it. Standards are also important in ensuring that products are compatible – that
paper is compatible with printers, cassette tapes with tape recorders. Only then
will either product be of any use and thus have a market. The benefits of standardization mean that standards do not have to be legally enforced for them to be
widely used: only in some product areas, such as children's toys, is it illegal to sell

products that do not conform to the relevant British Standard. However, claiming that a product conforms to a standard when it does not is an offence under trade descriptions legislation.

Many matters that are of concern to the producers and users of a product, such as its durability and energy efficiency, are also of wider concern. There is also scope for including matters that do not directly affect the producer and user, such as risks to others or to the environment. Standard setting could therefore be informed by the principles that I derived in Chapter 3. This would require limited organizational change, though it may increase the range of 'interested parties' who should be involved in standard setting. It would also involve recognition that the setting of standards is what Ulrich Beck calls an arena of 'sub-politics': though not part of the official government it is an arena of governance, in which the decisions made change the conditions of social life (Beck, 1992, p233) – in other words they change the world. British Standards are documents that are of public concern, so should not be commodities that the BSI sells: they should, like government documents, be available free on the internet. As an arena of sub-politics, standard setting is legitimately an area for political discussion and supervision.

Political supervision of technological development

Standards can obviously only be set for areas of technology that are reasonably established. They cannot direct the development of new technology. For this we need something akin to the planning system. Like the planning system, elected politicians should ultimately be the decision makers, not civil servants or committees of experts and industry representatives. Politicians have a legitimacy and accountability that comes from being elected. Politicians are more effectively bound by codes of conduct to act in the public interest than non-politicians and, unlike representatives of industry and (increasingly) scientists, do not generally have a greater interest in any particular technologies than that of the population as a whole. The politicians must make impartial, disinterested decisions, and their ability to do this may be greater if they are in the position of spectators of, rather than actors in, government (Arendt, 1982, p55), in other words that they are members of the legislature, but not of the executive. This would mirror the situation in planning, where local planning committees are not part of the executive of the local authority.

In the UK system, the politicians who make these decisions could be a cross-party committee of parliamentarians – a 'technology committee' – whose members are not required to stick to a party line. This committee should:

1   oversee the spending of research councils on areas relevant to technology;
2   make decisions about government funding for the development of new technologies and the provision of infrastructure for new technologies; and
3   make recommendations for legislative regulation of technologies, at UK and European levels.

Under the first function the committee could consider needs for research into the effects of a technology as well as research that may lead to technological developments.

The third function would apply to technologies that are potentially socially disruptive or that may have significant environmental impacts. Under this function the committee could make recommendations that standards be developed in particular areas of technology to address concerns that it identifies. It might also recommend a slowing down of the rate of technological change to allow social adjustment to it and for monitoring and evaluation of the effects of technological innovations. In all its functions the committee would have to consult widely, and, in coming to its decisions, have to take into account all factors which published policies say are 'material considerations'.

An independent commission of inquiry

At the end of Chapter 9 I suggested that we should devise methods for holding to account those who have made key decisions which affected the course of technological development. The aim of such holding to account would primarily be to learn from what happened in the past. Given the time it takes for effects to become apparent, this public accounting will probably have to concern itself with decisions made a reasonable distance in the past, perhaps a decade or more earlier. The process could consist of public inquiries into particular past technological choices, conducted by an organization that has a degree of independence from government, but whose recommendations the government, or the technology committee suggested above, would be required to respond to.

The reports from these inquiries would not only throw light on the process of decision making about technology, but may make recommendations on how existing technologies could be reconfigured so they better embody the principles set out in Chapter 3. In the UK a standing Royal Commission, similar to the Royal Commission on Environmental Pollution (RCEP), could provide the required independent organization. Its work would be assisted if it had the power to require people to give evidence to it, including employees of private companies. Although not having powers of sanction, it would be able to confront such people with the effects of the decisions they have made and require that they account for them. This possibility, that one may in the future have to account in public for what one does, may also have an influence on how decisions are made now.

Policy formation

The final element of the organizational structure is the formulation of policies to guide decisions on technology, made by the parliamentary committee and the standards-setting organization. No matter how good the institutional framework of decision making about technology, good, responsible decisions will not be the outcome if they are not made on the basis of good policies that set out what those making decisions have responsibility for and therefore what they must take into consideration.[5] The government executive should have responsibility for policy formation, but it should be the outcome of a process that enables and encourages public participation.

In Chapter 3 I argued that our goal when making decisions about technology should be to make the world a better home for human life on earth.

I then suggested that because of the sort of beings we are – biological organisms and moral persons with an aesthetic sense – the world should not significantly change the existing natural processes and cycles of the earth; it should be a place for responsible human action and it should be beautiful rather than ugly. Translating these requirements for the world into features that technology should have, I proposed the following as principles on which policies to inform decisions about technology should be based:

1 technology should use materials that can be incorporated into the natural cycles of the earth without changing those cycles or starting new 'natural' processes that would not exist without human action;
2 technology should not dislocate natural cycles but enable human activities to be accommodated within them;
3 technology should facilitate human interaction;
4 technology should allow for human unpredictability and fallibility – of designers, engineers and risk assessors, as well as of operators – and not have catastrophic consequences if people make mistakes or act maliciously;
5 technology should not make the world more risky, and thus restrict what it is safe for people to do;
6 technology should enable responsible individual action and should not enforce irresponsibility or increase dependency (of some people on others or on institutions and organizations); and
7 technology should produce and consist of durable, beautiful things.

These principles are not rules for decision making but are intended to give guidance as to the things that should be considered in making public decisions about technology. They concern the effects of technology on the nature of the world as a home for human life, and the impacts of that world on the earth. They are not concerned with aspects of a technology that are likely to be of interest to the individual (or organization) that buys or uses a technology, such as whether it makes life more comfortable or convenient or reduces the costs of producing other things. Judgement of these matters can be left to the individual or business and should not be the concern of public policy.

The Regulation of Chemicals

Chemicals as technology

Of the seven principles for decision making about technology that I suggested above, the first is of most direct relevance to chemicals, since chemicals are what materials are composed of. For the current regulatory system this means that a distinction should be made between chemicals that are found in nature and those that are not. In Chapter 7 I argued that non-nature-identical chemicals are more *risky* than nature-identical ones because we know less about their effects – unlike natural chemicals, they may have effects that we have not encountered before. I suggest that the regulatory system should be reformed to focus on *riskiness* rather than risk and below I suggest how such a system might work.

If we take a wider view of chemicals as technology, more of the principles that I set out above become relevant. The two definitions of technology that I put forward in Chapter 3 are first that technology is how we add things to the world, things being material objects, and second that technology is the things that we have added to the world that we use. There are thus two ways in which we could assess chemicals as technology: by assessing the world constituted by the technology that produces a chemical and by assessing the chemical in the context of a particular use.

Regulating on the basis of riskiness

The current regulatory system seeks to reduce risks from chemicals, but these risks are narrowly conceived as known risks: they are only recognized where there is good evidence that a chemical has the capacity to cause a particular type of harm. The extent to which we are ignorant about what the effects of a chemical are and the uncertainties about the effects that we do suspect are not taken fully into account. Focusing on the riskiness of the production and use of a chemical, rather than just on known risks, would reduce the expectation of precision while enlarging the scope of assessment so that it includes consideration of features such as novelty, persistence and mobility that affect how we should regard our knowledge of the capacity of a chemical to cause harm (see Chapter 7).

I suggest that regulation should aim to reduce the production and use of risky chemicals by requiring that the least risky substance or method is always used for any particular purpose. Any use of risky substances must be justifiable in terms of the public benefits of that use (not merely by private or commercial benefits). The more risky the chemical, the stronger the arguments in favour of using it would need to be. Such justifications could include reference to risks incurred if the chemical is not used. This will probably require a combination of legal and other measures, including authorization procedures (as in REACH), liability rules and the full disclosure of synthetic chemicals used in making products. A change in culture, not merely legal compliance, is what is required.

This approach to regulation should avoid the charges often levelled at those calling for a more precautionary approach in chemicals policy that bases regulation on hazards, rather than on risk. Opponents point to the relationship between effect and dose, some suggesting that almost any chemical can be harmful if the dose is high enough, and thus be deemed hazardous. This, they say, renders regulation on the basis of hazard, rather than risk, meaningless (see, for example, Nilsson, 1998). What I am suggesting would not mean that all hazardous chemicals would be banned, rather that there would need to be good reasons for their use. It would be clear that allowed uses of risky chemicals are not necessarily 'safe'. Rather, they involve taking some risks, but ones that have been judged as being justified. In contrast, the current system, through the idea of no-effect levels, suggests that exposures below those levels are safe, whereas in fact, as I showed in Chapter 7, there is very often a great deal of uncertainty as to whether this is the case or not.

Deciding which is the least risky substance or method in a particular situation is not necessarily a straightforward matter. I am not suggesting, for example, that it is possible to combine the four aspects that I have identified (in Chapter 7) as contributing to the riskiness of a chemical – the capacity to cause harm, novelty, persistence and mobility – in any straightforward way to provide a measure of riskiness along a single scale. Though it will be necessary to devise some sort of categorization of chemicals according to how risky they are, I do not propose to go into the details of such a classification scheme, merely to provide a few pointers as to how one could be constructed.

As a starting point, regulation should distinguish between chemicals that are found in nature and those that are not. Of course, it is not always clear whether a particular chemical is identical to one found in nature, and there are bound to be grey areas. There is a need, however, to put chemicals into a number of graded categories according to whether they are found in nature, and if so how common they are in particular environmental compartments. Legislation should contain lists of substances in each category. If it is not known in which category a chemical is it should be assumed to be non-naturally occurring. This system will therefore encourage investigation of the chemical constituents of the natural environment. The presence of a chemical in the environment cannot of course be taken as evidence that it is natural: the environment and living organisms are now contaminated by many non-natural chemicals produced by human industry or derived from such chemicals. What will be needed, in addition to analysis data, is a good understanding of biochemistry and biogeochemical processes. This will in turn increase understanding of what the effects of human production and use of chemicals might be.

Whether a chemical substance is naturally occurring should affect where the burden of proof lies. At one end of the scale are substances identical to common natural ones. For these the burden of proof should lie with the regulator to show that they have the capacity to cause harm. Regulatory controls on them should then depend on the nature of the harm that they have the capacity to cause. At the other end are chemicals that are clearly novel. These should be assumed to be risky unless there is good evidence that they are accommodated in natural processes without significantly changing those processes or causing harm.

Non-nature-identical chemicals should be further categorized according to what we know about how they fit into natural processes and cycles and according to their persistence and mobility. The latter characteristics both increase the riskiness of novel chemicals. It is less clear that they make a naturally occurring chemical more risky, however; rather they are properties that, like the other properties of the chemical, enable it to perform its function in natural systems and processes.

The types of harm that chemicals have the capacity to cause (in other words their hazards) are qualitatively different and not commensurate with each other. At one extreme are effects that require reasonably high concentrations of the substance, are immediate and localized (for example flammability, explosivity, corrosiveness and acute toxicity). The causal relationship between a particular chemical exposure and such effects is usually obvious, or at least easy to demonstrate. Those affected generally include those who deal directly with the chemical and it is often possible to handle and store the chemical in such a way that harm is avoided. The existing European Union (EU) regulatory system, dating from the 1967 'dangerous substances' directive (Council Directive 67/548/EEC) was clearly set up with this sort of hazard in mind. The focus of the 1967 directive was on the classification, packaging and labelling of substances according to 'categories of danger', to try to ensure that they were handled and stored safely.

At the other extreme are effects such as endocrine disruption, carcinogenicity, chronic toxicity and ozone depletion, which are not apparent to those who deal with the chemical. Causal relationships between specific chemicals and their effects are generally difficult to prove, perhaps because they occur remote from the site of use of the chemical, either in time or space, or because they are caused by very low concentrations, or perhaps only when other substances are also present. A much greater proportion of those who suffer from these effects than the first sort will not have had any dealings with the chemical as a chemical substance, so will be unaware of their exposure to it.

If it comes to a choice between a chemical that may have the latter type of property and a chemical thought to have only the former type, the presumption of public regulation should be that the chemical whose effects are immediate and localized should be used. Such chemicals may pose greater risks to those handling them, but the possible harms are ones they can avoid if they act in the right way, such as by following safety procedures. The immediacy and obviousness of the effects mean that precautions are likely to be followed. It is far more difficult to get people to take care and to follow strict procedures where the effects of not doing so are not obvious to them. Chemicals with chronic effects are also more likely to harm those not directly involved in handling the chemical. This, I would argue, is wrongful harm done to others by those who produce and use the chemical, and regulation is concerned with preventing people from wrongfully harming others, not just with reducing total harm.[6]

Assessing the world of chemical production

Chemical production processes constitute a world – of chemical manufacturing plants, storage tanks, tankers and so forth – in which people (employees, of course, but also people who live near chemical plants and those who visit them) live for all or part of their lives. That world can be compared with the world associated with alternative means of producing the same chemicals or material used for the same purpose, which it frequently destroys. For example, in the 19th century the industrial synthesis of the natural dyes alizarin and indigo from constituents of coal tar led, respectively, to the collapse of the French madder industry (the madder plant being the natural source of alizarin) and the Indian indigo industry (Williams, 1972, pp65–66). The introduction in the 1960s of plastic bobbins – products of the chemicals industry – caused the closure of many bobbin mills in the English Lake District that had made wooden bobbins from sustainably produced coppiced timber. The cessation of coppicing in these woodlands meant a reduction in their biodiversity and value for wildlife, so wildlife organizations now often fund the coppicing and woodland management that was previously part of a process of production (Bewley, 1998; Lake District National Park Authority, 2002). The current move towards the use of plastic rather than cork stoppers for wine bottles threatens the destruction of the cork oak forests of Portugal, which currently provide a sustainable livelihood for local communities as well as a valuable habitat for wildlife. As the market for cork is lost, these forests are being felled to make way for other economic activities (Goncalves, 2000).

In assessing synthetic chemicals, we could therefore compare the world constituted by the processes of industrial synthesis of those chemicals with those of alternative technologies, using the principles I suggested above. On the fourth and sixth of these principles chemical production plants are often to be found wanting. Chemical plants have little tolerance of human fallibility and unpredictability, in that if careful safety procedures are not followed accidents can lead to significant and widespread damage.[7] Compared to technologies based on natural processes, they involve much greater dependency of individuals on human institutions (see Chapman, 2005).

An important question to consider is whether synthetic chemical production processes have become more dominant because they can be done at a lower cost, as is the common view, or because the organizations that carry them out are more powerful. Processes based on natural systems are often more amenable to being carried out on a small scale, by individuals or small companies, which, as I pointed out in Chapter 8, only have any hope of dealing with large organizations on an equal footing if they join together to act in concert.[8] Thus government action to restrict chemical production processes or to promote alternative methods of production that constitute a better public world will not necessarily make the economy less efficient. Rather it may correct the distortion in market economies caused by the inequalities of power between large corporations and small producers.

Developing ethics of practices

Seeing chemicals as things that are used for particular purposes opens up the question of whether there are alternative, less risky means of fulfilling those purposes: other chemicals or other methods. For example, one can keep dust mites out of duvets by impregnating the cover with a chemical toxic to dust mites or by using a very finely woven material, which in itself presents no risks to human health. If we are at all uncertain about the effects of the toxic chemical, the second method is a great deal less risky than the first. We should therefore substitute the use of the chemical by the use of finely woven material, even if we cannot identify the risks of the chemical to organisms other than dust mites.

This principle of substitution could be extended to form part of something that could be termed an 'ethics of a practice'. By this I mean a set a principles that takes into account a wide variety of considerations, including (but not limited to) avoiding the use of risky chemicals, and gives guidance on how the various tasks that form part of a technical practice are to be carried out. The key example of an ethics of a practice is organic agriculture. Organic agriculture is not primarily about not using synthetic chemicals, but of working within natural systems to meet multiple objectives. These include high levels of animal welfare, provision of rural employment, and enhancement of the landscape and wildlife habitats, as well as the production of healthy food, the maintenance of soil fertility and a balanced ecosystem in which pest species do not proliferate.[9] Although minimum standards for organic production have been set at the EU level, technical committees of organic certification bodies, such as the Soil Association in the UK, continually revise what methods, practices and materials are acceptable and what are recommended in organic systems.[10] Chemical use is put within the wider context of the particular tasks that have to be done and problems that have to be solved. The aim is to solve those problems in ways that are not risk creating (that do not themselves result in further problems that have to be solved (Beck 1992, pp178–179)) and that result in positive benefits, perhaps for other aspects of the system. Similar standards and guidelines could be developed for many other areas that use chemicals, including textiles, furniture, computers and paints. These should have regard to the principles for decision making about technology that I set out above. Considering chemical use alone may result in the solutions creating problems in other areas.

Collective production of standards would reduce the burden on individual manufacturers[11] and could be accompanied by an accreditation system for products produced according to them. Such standards could be produced by industry organizations in collaboration with other interested parties, perhaps through the system for standards setting discussed earlier in this chapter, or their development could be made the responsibility of the regulator of the industry.[12] Their setting should be an open process that encourages public debate.

Enabling Individual Responsibility

No system for making decisions will automatically produce good results. No matter how well crafted the organizational arrangements or wise its animating principles, neither are a substitute for an active, engaged citizenry that takes responsibility for the public world that it shares. In Chapter 9 I discussed some of the structural blocks to individual responsibility in modern societies, but also pointed out ways in which individuals and organizations nonetheless attempt to ensure that they make responsible decisions about technology (such as what products to buy and how to use them).

This responsibility is only possible if people have a right to information about products: how they are made, what effects their production has, the chemicals they contain, and the effects of their use and disposal. This information is much wider than the information about risks which seems to be the limit of what government policy thinks consumers should be provided with (see Chapter 4). To make responsible decisions, people also need to have an appreciation of the value of things that a technology puts at risk. Information alone does not in itself indicate what should be done, but it is fuel for public debate on whether technologies make for a good world or not, and how they should be produced or used. Such debates currently take place in specific limited domains, among groups of activists, in campaigning organizations or within the pages of magazines such as the *Ethical Consumer*. Occasionally they break out into wider public view – most strikingly in recent times with the issue of genetically modified food: there was a week in February 1999 when the issue was on the front page of every national newspaper and discussed in every news bulletin in the UK. Enabling individual responsibility involves encouraging these debates and ensuring, through legislation, that the information needed for them to be informed is publicly available.

One specific way to encourage these debates would be public interest advertising: advertising that points out negative effects on the world and the earth that particular products or technologies have, as a counter to the commercial advertising currently done to sell products. Public interest advertising should be funded by a levy on commercial advertising to provide a pot of money that can be used by not-for-profit organizations to make their own advertisements. To give a fair playing field the levy should be 100 per cent, so that just as much money can be spent on criticizing as is spent on promoting products. These public interest advertisements should be subject to the same requirements of honesty and truthfulness as commercial advertising. Organizations making them should, for example, have to support the claims they make with evidence, and to present what they say in a way that is not misleading. By raising concerns about the effects of products on the world and the earth, public interest advertising could put pressure on businesses to make products and provide services that contribute to a good world for human life on earth. Achieving this by regulation would be complex and bureaucratic.

To be responsible one must have the power to act differently, not merely the knowledge of what the effects of one's actions are. The world – including technology – should be such that individual responsible action is possible. Government cannot force individuals to act responsibly, but it can and should ensure that it is reasonably possible for them to do so. For example, through regulations on the design of buildings, the energy consumption of products, the location of development and the nature of the transport infrastructure, government can ensure that it is possible to live a normal life as part of mainstream society without consuming more than one's fair share of energy or other resources. Government should publicize what a fair share is – of fossil fuel consumption, for example – and there should be mechanisms that inform individuals of how much they are consuming.[13]

In the chemicals arena, manufacturers and users have long argued that making information on the chemical composition of products publicly available breaches their right to commercial confidentiality (see Chapter 5). However, it seems to have been possible to label food products with their ingredients without giving away trade secrets. The same should be possible for products that use synthetic chemicals. If we are going to enable responsible purchasing decisions – by companies in the supply chain, including manufacturers and retailers, as well as by the eventual users of the product – there should be a right to know how a product has been produced, what synthetic chemicals it contains and what were used in the process of producing it. This right should mean that, where feasible, products are labelled with the chemicals that they contain or that were used in production. Where this is not feasible the information should be available on the internet. In addition, where 'ethics of practices' have been developed, products should be labelled to indicate whether their production conformed to the principles of such ethics.

who were required by law to dip their sheep in organophosphate insecticides. The replacements for organophosphates in sheep dips (synthetic pyrethroids) are now causing water pollution problems (RCEP, 2003, p132).

We are perhaps more likely to avoid new problems if, when assessing novel technologies, we consider not just what we know about their effects, but the extent to which we are ignorant or uncertain about what those effects will be. We should consider the riskiness, not just the currently known risks, of new technologies.

A third lesson is that we need to consider what we are doing from different perspectives. We should remember that we almost never do just one thing: the farmer is not just producing food but may also be polluting water supplies or maintaining the countryside; the doctor is caring for his or her patient, developing medical knowledge, performing a role within the institution of the hospital and earning a living; the company is a world in which its employees spend their working time, it provides livelihoods and it makes products or provides services that form part of the world outside the company; a house provides a home for those who live in it and is part of the shared public world of those outside it. 'Unintended side-effects' are a result of not being aware of all these different possible descriptions of what we are doing, an unawareness that may be a deliberate turning of a blind eye so as to disown responsibility.

Hannah Arendt's categories of labour, work and action are the three basic things that we do in the active part of our lives, the doing of each of which may coincide with the doing of others (Arendt, 1958). Arendt makes it clear that they have different purposes and functions as well as conditions, and therefore should be judged by different criteria: labour by whether it provides for the necessities of life and cares for the world; work by whether it builds a durable, stable world that is a home for human life; and action by whether it reveals who the actor is and establishes human relationships. In addition, the scale and novelty of modern technology mean that now we also have to consider whether what we do impairs the ability of the earth to sustain life. A focus on just one of these results not only in unexpected problems, but in a dangerous imbalance in the different conditions needed to live a good human life on earth.

It may seem that meeting many different objectives at once is to ask too much, but this is what we are all used to doing in everyday life. Important life choices are not made on the basis of single criteria, but by considering the available options from all the different perspectives and coming to a decision about what, on the whole, is the best given all the different things that are important and deserve consideration. Human life has multiple conditions and for human life to be lived well many different conditions must be met. In recent times, massive economic growth can be regarded as driven by the desire to meet the biological needs of human beings – for food, warmth and comfort – to the extent that the process has developed its own momentum and is now unrelated to those needs. The provision of material comfort and convenience, for the few at least, has been at the expense of a world in which responsible human action is possible. It has also meant that we are living in a way that cannot be sustained on this earth.

Unlike the dangers inherent in nature, we are responsible, and have responsibility for technology. Technological change is not an autonomous, automatic process beyond our control but the result of human decisions. It only looks like an

Conclusion: Lessons from Synthetic Chemicals

What lessons can be learned from our experience of producing, using and regula
ing synthetic chemicals? The first is the limits of our knowledge: we cannot ha
a complete intellectual grasp of the world. Therefore, if we introduce novel thin
into the world, we cannot know what will happen. Part of why we cannot kno
is that we cannot predict how humans will behave in specific instances. A ne
source of unpredictability – new in human history – is our creation of things tha
are novel with respect to the materials of the earth. These may start new processe
in nature, by interaction with natural materials and processes, the outcome o
which is unpredictable, in the same way as are human affairs. In human affairs
(the realm constituted by human relationships), however, we can make promises
to each other to make the future more certain, and can break chains of action and
reaction by forgiveness; these remedies are not available to manage the unpredictability of creating novel matter.

Reassurances of the safety of novel technologies based on risk assessment
falsely imply that we can know what effects the novel thing created by the technology will have, or that at least we will be able to undo the technology if it does
turn out to cause harm. The production and use of a novel synthetic chemical is
regarded as akin to the making of a table, which can be destroyed and removed
from the world after we have made it. That this is not the case, and that the processes set in motion by a technology are irreversible, has been a concern raised in
the debate about genetic engineering. For example, one of Jeremy Rifkin's arguments against genetic engineering in agriculture is that as the products of genetic
engineering are alive, they reproduce, grow and may spread from one place to
another: once released, genetically engineered organisms cannot be constrained
or recalled (Rifkin, 1985, pp47–48). These arguments, which apply to some types
of genetically modified organisms more than others, are also relevant for synthetic
chemicals. Though they are not alive, many chemical substances do migrate in
the environment, and cannot be recalled. If they are persistent, their presence in
the environment is irreversible.

A second lesson is that we should avoid solving old problems in ways that create new ones. Many novel synthetic chemicals have been welcomed as removing
the hazards or drawbacks of the previously used substances or methods, only to
find, some decades after their introduction, that they had serious consequences of
a different kind. Thus chlorofluorocarbon (CFC) refrigerants are not flammable
or toxic, the drawbacks of the previously available refrigerants; organochlorine
pesticides did not result in the acute poisoning episodes seen with the previous
arsenical insecticides. But after using these chemicals for decades, we found out
that CFCs were destroying the ozone layer and that organochlorine pesticides
prevented the successful breeding of birds of prey. The search for alternative refrigerants has, eventually, taken us back to using ammonia – the toxic gas (which
in a closely related, cationic form is prevalent in soils) that CFCs were seen as
being superior to. In contrast, organochlorine pesticides were often replaced by
shorter-lived organophosphates, a different class of non-nature-identical synthetic
chemicals, which have turned out to have complex neurotoxic effects. They are
thought to be responsible for the chronic debilitation of many UK sheep farmers,

automatic process if we adopt a viewpoint that is far removed from human experience in the world (Arendt, 1958, p323). If, instead of observing from the outside, we pay attention to what we do in the world, we realize that we do have the power to change that world and to make it a fit home for human life on earth.

Notes

1   PPS stands for planning policy statement. These are revisions of the previous planning policy guidance notes (PPGs), of which there were 25. They are statements of national policy on various aspects of planning in England. Each covers either a particular type of development (for example housing or retail) or a topic relevant to planning (for example archaeology or flood risk). They are available at www.communities.gov.uk (accessed December 2006).

2   Cases where decision makers have made decisions on the basis of their private interests (generated, for example, by bribes from developers) do not refute this, since such practices are recognized as corrupt and contrary to how the decisions should be made. Those who make planning decisions have to abide by a code of conduct which requires that they declare if they have a personal interest in the matter and withdraw from the discussion and decision if that interest could be considered to be 'prejudicial' (Committee on Standards in Public Life, 1997).

3   Information about the British Standards Institute has been obtained from their website, www.bsi-global.com (accessed December 2006).

4   Royal Charters are given to bodies that work in the public interest and can demonstrate pre-eminence, stability and permanence in their particular field. Several professional institutions, long-established universities and the BBC have Royal Charters.

5   The importance of policy can be seen in what happened to the UK planning system under the Thatcher government of the 1980s. The system itself was not changed, but the content of the policies was, so that planning authorities were forced into having to allow whatever developments business proposed (see Taylor 1998, pp137–138).

6   I am grateful to Jonathan Wolff for this insight.

7   The best known accident at a chemical plant was at the Union Carbide plant in Bhopal, India, in 1984. The release of a massive quantity of lethal gas was caused by a disgruntled employee spoiling a batch of methyl isocyanate by adding water to a storage tank (Browning, 1993). A key accident in the UK, which led to legislation on hazardous installations, occurred at Flixborough in 1974. Flammable gas was released following the failure of pipework that had been installed a few months before to replace a leaking reactor (Health and Safety Executive, 1975).

8   There are many small companies (though probably not individuals) in chemicals manufacturing, but the heart of the industry is the large chemical companies. Large organizations, including government, were key in its development. The two world wars, with their increased government intervention in industry, provided important boosts to the chemicals industry: after the war products manufactured for war purposes had to find civilian uses. For example, nerve gases became pesticides and ammonia for explosives found a use in fertilizers (see Steingraber, 1998, pp94–99).

9   See Conford (2001) on the original concerns about the health of the soil, people and nation that led to the organic movement and the website of the Soil Association (www.soilassociation.org.uk) on current aims. The increase in the market for organic food in the last decade and the growing role of conventional agribusiness and retailers has led some to question whether 'organic' means sustainable. Much of the organic produce for sale in UK supermarkets, for example, is imported from the South: the amount of energy the transport consumes contributes to unsustainability, and production in the South tends to be dominated by large scale farming interests, who drive out sustainable small scale farmers (Rigby and Brown, 2003). However, the important point from my perspective is that this critique comes from within the organic movement as much as from outside it. This illustrates how what I have called the 'organic ethic' is a holistic ethic, concerned with all the many aspects of farming systems – social and environmental – not just with the use of chemicals.

10   For example, guidelines for organic gardening produced by the Henry Doubleday Research Association (HDRA) set out for various tasks what materials and methods constitute best practice, what are acceptable but not ideal, what may be used by those moving towards an organic gardening regime to help deal with particular problems, and what is not acceptable (HDRA, 1995).

11   This burden can be considerable, as illustrated by the example given by Colborn et al (1996, p228) of the redesign of a line of upholstery fabric so that the manufacturing process and the final product were free of hazardous chemicals; 7500 chemicals used to dye or process fabrics had to be surveyed.

12   For example, the Environment Agency, the regulator in England and Wales of complex industrial processes that are covered by the EU Directive on Integrated Pollution Prevention and Control (IPPC), produces technical guidance documents for each industry to assist in identifying what is considered the 'best available technique' for that process under various circumstances. To obtain a permit to operate an IPPC process, the operator has to show that they have 'systematically developed proposals to apply the best available technique' (see www. environment-agency.gov.uk). What I have in mind could be similar, but take into consideration a wider range of issues than just pollution, which is the concern of IPPC.

13   Tradable quota systems for carbon emissions, where individuals are given an allocation of quota, do this for fossil fuel consumption (see policy C3 of the Green Party Manifesto for a Sustainable Society at http://policy.greenparty.org.uk/mfss (accessed November 2006) or the Tyndall Centre proposals for domestic tradable quotas (Starkey and Anderson, 2005).

References

Arendt, H. (1958) *The Human Condition*, University of Chicago Press, Chicago, IL

Arendt, H. (1982) *Lectures on Kant's Political Philosophy*, Harvester Press, Brighton

Beck, U. (1992) *Risk Society: Towards a New Modernity*, trans. M. Ritter, Sage Publications, London

Bewley, B. (1998) 'From Buttermere to the bobbin factory', *British Archaeology*, no 37

Browning, J. B. (1993) 'Union Carbide disaster at Bhopal', in J. A. Gottshalk (ed) *Crisis Response: Inside Stories on Managing Under Siege*, Visible Ink Press, Detroit, MI

BSI (2005) *A Standard for Standards, BS 0:2005*, BSI British Standards, London

Chapman, A. (2005) 'Genetic engineering: The unnatural argument', *Techne*, vol 9, no 2, pp81–93

Colborn, T., Dumanoski, D. and Myers, J. P. (1996) *Our Stolen Future*, Little Brown and Company, London

Committee on Standards in Public Life (1997) 'Third report: Standards of conduct in local government in England, Scotland and Wales', Stationery Office, London

Conford, P. (2001) *The Origins of the Organic Movement*, Floris Books, Edinburgh

Dagger, R. (2003) 'Stopping sprawl for the good of all: The case for civic environmentalism', *Journal of Social Philosophy*, vol 34, no 1, pp44–63

Gonclaves, E. (2000) *The Cork Report – A Study on the Economics of Cork*, RSPB, Sandy, Bedfordshire

HDRA (Henry Doubleday Research Association) (1995) 'The Henry Doubleday Research Association's guidelines for organic gardening', HDRA, Coventry

Healey, P. (1997) *Collaborative Planning: Shaping Places in Fragmented Societies*, Macmillan Press, London

Health and Safety Executive (1975) 'The Flixborough disaster: Report of the Court of Inquiry', HMSO, London

Lake District National Park Authority (2002) 'Habitats of the Lake District', Education Service Factsheet, Lake District National Park Authority, Kendal

Light, A. (2003) 'Urban ecological citizenship', *Journal of Social Philosophy*, vol 34, no 1, pp44–63

Nilsson, R. (1998) 'Integrating Sweden into the European Union: Problems concerning chemicals control', in R. Bal and W. Halffman (eds) *The Politics of Chemical Risk*, Kluwer Academic Publishers, Dordrecht, pp159–171

ODPM (Office of the Deputy Prime Minister) (2005) 'The planning system: General principles', published alongside PPS1, www.communities.gov.uk, accessed December 2006

RCEP (Royal Commission on Environmental Pollution) (2003) 'Twenty-fourth report: Chemicals in products: Safeguarding the environment and human health', Stationery Office, London

Rifkin, J. (1985) *Declaration of a Heretic*, Routledge and Kegan Paul, Boston, MA

Rigby, D. and Brown, S. (2003) 'Organic food and global trade: Is the market delivering sustainability?', Discussion Paper Series No 0326, School of Economic Science, University of Manchester, Manchester

Starkey, R. and Anderson, K. (2005) 'Domestic tradeable quotas: A policy instrument for reducing greenhouse gas emissions from energy use', Tyndall Centre Technical Report 39, www.tyndall.ac.uk/publications, accessed December 2006

Steingraber, S. (1998) *Living Downstream: An Ecologist Looks at Cancer and the Environment*, Virago Press, London

Taylor, N. (1998) *Urban Planning Theory since 1945*, Sage Publications, London

Williams, T. I. (1972) *The Chemical Industry*, EP Publishing Ltd, Wakefield

EU directives

Council Directive 67/548/EEC on the approximation of the laws, regulations and administrative provisions relating to the classification, packaging and labelling of dangerous substances, *Official Journal*, L196, 16.8.1967, p1

Index